VICKSBURG 1863

Recent Titles in
Battles and Leaders of the American Civil War
John David Smith, Series Editor

The Seven Days' Battles: The War Begins Anew
Judkin Browning

Antietam 1862: Gateway to Emancipation
T. Stephen Whitman

Chickamauga 1863: Rebel Breakthrough
Alexander Mendoza

Shiloh: Confederate High Tide in the Heartland
Steven E. Woodworth

The Richmond-Petersburg Campaign, 1864–65
Charles R. Bowery Jr.

The 1864 Franklin-Nashville Campaign: The Finishing Stroke
Michael Thomas Smith

VICKSBURG 1863

The Deepest Wound

Steven Nathaniel Dossman

Battles and Leaders of the American Civil War
John David Smith, Series Editor

 PRAEGER

AN IMPRINT OF ABC-CLIO, LLC
Santa Barbara, California • Denver, Colorado • Oxford, England

973.7344
Dos

Library of Congress Cataloging-in-Publication Data

Dossman, Steven Nathaniel.
  Vicksburg 1863 : the deepest wound / Steven Nathaniel Dossman.
    pages cm. — (Battles and leaders of the American Civil War)
  Includes bibliographical references and index.
  ISBN 978–0–313–39601–4 (cloth : acid-free paper) — ISBN 978–0–313–39602–1 (ebook) 1. Vicksburg (Miss.)—History—Siege, 1863. 2. Vicksburg (Miss.)—History—Civil War, 1861–1865. 3. United States—History—Civil War, 1861–1865—Campaigns. I. Title.
  E475.27.D67   2014
  973.7'344—dc23   2014018473

ISBN: 978–0–313–39601–4
EISBN: 978–0–313–39602–1

18 17 16 15 14   1 2 3 4 5

This book is also available on the World Wide Web as an eBook.
Visit www.abc-clio.com for details.

Praeger
An Imprint of ABC-CLIO, LLC

ABC-CLIO, LLC
130 Cremona Drive, P.O. Box 1911
Santa Barbara, California 93116-1911

This book is printed on acid-free paper (∞)

Manufactured in the United States of America

Publ 9/28/14

$48

This book is dedicated to the men and women who sacrificed and suffered during the Vicksburg campaign.

And to Andrea,

"Behold, you are beautiful, my beloved, truly lovely."

Song of Solomon, 1:16

Contents

Illustrations   ix

Maps   xi

Series Foreword   xiii

Acknowledgments   xv

1. "The Mississippi is the backbone of the Rebellion"   1

2. "A series of experiments"   19

3. "The road to Vicksburg is open"   47

4. "Time is all-important"   65

5. "Vicksburg or hell!"   91

6. "The most valuable conquest of the war"   117

7. "The death knell of the beloved Confederacy"   137

Notes   149

Bibliographical Essay   181

Index   185

Illustrations

Photo essay follows page 116

Major General Ulysses S. Grant

Major General William T. Sherman

Lieutenant General John C. Pemberton

General Joseph E. Johnston

Major General James McPherson

Major General John McClernand

Admiral David Dixon Porter

Major General John S. Bowen

Brigadier General John Gregg

Major General Martin L. Smith

Major General John H. Forney

Major General Carter L. Stevenson

Illustration of the surrender interview between Grant and Pemberton, July 3, 1863

The Shirley House during the siege of Vicksburg

Fighting in the crater created after the explosion of the mine under the Third Louisiana Redan on June 25, 1863

The Texas Monument at Vicksburg National Military Park

Maps

The First Union Attempts to Capture Vicksburg   23

The Bayous and the Canal   37

The Vicksburg Campaign, April 29–May 14, 1863   51

The Vicksburg Campaign, May 15–19, 1863   78

The Second Assault on Vicksburg, May 22, 1863   97

The Pursuit of Johnston, July 4–10, 1863   138

Series Foreword

In October 1864 Confederate President Jefferson Davis sought to rally increasingly demoralized southerners, declaring "by fighting alone can independence be gained." Months later, in his Second Inaugural Address, President Abraham Lincoln reminded northerners that "the progress of our arms, upon which all else chiefly depends, is as well known to the public as to myself; and it is, I trust, reasonably satisfactory and encouraging to all."

Though historians have debated endlessly about the causes of Union victory and Confederate defeat in the American Civil War, the North proved triumphant on the battlefield not because of its population advantage, its manufacturing superiority, or because of internal divisions in Dixie. Above all else, Southern hopes for independence and European recognition hinged on battlefield victories; Northern success ultimately resulted from combat victories and superior leadership.

The books in Praeger's *Battles and Leaders of the American Civil War* series focus closely on key Civil War battles and the leaders who led their men into the fight. The books treat major battles and examine minutely how the outcome of the battles depended on the abilities, skills, triumphs, and failures of commanders who orchestrated the campaigns. Each book underscores the nexus between military outcome and command decisions, including political implications, supply, tactics, and strategy. The authors emphasize contingencies that influenced battle outcomes. They also consider the social, political, and geographic context of each battle and the background and personalities of the commanders.

With more than 620,000 deaths, the Civil War was the bloodiest conflict on American soil. Books in *Battles and Leaders of the American Civil
War* interpret the war's combat and its leadership as central to its meaning.
Readers will find the volumes fast-paced, up-to-date, well-researched, and
valuable guides as they ponder the war's triumphs and tragedies.

John David Smith

Charles H. Stone Distinguished Professor of American History
The University of North Carolina at Charlotte

Acknowledgments

Appreciation and gratitude must be extended to all who helped in the creation of this book. I would like to thank Michael Millman, John David Smith, and all the staff at ABC-CLIO for their patience and assistance in editing the manuscript. I also would like to thank Dr. Charles D. Grear for providing me with the opportunity to write this project. Dr. Steven Woodworth, Dr. Donald Frazier, and Dr. Robert F. Pace must be recognized as the mentors who taught me to be a historian. Many dedicated archivists assisted in the research that is found within these pages. I would like to thank all the archivists and staff who aided my research at the following institutions: the Mississippi Department of Archives and History, the Abraham Lincoln Presidential Library, the Chicago History Museum, the Wisconsin Historical Society, the Ohio Historical Society, the Indiana Historical Society, the Library of Congress, the Pearce Civil War Collection at Navarro College, and the Old Court House Museum in Vicksburg. I must also thank my wife Andrea for her love and support throughout the writing process.

1

———∞∞∞———

"The Mississippi is the backbone of the Rebellion"

Confederate President Jefferson Davis could barely stand the strain. Physically and mentally exhausted by months of anxiety and overwork, his fragile health had suffered severely from the stress of war. By June 1863, Union soldiers had occupied Davis's own plantation along the Mississippi River, Briarfield, and ransacked many of his personal possessions. On July 2, 1863, an unidentified malady sent him to his sickbed. On July 6, Davis recovered enough to return to work, still hoping that a miracle might occur in his beloved home, the state of Mississippi. Then, the disastrous news crashed upon him. The fortress at Vicksburg, Mississippi, and the entire army defending it had surrendered on the Fourth of July to Major General Ulysses S. Grant and his Army of the Tennessee.[1] The fall of Vicksburg ensured the surrender of the Confederate garrison at Port Hudson, Louisiana, and when it capitulated on July 9, the Union controlled the length of the Mississippi River, fatally dividing the Confederacy. Only months before at the beginning of the year, Vicksburg had appeared as an impregnable symbol of southern resistance, defiantly repulsing repeated Federal advances. Now the "Gibraltar of the West" lay in Yankee hands.[2] From then on until the day he died, Davis would wage a war of words over how this disaster occurred and who bore responsibility.[3]

The national survival of the Confederacy depended upon control of the Mississippi River. The river divided the South in twain, and Union supremacy along the Mississippi would prevent vital logistical and manpower transport from the west bank to the east, reducing the

Trans-Mississippi theater to an isolated region of the Confederacy unable to influence the outcome of the war. The state of Texas contained the Confederacy's only international border apart from the United States, and as the northern blockade gradually constricted access to southern ports, the European trade from Matamoras, Mexico, into Texas became increasingly essential to the Confederate war effort. The river represented a natural invasion route that would allow the Union to separate the South and deny the flow of critical supplies such as livestock, salt, and sugar to the hard-pressed Army of Tennessee and Army of Northern Virginia.[4] In 1861, President Abraham Lincoln observed, "The Mississippi is the backbone of the Rebellion; it is the key to the whole situation. While the Confederates hold it they can obtain supplies of all kinds, and it is a barrier against our forces."[5] Union Major General William T. Sherman agreed, writing in a dispatch to Major General Henry W. Halleck, "The man who at the end of this war holds the military control of the Valley of the Mississippi will be the man."[6]

Successful secession would also obstruct midwestern trade from using the river to access foreign markets, forcing the commerce of the Old Northwest to divert along railroads and canals to the Atlantic Ocean. The defense of the Mississippi promised invaluable returns to the Confederacy as an economic and propaganda weapon that could undermine the will to wage war and stimulate opposition to the Lincoln administration within the northern states west of the Appalachian Mountains. Rebel supremacy along the river preserved the geographic unity of the Confederacy and encouraged its population to persevere in the struggle, presenting a key symbolic stronghold against the North, while a triumphant Union conquest of the Mississippi would permanently weaken the Confederacy's diplomatic stature and seriously damage morale throughout the South. In the course of the Civil War, the Mississippi River occupied a unique position as the Confederacy's greatest weapon and its greatest weakness.[7] Unrestricted access to the river was so critical to the northern economy that Sherman proclaimed, "To secure the safety of the navigation of the Mississippi River I would slay millions. On that point I am not only insane, but mad."[8]

The citizens of the Trans-Mississippi theater held the same opinion as Sherman, realizing that Confederate fortifications on the river protected their own homes from Federal invasion. Texan Colonel William H. Parsons wrote after the war that "the point . . . of perpetual menace and vital danger, especially to Texas, was the proximity of powerful Federal armies on the Mississippi front of the State of Arkansas," where "that inland sea" served as "their base of operations, by fleets connecting with the very heart of their overwhelming resources."[9] Parsons wisely observed, "Our lines once broken, whether on the Mississippi or the Arkansas, or the Red River, would have thrown open the approach to the invasion of Texas, by an ever alert and powerful foe."[10] Uninterrupted access to the eastern shore of the waterway maintained the Trans-Mississippi's strategic role in the war. The Mississippi River defenses provided protection for the significant logistical traffic along the Arkansas and Red Rivers, which presented potential aquatic highways for Union armies to threaten and invade Arkansas, western Louisiana, and Texas. The enormous manpower demand of the northern effort to open the Mississippi River reduced the number of Federal troops available for offensive operations elsewhere against the interior of the Trans-Mississippi, especially along the Texas coast. The defense of the seceded states west of the river and their vast agricultural resources depended upon Confederate possession of what one contemporary observer labeled as the "spinal column of America."[11] While the legendary battles of Ulysses S. Grant's epic conquest of Vicksburg are internationally renowned, the role played by Texans and other Trans-Mississippi soldiers in the defense of the southern citadel remains largely forgotten. Altogether, some 30 Lone Star units served in the defense of Fortress Vicksburg on both sides of the Mississippi River, providing one of the largest concentrations of Texans seen in a single campaign during the war. An estimated 38 units participated in the campaign from Arkansas, along with 35 from Louisiana and at least 28 from Missouri.[12]

In 1860, Vicksburg, Mississippi, was the second-largest city in Mississippi with a population of 4,591 residents, consisting of "3,158 whites, 31 free blacks, and 1,402 slaves."[13] Due to the prosperous river trade, the town contained a sizable number of northern merchants and European immigrants, and "only about one-third of its adult population was Southern-born."[14] The steep bluffs of the area had inspired the Spanish to construct Fort Nogales near the future site of Vicksburg, which later American settlers founded in 1825 and named in honor of the Reverend Newitt Vick. When Mississippi's secession convention convened, Vicksburg and many of the towns along the Mississippi River voted for Unionist delegates as the river economy relied upon commerce with the North. The counties farther inland strongly supported secession, as the elite plantation owners of Central Mississippi would not accept the election of a Republican candidate as president.[15]

Early in the war, President Lincoln pointed at a map of the region in a meeting with his commanders and noted, "Vicksburg is the key. Here is Red River, which will supply the Confederates with cattle and corn to feed their armies. There are the Arkansas and White Rivers, which can supply cattle and hogs by the thousand. From Vicksburg these supplies can be distributed by rail all over the Confederacy." The president continued, "Then there is that great depot of supplies on the Yazoo. Let us get Vicksburg and all that country is ours. The war can never be brought to a close until that key is in our pocket." Lincoln had traveled down the Mississippi River in a flatboat during his youth, and drawing from these experiences, he declared, "I am acquainted with that region and know what I am talking about, and, valuable as New Orleans will be to us, Vicksburg will be more so. We may take all the northern ports of the Confederacy, and they can still defy us from Vicksburg." In Lincoln's opinion, Confederate supremacy of the Mississippi River "means hog and hominy without limit, fresh troops from all the states of the far South, and a cotton country where they can raise the staple without interference."[16] His opponent, Confederate President Jefferson Davis, described Vicksburg as "the nailhead that held the South's two halves together."[17] Grant's campaign for Vicksburg would ultimately deal a decisive blow to the Confederacy and drastically alter the nature of warfare in the Civil War.

At the outbreak of the war, the North immediately recognized the immense importance of the Mississippi River. In May 1861, Union General in Chief Winfield Scott proposed an invasion down the river to divide the Confederacy combined with a naval blockade of southern ports to slowly strangle the South into submission. Once the South had been divided, Scott believed that Union forces could fortify their positions and wait for the southern population to repudiate secession and rejoin the Union. Although Scott's "Anaconda Plan" met with ridicule in the northern press and underestimated the amount of popular support throughout the South for secession, many aspects of the plan would later be put into practice by Union commanders.[18] On April 19, 1861, Lincoln implemented one element of the Anaconda Plan by proclaiming a blockade of the southern coast, and preparations soon began to commence the conquest of the Mississippi River valley. Later that year, James Buchanan Eads, a successful businessman and inventor with years of experience on the Mississippi, won a contract to produce seven gunboats for the U.S. Navy. Working with ship designer Samuel Pook, Eads constructed the famous ironclad gunboats known as "Pook Turtles." The Union also purchased a large number of river steamers and converted them to military vessels by adding wooden or iron armor. By February 1862, the Union's Western Gunboat Flotilla possessed a growing fleet of both ironclad and timberclad gunboats to operate on the "brown water" of the inland rivers.[19]

Defending the heartland of the Confederacy presented Davis and his commanders with several severe disadvantages. In the eastern theater, the major rivers flowed from west to east, providing a series of natural defensive lines that could protect against any invading army. In contrast, in the western theater, the large navigable rivers ran north and south, allowing the Union to potentially cut the Confederacy into pieces. Along with the Mississippi River, the Tennessee and Cumberland Rivers flowed through the South like twin blades of a geographical sword of Damocles. The region contained few major roads and railroads, and, worse still, most of its major transportation and manufacturing resources lay in vulnerable locations on the periphery of the Confederacy or on the major rivers. Northern firms owned most of the steamboats that sailed on those rivers, and most of these had northern crews who sailed home after secession, leaving only a few vessels to fall into Confederate hands at the beginning of the war. Since the infant nation lacked the industrial capacity to construct a large navy to challenge the Union fleet, the Confederacy would have to rely upon fixed fortifications and channel obstructions to prevent Union incursions along the waterways, such as Island No. 10 on the Mississippi, Fort Henry on the east bank of the Tennessee River, and Fort Donelson on the west bank of the Cumberland River.[20]

Fortunately for Davis and his generals, the state of Kentucky declared neutrality at the beginning of hostilities. While this ultimately futile policy existed, it presented a crucial shield that protected much of the western Confederacy from any possible Union offensive. In order to respect Kentucky's neutrality in the summer of 1861, Confederate authorities established Forts Henry and Donelson in Tennessee, though Kentucky contained far stronger positions for the defense of the twin rivers. The two forts, christened Fort Henry in honor of Tennessee's Confederate Senator Gustavus A. Henry and Fort Donelson after Tennessee's attorney general Daniel S. Donelson, lay too far apart to be mutually supportive. In addition to this inherent weakness, Confederate engineers placed Fort Henry in such a poor location that the stronghold was in danger of flooding.[21]

These early blunders might have been rectified with enough time and leadership. Unfortunately for the South, the western Confederacy had little of either in early 1861. On September 4, 1861, Major General Leonidas Polk rashly occupied Columbus, Kentucky, on his own authority to gain possession of high bluffs located on a bend in the Mississippi River. This political miscalculation persuaded the majority of Kentuckians to remain loyal to the federal government and immediately opened the state to Union forces. Polk's reckless infringement on Kentucky's neutrality

resonates as one of the worst decisions made by any Confederate commander during the war. On September 6, in response to Polk's incursion,
a little-known Illinois brigadier general named Ulysses S. Grant seized
control of Paducah, Kentucky, at the mouth of the Tennessee River,
allowing the Federals to outflank the Confederate position at Columbus.
Faced with a growing crisis in the West, Jefferson Davis appointed
his old friend and new Confederate General Albert Sidney Johnston as
commander of the enormous Department Number Two on September 10,
1861.[22]

Department Number Two eventually ranged from the Appalachian
Mountains to Indian Territory, containing the states of Kentucky, Tennessee, Arkansas, Missouri, the Indian Territory, and the western half of Mississippi. Johnston struggled vigorously against chronic shortages of men,
arms, and equipment in his immense department and by January 1862
had pieced together a thin defensive line stretching from southern Missouri across the Mississippi River to Columbus, Kentucky. From there,
the Confederate frontier turned south to Forts Henry and Donelson in
Tennessee, then up to Bowling Green, Kentucky, before ending near the
Cumberland Gap in the mountains of eastern Kentucky. In a few months,
Johnston had organized an improvised army of some 67,500 inexperienced
and ill-equipped soldiers, while his subordinate Major General Earl Van
Dorn mustered nearly 20,000 more in Arkansas and Missouri. On November 7, 1861, Polk repulsed an attack made by a small force under Grant in
the Battle of Belmont, Missouri, but Johnston knew his overextended com-
mand had too few reserves to contain any serious penetration of the
Confederate line should any segment of the 1,000-mile front be breached.[23]

While the Confederacy strained to create an army from scratch, the
North mobilized rapidly to secure the western rivers with an army roughly
twice the size of Johnston's and a growing armada of gunboats. Two funda-
mental goals governed the Union war effort and dictated the course of
operations in the western theater. The North's first objective, seizing control of the region's major rivers, would be executed in conjunction with a
simultaneous effort to capture the critical railroad and industrial centers
of the western Confederacy, such as Corinth, Mississippi; Chattanooga,
Tennessee; and Atlanta, Georgia. On January 19, 1862, Brigadier General
George Thomas routed the small Rebel force that held Johnston's eastern
flank at the Battle of Mill Springs, Kentucky, leaving largely Unionist East
Tennessee exposed to a Federal advance.[24] Before Johnston could react to
this threat to his right, on February 2, 1862, Ulysses S. Grant initiated a
combined army–navy expedition to capture Forts Henry and Donelson
on the vulnerable Tennessee and Cumberland Rivers.[25]

Up to this point in the war, Grant had seen little action other than the skirmish at Belmont and seemed likely to play only a minor role in the Union's grand effort to suppress the rebellion. Born in Ohio, Grant graduated from the U.S. Military Academy in 1843 and had seen considerable action in the Mexican War. There he acquired a reputation for bravery and an everlasting admiration for Major General Zachery Taylor, who became his role model as a commander. After the Mexican War, Grant languished in the dullness of peacetime duty and found himself battling boredom in a series of frontier assignments. Separated from his beloved wife and family, Grant drowned his sorrows in alcohol. Although the extent of Grant's fondness for the bottle is still debated amongst historians to this day, he had to resign from the army in 1853 in order to avoid a court-martial for excessive drinking. Finding little success as a civilian, Grant failed in various business pursuits and eventually found himself reduced to working as a clerk in his father's store in Galena, Illinois. At the outbreak of war in 1861, he received command of the 21st Illinois Infantry and, with the patronage of Congressman Elihu Washburne and Illinois Governor Richard Yates, soon acquired a promotion to brigadier general and command of the District of Cairo in Halleck's Department of the Missouri.[26]

Fort Henry's commander, Brigadier General Lloyd Tilghman, sent most of his 3,400-man force to Fort Donelson before Grant's army attacked and remained behind with only a skeleton gun crew to battle Flag Officer Andrew H. Foote's Western Gunboat Flotilla of seven gunboats. On February 6, the U.S. Navy battered Fort Henry into submission after nearly an hour and a half of shelling, and Tilghman surrendered his command to Foote before Grant's army arrived. The brief battle cost the Union 11 killed, 31 wounded, and five missing while the Confederacy suffered five killed, 11 wounded, and 94 captured. The fall of Fort Henry opened the Tennessee River to Union navigation, and soon Foote's gunboats had steamed as far south as Muscle Shoals, Alabama, destroying a key railroad bridge and other badly needed supplies along the way. Foote's squadron also captured the incomplete Confederate ironclad *Eastport* and unleashed panic throughout the region with their display of northern naval superiority.[27]

Grant did not stop to rest on his laurels after taking Fort Henry. Instead, he immediately marched his army to attack Fort Donelson while Foote's gunboats steamed back north to enter the Cumberland River. Upon learning of the surrender of Fort Henry, Johnston rushed some 12,000 reinforcements to Fort Donelson in hopes of either defeating Grant's army or at least buying enough time for the rest of Confederate forces to evacuate

Bowling Green, Kentucky. In a move that would later prove extremely costly, Johnston also ordered Brigadier General John B. Floyd of Virginia to command the fort with Brigadier General Gideon J. Pillow of Tennessee as his second in command. Both Floyd and Pillow had received their rank as political generals and outranked the third-highest-ranking Confederate officer at the fort, West Point–trained Kentuckian Brigadier General Simon B. Buckner. On February 14, the guns of Fort Donelson withstood a bombardment from Foote's flotilla for an hour and a half and, to the surprise of observers on both sides, inflicted serious damage on the gunboats. During the night, at a council of war, the senior commanders of the fort decided to attempt to break out of the Federal siege the next day and rejoin Johnston's army. Early on the morning of February 15, the Rebels surprised Brigadier General John McClernand's division and drove the Federals back, opening a clear evacuation route to rejoin the rest of Johnston's retreating army.[28]

However, the poorly planned escape attempt failed when Floyd and Pillow became confused and ordered their men to return to their original positions rather than begin the necessary march, allowing the Federals to regain the lost ground. Soon thereafter, Grant ordered a counterattack by Brigadier General Charles F. Smith's division that gained control of part of the defensive line held by Buckner's men. That night in another council of war, the three fractious Confederate generals determined that the fort could not be held despite the fact that the fort contained enough supplies to hold out for a considerable amount of time and that reinforcements could still arrive from across the Cumberland River. After agreeing to the council's decision, Floyd refused to surrender to Grant's army, as he feared arrest for embezzlement while serving as secretary of war in the Buchannan administration, and relinquished his command to Pillow. Pillow likewise refused to surrender the post, and both he and Floyd fled ignominiously, leaving Buckner to endure the humiliation of capitulation. On the morning of February 16, Buckner surrendered 14,623 men, 57 cannon, and a large amount of badly needed equipment and supplies to Grant, his old classmate from West Point. Perhaps 5,000 Confederates, including 500 men led by Colonel Nathan Bedford Forrest, refused to surrender and escaped through gaps in the Federal lines. The fighting at Fort Donelson cost Grant's army 500 killed, 2,108 wounded, and 221 missing, while the Confederates lost perhaps 2,000 killed and wounded. On February 23, the Union Army of the Ohio under Major General Don Carlos Buell captured Nashville, the first southern state capital to fall outside of the Border States.[29]

Grant's triumphs gave the Union its first major victories of the war. Grant instantly became a national hero and won a promotion to major general, while the northern press rechristened his first two initials to stand for "Unconditional Surrender" Grant.[30] The fall of the two forts cost the Confederacy dearly. The stunning defeats eliminated roughly a third of Johnston's forces and resulted in the loss of the irreplaceable Cumberland Iron Works at Clarksville, Tennessee, exceeded only by Richmond's Tredegar Iron Works in production, and Nashville, a critical rail and manufacturing center that had already produced more than 100,000 pounds of gunpowder for Confederate armies. The retreating Rebels had to abandon most of the rich agricultural area of Middle and West Tennessee, and Grant's victories also threatened to cut off Polk's garrison at Columbus, Kentucky, which had been so costly to occupy in the first place. The evacuation of Columbus opened the Mississippi River free to Union navigation as far south as the Confederate bastion on Island No. 10 in the Missouri boothill.[31]

At the same time across the river, in the first two months of 1862, the Union Army of the Southwest under Brigadier General Samuel R. Curtis drove Major General Sterling Price's Missouri State Guard out of the southwestern corner of Missouri and into northwestern Arkansas. Uniting with a separate Confederate army under Brigadier General Benjamin McCulloch and under the overall command of Van Dorn, the hastily created Confederate Army of the West audaciously attacked Curtis on March 7–8 at the Battle of Pea Ridge (or Elkhorn Tavern), Arkansas. Curtis repulsed Van Dorn's ill-planned offensive and won a decisive victory that saved Missouri for the Union. Curtis's stubborn stand at Pea Ridge allowed the riverine invasions to continue east of the Mississippi River and enabled his army to secure the northern half of Arkansas.[32]

After Grant had captured the forts that defended the core area of the Confederacy west of the Appalachians, he commanded the resulting Union advance down the Tennessee River upon the critical rail junction of Corinth, Mississippi. Corinth contained the sole intersection of the Memphis and Charleston Railroad, labeled the "vertebrae of the Confederacy" by Confederate Secretary of War Leroy Walker, with the Mobile and Ohio Railroad, which provided a valuable link to the southern Gulf coast.[33] The crossroads at Corinth were indispensable to the transport of supplies from the Trans-Mississippi region to the eastern half of the Confederacy and would present a key supply base for the North to continue their offensive into the Mississippi River valley. In a desperate gamble to halt the threatening Union invasion and regain lost territory, Johnston concentrated some 43,968 men at Corinth to attack Grant's 39,830 Federals encamped nearby at Pittsburg Landing, Tennessee, hoping to strike before the Army of the Tennessee could be reinforced by Buell's

35,000-man Army of the Ohio. On April 6, Johnston's Army of the Mississippi attacked and caught the Yankees completely by surprise, capturing several Union camps and thousands of prisoners before driving the remainder of Grant's army back to a final defensive line protecting Pittsburg Landing and the precious link to Buell's rapidly arriving army across the Tennessee River. The fateful death of Johnston and the inevitable confusion of war prevented a final assault that might have captured the landing before nightfall, and on the ensuing second day of battle, the heavily reinforced Union army counterattacked and drove back the exhausted Confederates. The Army of the Mississippi, now led by Johnston's second in command General Pierre G. T. Beauregard, limped back to Corinth after enduring some 10,699 killed, wounded, and missing. The Federals, having lost 13,047 men, gave only a halfhearted pursuit and allowed the retreating Rebels to escape.[34]

The battle of Shiloh nearly destroyed Grant's Army of the Tennessee, but a heroic defense and the timely arrival of the Army of the Ohio saved Union forces from destruction. Shiloh was the first battle of the Civil War to claim more than 23,000 casualties, more than had been lost in all previous American Wars. The carnage of the battle stunned the nation and proved to all observers that the war would be long and costly. The near disaster also almost ended Grant's career, whom the capricious press now named "Ulysses Surprise Grant" and severely criticized for his failure in preparing an adequate defense against a possible Confederate assault.[35] Following the battle, Halleck arrived and took personal command of the combined Union armies advancing upon Corinth, leaving Grant regulated as a nominal second in command with little to do. As Grant recalled in his memoirs, "For myself I was little more than an observer. Orders were sent direct to the right wing or the reserve, ignoring me, and advances were made from one line of intrenchments to another without notifying me." Grant admitted after the war that "my position was so embarrassing in fact that I made several applications during the siege to be relieved."[36]

On May 29, Beauregard evacuated Corinth after an extended siege. A few days after the Union army occupied the crucial rail junction, Sherman learned that Grant had requested a 30-day leave. As Grant prepared to embark for St. Louis, Sherman asked his old friend why he was leaving. Grant answered, " 'Sherman, you know. You know that I am in the way here. I have stood it as long as I can, and can endure it no longer.' " When Sherman asked if Grant had any "business" in St. Louis, Grant replied, " 'Not a bit.' "[37] Sherman reminded Grant of his own previous troubles with the press and persuaded his fellow Ohioan to forestall his leave to see if his fortunes would improve. A few days later, when Grant informed

Sherman of his decision to remain with the army, Sherman wrote in his reply, "You could not be quiet at home for a week when armies were moving, and rest could not relieve your mind of the gnawing sensation that injustice had been done you."[38] In Washington, public outcry over the bloodshed of Shiloh resulted in a chorus of detractors calling for Grant's removal from command. Despite the criticism, President Lincoln wisely retained the aggressive general, saying, " 'I can't spare this man; he fights.' "[39]

Meanwhile, the Western Gunboat Flotilla continued their assault down the Mississippi River. On March 14, Union Major General John Pope and his 20,000-man Army of the Mississippi captured New Madrid, Missouri, threatening the Confederate defenses at Island No. 10. Pope lacked the means to land on the Tennessee shore until Union Colonel J. W. Bissel discovered that the adjacent Wilson's Bayou could be lengthened into a canal that would enable the necessary transports to bypass the Confederate batteries. Since the heavier gunboats could not clear the shallow water of the canal, on the night of April 4, the ironclad *Carodelet* successfully steamed past the guns defending Island No. 10, and on April 6, the *Pittsburg* did the same, allowing the Federals to cut off the escape of some 7,000 Confederate defenders. On April 7, the stronghold surrendered to Foote, which opened the river as far south as Fort Pillow, 40 miles north of Memphis. By June 3, Fort Pillow had been evacuated, and on June 6, the Union fleet crushed a small flotilla of Rebel "cottonclads" in the naval battle of Memphis. Memphis surrendered that same day to the Union fleet now under Captain Charles H. Davis, as by this point Foote had departed on medical leave. The hero of Fort Henry and the early river battles died from Bright's disease on June 26, leaving Davis to carry on the campaign to conquer the mighty Mississippi River. Soon thereafter, Curtis's Union Army of the Southwest captured the river port of Helena, Arkansas, on July 12, 1862, leaving no other major Confederate defenses upstream of Vicksburg.[40]

The U.S. Navy had also been active along the southern end of the Mississippi River. In 1862, the city of New Orleans contained a population approaching 170,000 citizens, making it the principal metropolis and most important port in the Confederacy. Its yearly trade surpassed $185,000,000, and in the entire United States, only New York City's harbor saw more business than the docks of New Orleans. In addition to commerce, the Crescent City contained several vital industrial resources the Confederacy needed for survival, such as manufacturing and shipbuilding facilities. Downstream of New Orleans, two outdated brick forts, Forts Jackson and St. Philip, stood guard along with a small makeshift naval fleet of a few small boats and two unfinished ironclads, the *Louisiana* and *Mississippi*. Between the two forts lay an obstruction of chains, timber, and debris designed to prevent Union warships from repeating Foote's tactic at Island No. 10 of sailing through the defending artillery barrage. After months of preparations, Flag Officer David G. Farragut and the warships of the West Gulf Blockading Squadron ascended the mouth of the Mississippi River to attack the largest city in the Confederacy. On April 18, the guns of Farragut's mortar schooners began bombarding the two forts, and on the night of April 20, Farragut's forces attempted to rupture the barrier but ultimately failed and retreated. On the night of April 24, Farragut's fleet once again assaulted the channel obstruction and this time successfully breeched the barrier, opening the way for the squadron to steam past the forts. After enduring a thrilling nocturnal battle, by 4:40 A.M. on April 25, Farragut's flotilla had survived the gauntlet of fire and arrived upstream of the forts with the loss of only one gunboat, the *Varuna*. The opposing Confederate fleet had been totally destroyed. On April 29, the city of New Orleans surrendered to Farragut, and on May 1, a Union occupation force of 15,000 soldiers arrived under Major General Benjamin Butler. From there, the West Gulf Blockading Squadron sailed upriver to Baton Rouge, capturing the Louisiana state capital on May 9 and Natchez, Mississippi, on May 12.[41]

On May 18, 1862, Farragut's seemingly unstoppable fleet appeared below Vicksburg, Mississippi. When Farragut demanded the city's surrender, the military governor of Vicksburg, Lieutenant Colonel James L. Autrey, declared, "Mississippians don't know, and refuse to learn, how to surrender to an enemy. If Commodore Farragut or Brigadier-General [Benjamin F.] Butler can teach them, let them come and try."[42] The Confederates had only recently begun constructing defenses at Vicksburg, which contained the only defensible position on the Mississippi River south of Memphis. The city's 250-foot bluffs dominated a horseshoe bend of the river, meaning that Union warships would have to fight the current of the Mississippi River in order to navigate a 180-degree turn around De Soto Point while under fire from Confederate batteries. To the east from Vicksburg ran the Southern Railroad of Mississippi, which connected the city to the state capital of Jackson and from there to the major armies of the Confederacy. To the west across De Soto Point ran the Vicksburg, Shreveport, and Texas Railroad, which had been completed as far as Monroe, Louisiana. The river port also contained the A. M. Paxton and A. B. Reading foundries, two essential resources that produced cannon and munitions for the southern war effort. Although the commander of Vicksburg, Brigadier General Martin L. Smith, had only 18 cannon and some

3,600 men when Farragut arrived, work parties labored furiously to add more as reinforcements arrived, and eventually the "Hill City" would boast 50 cannon trained on the river. Farragut, realizing that he had reached the end of his logistical rope and lacked the manpower to attack the city, reluctantly retreated to New Orleans on May 26.[43]

The defenders of Vicksburg did not have to wait long for the Union navy to return. On June 18, Farragut's fleet once again sallied forth against the southern citadel, reinforced by the mortar flotilla under Commander David Dixon Porter and some 3,300 men commanded by Brigadier General Thomas Williams. Farragut immediately began a sporadic shelling of the city, and on June 27, Williams's men began digging a canal across De Soto Point in an effort to bypass the heavily fortified Vicksburg bluffs. Although Williams added more than 1,000 freed slaves to the work parties, the canal operation collapsed when water levels in the river dropped due to a lengthy drought across the region and large numbers of laborers fell victim to the pestilential fevers native to the area. With too few soldiers to either complete the canal or attempt an amphibious assault on Vicksburg, Williams suspended the effort on July 24. Still, the failed canal operation did sever the railroad across De Soto Point, forcing future supplies from the Trans-Mississippi to be transported down the Red River to Vicksburg. While Farragut bombarded Vicksburg from downstream, a portion of Davis's gunboat squadron arrived upstream of the city on June 24. Excited by the prospect of conquering the entire river, Farragut determined to repeat his New Orleans tactic of steaming his ships past the Confederate batteries. In the predawn darkness of June 28, a few of Farragut's saltwater warships survived an intense barrage of fire from the Vicksburg river defenses and safely sailed alongside the distinctive gunboats. The brown-water navy of the Western Gunboat Flotilla had finally made contact with the blue-water navy of the West Gulf Blockading Squadron. Still, despite Farragut's bombardments and dramatic exploits, the defenders of Vicksburg stubbornly refused to surrender.[44]

On the day before Farragut's ships raced past the batteries, Major General Earl Van Dorn arrived to assume command of the Vicksburg defenses. A native of Port Gibson, Mississippi, Van Dorn now commanded Confederate forces 27 miles away from his birthplace. In January, Davis had appointed him commander of the District of the Trans-Mississippi, where he had rashly marched to catastrophe at the Battle of Pea Ridge. After the Pea Ridge debacle, Van Dorn heeded Beauregard's request for reinforcements for the Army of the Mississippi then assembling at Corinth and promptly transferred his army across the Mississippi. Seeking to remove the stain of Pea Ridge from his military reputation, Van Dorn immediately began preparations to drive the invaders away from his home. Fortunately for the Confederacy, an unfinished ironclad, the CSS *Arkansas*, had been rescued from Memphis before it fell to Federal gunboats. After being relocated to the Yazoo River, Confederate shipbuilders finished the warship with rustic ingenuity. The *Arkansas* mounted 10 guns secured behind ersatz armor of railroad iron but relied upon recycled and unreliable engines to power the ship. In late June, Lieutenant Isaac Brown determined to give his ship a trial run by storming through the 33 Union ships besieging Vicksburg.[45]

On July 15, Brown finished his preparations and ordered the *Arkansas* to steam to Vicksburg. As the *Arkansas* sailed down the Yazoo River, three Union vessels—the ironclad *Carondelet*, the timberclad *Tyler*, and the ram *Queen of the West*—challenged the Confederate monster. In a brief battle, the *Arkansas* quickly ran the *Carondelet* aground and forced the other two remaining gunboats to beat a hasty retreat back to the unsuspecting Union fleet. The *Arkansas* pursued the fleeing Federal warships into the Mississippi River and then turned south, sailing through the midst of Farragut's astounded armada. After a furious battle, Brown and his crew arrived safely under the protection of the Vicksburg river batteries. An infuriated Farragut attempted to attack the *Arkansas* at Vicksburg on July 22, but the defending Confederate artillery drove back the northern assault. Southern morale soared when soldiers and civilians on the hills of Vicksburg witnessed the *Arkansas*'s fiery passage through a floating inferno. Farragut's fleet, embarrassed by the *Arkansas* affair, threatened by falling water levels, and ravaged by disease, retreated southward on July 24. The Western Gunboat Flotilla returned north soon after, and the naval siege of Vicksburg ended in a Confederate triumph.[46]

When the Federal navy abandoned their aquatic assault on Vicksburg, Van Dorn instantly initiated a counteroffensive to recapture Baton Rouge. Now commanding a reinforced army of 15,000, Van Dorn ordered Major General John C. Breckinridge to take 4,000 men to liberate the Louisiana state capital while the *Arkansas* sailed downstream to provide naval support. If the Confederate offensive succeeded, a new defensive barrier on the Mississippi River would be established below Vicksburg, and perhaps even New Orleans might be retaken as well. However, Breckinridge's march bogged down in the swamps, and soon almost half of his command had fallen ill with the same deadly fevers that had afflicted the Federals. On August 3, the *Arkansas* proceeded southward to cooperate with Breckinridge, but its secondhand engines failed before the ironclad ever reached Baton Rouge, and the vessel had to be scuttled to prevent its capture by Union gunboats. On August 5, Breckinridge assaulted General Williams and his roughly 2,500-man garrison of Baton Rouge. Although the Union commander died in the battle, without the *Arkansas*, the Rebels had to fall back after bitter fighting. Despite the abortive attack, Van Dorn did fortify the bluffs near Port Hudson, Louisiana, which provided a critical stronghold south of Vicksburg and the mouth of the Red River. As long the Confederates could keep the Union navy from threatening this stretch of the river, the vital flow of supplies from the Trans-Mississippi would continue.[47]

The seemingly endless series of Confederate military disasters in early 1862, culminating in the devastating loss of New Orleans and the abandonment of Corinth, combined with Union Major General George McClellan's peninsula campaign in Virginia, pressed the Confederacy to the brink of total defeat. To many observers, the end of the war was in sight. By the late summer of 1862, the Confederacy possessed only a precarious 100-mile section of the Mississippi River between Vicksburg and Port Hudson. Grant recalled after the war that by this point, "the Confederates at the west were narrowed down for all communications with Richmond to the single line of road running east from Vicksburg. To dispossess them of this, therefore, became a matter of the first importance." As the Union general affirmed, "The possession of the Mississippi by us from Memphis to Baton Rouge was also a most important object. It would be equal to the amputation of a limb in its weakening effects upon the enemy."[48]

For the Confederacy, reversing this tide of defeat would take inspired leadership, brilliant strategy, and quite a bit of luck. In the eastern theater, Davis appointed his senior military adviser General Robert E. Lee to replace a wounded General Joseph E. Johnston in command of the Army of Northern Virginia opposing McClellan's Army of the Potomac outside of Richmond. In the western theater, the Confederate president promoted General Braxton Bragg to command the Army of the Mississippi after the evacuation from Corinth when Beauregard left active duty temporarily due to ill health. Bragg reorganized and restored the army to effective fighting condition after it had endured the slaughter of Shiloh and the scourge of disease in Corinth. In late July, as the triumphant Federals diverted their attention to seizing Chattanooga and repairing damaged railroads, Confederate cavalry raids by Colonel John Hunt Morgan and Brigadier General Nathan Bedford Forrest unleashed havoc on Union supply lines. When Buell's advance on Chattanooga stalled, Bragg boldly divided his forces in an attempt to regain the strategic initiative. In one of the most impressive logistical operations of the war, Bragg transported more than 30,000 men by rail 776 miles to East Tennessee and soon began a daring invasion of Kentucky in collaboration with an 18,000-man army commanded by Major General Edmund Kirby Smith. The ambitious incursion into Kentucky occurred in conjunction with General Robert E. Lee's invasion of Maryland after his victory at the Battle of Second Manassas. At the same time, a separate Confederate army under Van Dorn and Sterling Price embarked upon a counteroffensive in northern Mississippi in an attempt to prevent Union reinforcements from being sent to oppose Bragg and recapture the important crossroads at Corinth. For the only time during the war, the Confederacy attempted to coordinate multiple offensives across the continent. In one of the most dramatic reversals of the war, over the summer of 1862, the Confederacy rose like a phoenix from the brink of defeat to the edge of victory.[49]

On September 19, a combined Union expedition under Grant and Major General William S. Rosecrans confronted Sterling Price's two divisions at Iuka, Mississippi, and in a savage battle, both sides suffered serious losses. Grant and Rosecrans reported their loss as 141 killed, 613 wounded, and 36 missing, which equaled 790 total casualties. Price admitted 85 killed, 410 wounded, and 157 missing, but Union burial parties documented 265 Rebel dead on the battlefield. This testimony, when combined with evidence from other sources, raises estimated Confederate casualties to 1,000 or more. In late September, Van Dorn and Price united their forces in the optimistically named Army of West Tennessee for an assault on Corinth. Van Dorn's recently created army contained a large number of regiments from the Trans-Mississippi states, including many veterans of Wilson's Creek, Pea Ridge, and Iuka. On October 3, Van Dorn attacked and drove Union defenders from two outer defensive lines to a final line surrounding the town. On the battle's second day, the Magnolia State native ordered a desperate frontal assault on elaborately prepared Federal fortifications that came tantalizingly close to success but ultimately ended in bloody failure. The Battle of Corinth took a deadly toll on both sides. Rosecrans recorded 355 men killed, 1,841 wounded, and 324 missing in the battle, or 2,520 total casualties. Exact Confederate losses are unknown but are estimated to be around 505 men killed, 2,150 wounded, and 2,183 missing, with perhaps 400 to 500 casualties incurred on the retreat from Corinth. Van Dorn's impetuous assaults cost his army roughly 5,000 men out of the 22,000 soldiers who marched to Corinth, for a casualty rate of over 20 percent. In certain units, the sacrifice reached appalling levels. Brigadier General John C. Moore's brigade endured 1,295 casualties out of 1,892 present for duty, or just over 60 percent of the brigade's strength. After engaging in intense fighting on the first day of the battle and spearheading a forlorn charge against Battery

Robinett on October 4, the 2nd Texas Infantry tallied a butcher's bill of roughly 200 men out of 324 taken into combat.[50]

The carnage at Corinth devastated the Confederate army in Mississippi, which never fully recovered from the defeat in terms of manpower or morale.[51] After the war, Sherman asserted that the Battle of Corinth was "a decisive blow to the Confederate cause in our quarter, and changed the whole aspect of affairs in West Tennessee. . . . In Memphis I could see its effects upon the citizens, and they openly admitted that their cause had sustained a death-blow."[52] After the battle, Louisiana Sergeant Edwin H. Fay wrote to his wife, "I think the cause of the Confederacy is lost in this West. . . . I am almost in despair as regards our cause. . . . I tell you Sarah that I am whipped now."[53] While initially successful in endangering Union control of the Border States, all of the simultaneous Confederate offensives in the fall of 1862 ended in defeat at the brutal battles at Antietam (or Sharpsburg), Maryland; Corinth, Mississippi; and Perryville, Kentucky. After so much incredible hardship and staggering bloodshed, the Rebels had gained little but glory and new battle honors to inscribe on their war-torn flags.[54]

The Battle of Corinth firmly yielded the strategic initiative to the Union in the Mississippi River valley. As Grant noted in his memoirs, the Battle of Corinth "relieved me from any further anxiety for the safety of the territory within my jurisdiction, and soon after receiving reinforcements I suggested to the general-in-chief [Major General Henry W. Halleck] a forward movement against Vicksburg."[55] On October 16, 1862, Grant received command of the recently created Union Department of the Tennessee, with authority to requisition reinforcements and supplies from the Department of the Missouri across the Mississippi River. On November 26, 1862, he launched his first campaign to capture Vicksburg by marching southward along the Mississippi Central Railroad from northern Mississippi.[56] The Rebels in Mississippi would soon prove that Vicksburg would not be taken without a desperate struggle.

2

—∞∞∞—

"A series of experiments"

On October 14, 1862, President Jefferson Davis appointed Lieutenant General John C. Pemberton to command of the Department of Mississippi and East Louisiana. Van Dorn, infuriated at being removed as army commander, demanded a court of inquiry to restore his reputation after the Battle of Corinth. Although eventually acquitted by the court, Van Dorn never again led an army in the field. In December, Pemberton reassigned the impulsive Mississippian to lead a cavalry division, where Van Dorn finally found a position far better suited to his martial abilities. Pemberton, a Philadelphian by birth and 1837 graduate of the United States Military Academy, cast his lot with the Confederacy in 1861 while his two younger brothers served in the Union army. Although he had married into a prominent Virginia family and considered the Old Dominion State his adopted home, Pemberton's subordinates and many civilians in Vicksburg never fully trusted the Pennsylvania Rebel due to his northern birth. Pemberton had seen extensive combat in the Mexican War but had never before commanded an army in a major battle. Nonetheless, Davis entrusted Pemberton to defend one of the most important positions in the Confederacy. In contrast to Van Dorn's reckless nature, Pemberton acquired a reputation as an able administrator but cautious commander.[1]

When Bragg had succeeded Beauregard as commander of the Army of the Mississippi, Davis had separated the states west of the Mississippi River from his authority by creating the Department of the Trans-Mississippi and replacing the previous commander of the region, Van Dorn, with Major

General Theophilus Holmes. An aged officer of 58 years, Holmes had previously performed poorly in the Seven Days campaign outside of Richmond, and like so many other Confederate officers who had failed to distinguish themselves in Virginia, he received a transfer to the West. Shortly after promoting Pemberton to command Vicksburg, Davis appointed General Joseph E. Johnston to command the newly created Department of the West on November 24. Johnston had been one of the heroes of First Manassas in 1861 and had commanded the Army of Northern Virginia until his wounding at Seven Pines. Now recovered, Johnston returned to duty to provide Davis with the unified command of the Confederate armies in the western theater that had been lacking since the death of Albert Sidney Johnston. As the ranking general in the theater, Johnston had the ability to transfer men from Bragg or Pemberton and to command either army in person if he so desired. However, Johnston approached his new assignment with hesitation and a seething resentment of Davis, with whom he had maintained a long-standing feud since the beginning of the war. Unlike Albert Sidney Johnston, neither Joseph E. Johnston nor Pemberton had the ability to command Holmes's forces or order him to transport reinforcements across the Mississippi River. Establishing the Mississippi River as a boundary between competing departments hampered cooperation between Confederate armies on either side and would later play a key role in the Vicksburg campaign. Fortunately for the Union, Lincoln did not make the same mistake Davis did.[2]

Pemberton's department contained an estimated 43,000 men, scattered in various garrisons and comprised of men from the states of Mississippi, Louisiana, Tennessee, Alabama, Georgia, Arkansas, Missouri, Texas, Maryland, and Virginia. While several of these units, such as the 2nd Texas Infantry, the 3rd Louisiana Infantry, and the First Missouri Brigade, could claim elite status, Pemberton's command also contained multiple elements with poor morale and inadequate training. Undoubtedly, the chronic infighting that arose among the higher-ranking officers and Pemberton's inability to unite his fractious subordinates represented the Pennsylvanian's greatest weakness. Ultimately, such backbiting and bickering would grievously affect the army in subsequent battles. Although it took some time for him to become familiar with his new department, by the early spring of 1863 Pemberton had organized the Army of Vicksburg into five divisions, led by Major Generals Martin L. Smith, Carter L. Stevenson, John H. Forney, John S. Bowen, and William W. Loring, along with the Vicksburg river battery defenses under Colonel Edward Higgins.[3] Pemberton's arrival, though celebrated in the newspapers, did not inspire confidence among the enlisted men. On December 9, Louisianan Sergeant

Edwin Fay informed his wife that Pemberton "is the most insignificant 'puke' I ever saw and will be very unpopular as soon as known. His head cannot contain sense enough to command a Regt. much less a Corps. Oh what will our Country come to, when we are cursed with such worthless Commanders."[4] A few days later, Fay complained that General Pemberton had "the most unintellectual *pukish* countenance of any man in the army" and that "he is not worth shucks. He has not sense enough to command a company, judging by his looks. Our army is disgracefully treated by being put under such commanders as Pemberton and Van Dorn."[5]

Pemberton did have the advantage of defending one of the most heavily fortified cities in the Confederacy. In June 1862, Major Samuel Lockett entered Vicksburg to serve as an engineer under General Martin L. Smith and on November 1 became the chief engineer of the Department of Mississippi and East Louisiana. Lockett, who graduated second in the West Point class of 1859, spent a month examining the series of hills, hollows, and ravines surrounding the town and devised a complex defensive line bristling with artillery along the ridges surrounding the eastward approaches to Vicksburg.[6] As he recalled, "No greater topographical puzzle was ever presented to an engineer. . . . At first it seemed impossible to find anything like a general line of commanding ground surrounding the city; but careful study gradually worked out the problem."[7] Most of the rolling terrain outside of Vicksburg had never been cleared of magnolia forests and wild canebrakes, which made Lockett's mission even more challenging. Beginning on September 1, work parties of slaves and free blacks cleared the land and constructed an elaborate series of fortifications stretching some eight miles around Vicksburg, consisting of nine strong-points with clear fields of fire protected by abatis and other obstructions. Lockett designed "a system of redoubts, redans, lunettes, and small-field-works" connected by trenches "to give a continuous line of defense" with both flanks secured by the Mississippi River.[8] Lockett also oversaw the building of fortifications along the bluffs north of town and at Warrenton, Mississippi, five miles downstream of Vicksburg.[9]

In November, Grant began his first offensive to capture Vicksburg by marching south from Grand Junction, Tennessee, with an army of 40,000 men. Grant's route would take the Army of the Tennessee down the Mississippi Central Railroad south to Jackson, from which he would turn west to attack Vicksburg from the rear. Grant intended to repair and utilize the railroad to maintain his supply lines, and the Union advance quickly drove Pemberton back behind the Tallahatchie River. In late November, Brigadier General Alvin Hovey and 7,000 men from the Department of the Missouri crossed the Mississippi River at Helena in a raid intended to damage the Mississippi Central Railroad and disrupt Pemberton's supply lines. Hovey's incursion failed to destroy the railroad bridge over the Yalobusha River but did persuade Pemberton to retreat from the Tallahatchie 60 miles to Grenada, south of the Yalobusha.[10]

That November, Grant also learned that his subordinate, Major General John McClernand, had obtained permission from President Lincoln the month before to raise an army from the midwestern states to complete the conquest of the Mississippi River. McClernand, a Democratic congressman from Lincoln's own district in Illinois, owed his rank to his political connections rather than his abilities as a commander. McClernand, like Lincoln, had served as a volunteer in the Black Hawk War, but the Illinois Democrat had no other professional military training. Despite his lack of martial education, McClernand had fought bravely, if not brilliantly, under Grant at Fort Donelson and Shiloh. After the battle of Shiloh, the ambitious McClernand began scheming to gain command of an expedition to capture Vicksburg. While Halleck had distrusted Grant after Shiloh, the general in chief had less respect for the inexperienced McClernand, whose vain personality won few friends among the West Pointed–trained officer class. As McClernand traveled the Old Northwest on a recruiting tour, he dispatched his hastily raised regiments to Memphis, in Grant's department.[11] When Grant wired Washington to clarify if he did indeed command the recently arrived regiments, Halleck replied on November 11, "You have command of all troops sent to your Department, and have permission to fight the enemy when you please."[12] Grant, who outranked McClernand, quickly organized and ordered the new regiments into the field.[13]

Pleased by his support from Halleck, Grant pushed on southward into the interior of Mississippi and its defiant population. Sergeant Ira Blanchard, a soldier in the 20th Illinois Infantry, recalled, "The people along the road displayed the white flag from their houses in token of submission, but if a soldier should approach a dwelling the women would almost invariably cry from the windows, 'Smallpox here, dare you come in?' "[14] Blanchard and his comrades soon "caught on to the dodge" and would forage for food at civilian residences regardless of the supposed quarantine. Blanchard frankly admitted that "if they had any hams in the smokehouse, or any chickens, they were very apt to suffer."[15] On December 8, Grant ordered his most trusted subordinate, Sherman, to lead an assault from the Yazoo River on the bluffs north of Vicksburg with 32,000 men before McClernand arrived. Sherman would take one division of his own command and the unbloodied regiments gathered in Memphis, along with some 13,000 soldiers stationed in Helena.[16] On December 6, Sherman

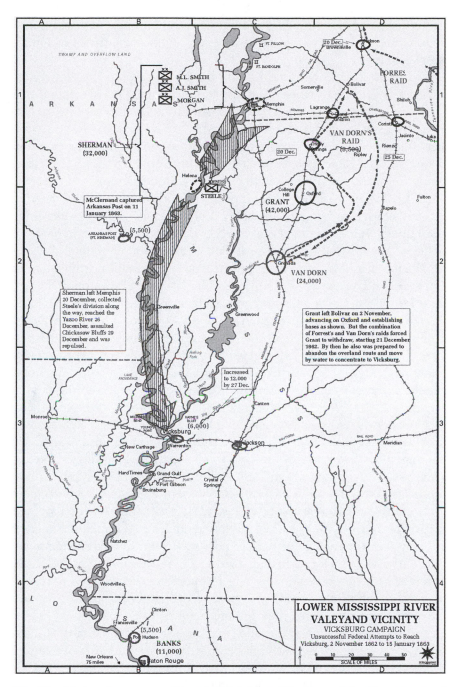

The First Union Attempts to Capture Vicksburg. (Courtesy of the Department of History, United States Military Academy)

had written to his brother of the importance of eliminating the Red River supply line, which would sever "the Texas supplies of cattle of which we find some here."[17]

While Sherman organized his amphibious invasion, Braxton Bragg unleashed Brigadier General Nathan Bedford Forrest on his second raid into West Tennessee, which caused chaos along Grant's supply lines on the Mississippi Central and Mobile and Ohio Railroads. From December 15 until New Year's Day, Forrest's cavalry stormed throughout western Tennessee and Kentucky, destroying track, burning supplies, severing telegraph lines, and inflicting more than 1,500 Union casualties. At the same time, Lieutenant Colonel John Griffin of the 6th Texas Cavalry reported to Pemberton that Grant's vast supply depot at Holly Springs, Mississippi, presented a vulnerable target for another daring cavalry raid. Pemberton assigned the mission to Van Dorn, who rode with a 3,500-man division of Texans, Tennesseans, Mississippians, and Missourians northward from Grenada on December 17. On December 20, Van Dorn's men charged into Holly Springs at sunrise, completely surprising the defenders and capturing nearly the entire garrison of 1,500 men. The mountain of Federal supplies at the well-stocked depot stunned the ill-fed and thread-bare Rebels. As Private Samuel Barron of the 3rd Texas Cavalry remembered, "A mere glace at the stores—heaps upon heaps of clothing, blankets, provisions, arms, ammunition, medicines, and hospital supplies for the winter, all for the use and comfort of a vast army—was overwhelming to us. We had never seen anything like it before."[18] For 10 hours, the Confederates labored to demolish the supply base, and Van Dorn estimated the damage they inflicted to be worth $1.5 million. After the capture of Holly Springs, Van Dorn continued his raid into West Tennessee before escaping south back into Confederate lines to much acclaim. Van Dorn had finally won an impressive victory, and the dramatic raid somewhat restored his tarnished military reputation.[19] As Grant stated in his memoirs, the twin Confederate raids "cut me off from all communication with the north for more than a week, and it was more than two weeks before rations or forage could be issued from stores obtained in the regular way."[20] After such a stunning display of the effectiveness of southern cavalry, Grant abandoned the overland campaign.[21]

Still, despite the retreat, the failed offensive enlightened Grant with the ability of his army to sustain itself by foraging from the local community. Rather than be limited by tenuous supply lines for provisions and forage, Grant learned that he could rely upon civilian resources to feed his army temporarily. This insight significantly increased the mobility of the Army of the Tennessee and had a tremendous impact upon his future operations.

Although Samuel Curtis's Army of the Southwest had survived off the Arkansas countryside for two weeks in the summer of 1862, Grant apparently had been unaware of Curtis's accomplishment or may have remained skeptical of such irregular logistical practices until he witnessed their value firsthand.[22] Grant's soldiers had long been supplementing their rations by foraging even before Van Dorn destroyed the Holly Springs depot. A newspaper correspondent from the *New York Herald*, Thomas W. Knox, reported that "our soldiers foraged at will on the plantations near our camp. The quantities of supplies that were brought in did not argue that the country had been previously visited by an army. Mules, horses, cattle, hogs, sheep, chickens, and other things used by an army, were found in abundance."[23] Grant gained valuable experience during those two weeks his army foraged for sustenance that he would later utilize in the following year. He declared after the war that "I was amazed at the quantity of supplies the country afforded. It showed we could have subsisted off the country for two months instead of two weeks without going beyond the limits designated." Grant observed, "Our loss of supplies was great at Holly Springs, but it was more than compensated for by those taken from the country and by the lesson taught."[24] Van Dorn's Holly Springs raid may have been a southern strategic success, but the victory would ultimately have ruinous consequences for both Mississippi's civilian population and the Army of Vicksburg.

While Grant's army marched through the growing chill of December, Sherman's hastily organized assault force sailed southward from Memphis on December 20. On the same day, Van Dorn captured Holly Springs, which ended the overland campaign that Sherman relied upon to distract Pemberton. Now Sherman would have to fight on his own to subdue Fortress Vicksburg against an enemy that could use interior lines to rush reinforcements to an already heavily fortified position. At the same time, a very anxious Jefferson Davis arrived in Vicksburg on an inspection tour of the western theater. Already, Davis and the new commander of the Department of the West, General Joseph E. Johnston, had visited the Army of Tennessee in Murfreesboro. There, Davis refused to heed Johnston's and Bragg's recommendations and ordered Major General Carter Stevenson's 9,000-man division transferred to Pemberton's army, though it would be weeks before Stevenson could unite with his new superior.[25] Davis also sent a forceful request to Holmes for reinforcements to be sent to Vicksburg from the Trans-Mississippi. "Nothing will so certainly conduce to peace as the conclusive exhibition of our power to hold the Mississippi river," argued Davis, "and nothing so diminish our capacity to defend the Trans-Missi. States as the loss of communication between the

States on the Eastern and Western sides of the river."[26] But while Davis had not hesitated to use his authority to overrule Johnston and Bragg to dispatch soldiers from the Army of Tennessee, he did not issue a direct order to Holmes to send troops across the Mississippi River, though the Trans-Mississippi soldiers had less distance to travel than Stevenson's men. Holmes had recently suffered serious losses in the Battle of Prairie Grove on December 7 and refused to transfer manpower across the river, as he could barely maintain control over what Confederate territory remained in Arkansas. Arkansas had already been abandoned once before by Van Dorn during the previous April when he marched to Corinth with the Army of the West along with virtually all stockpiled supplies, weapons, equipment, and machinery in the state. Van Dorn's stripping of the state's defenses had so infuriated Arkansas governor Henry M. Rector that he threatened to secede from the Confederacy. Both Holmes and Davis realized that it would be politically impossible to leave Arkansas undefended again, which meant that little help would be forthcoming from the region to aid Pemberton. Johnston already had a strained relationship with Davis, and as both Bragg and Pemberton continued to report directly to Richmond as well as to Johnston, confusion over conflicting orders and overlapping authority invariably followed. As it turned out, only two of Stevenson's four brigades arrived in time to aid Pemberton, but his 9,000 men would be sorely missed when Bragg challenged Rosecrans at the Battle of Stone's River (or Murfreesboro) at the end of the month.[27]

Earlier that year in October, the Western Gunboat Flotilla had been reorganized as the Mississippi Squadron. On October 15, Commander David Dixon Porter, the adopted brother of Rear Admiral David Farragut, took command of the Union's brown-water navy. To prepare for Sherman's amphibious landing, the Mississippi Squadron entered the Yazoo River on December 12 to clear the waterway of Rebel mines, known during the war as "torpedoes." The operation soon proved costly when one of the ironclads, the USS *Cairo*, struck on of the "infernal machines" and sank in the Yazoo. The crew of the *Cairo* escaped without loss of life, but the ill-fated ironclad had earned the dubious distinction of being the first warship sunk by an electronically detonated mine in naval history.[28] On December 24, urgent reports of a Federal invasion force sailing southward interrupted a Confederate Christmas ball at the Balfour house in Vicksburg, and well-dressed officers rushed from the dance to ready their commands for battle. Porter's gunboats provided naval support for Sherman's transports as they traveled down the Mississippi, and since the pervasive mines prevented a landing at Haynes' Bluff, Sherman disembarked in front of Walnut Hills just north of the city on December 26.

Pemberton remained in overall command at Vicksburg, but he allowed his subordinate Brigadier General Stephen Dill Lee to have tactical control against the Federal onslaught. Lee had recently been transferred west from the Army of Northern Virginia, where the West Point trained artilleryman had proven himself an able and efficient gunner. When Sherman's men reached the shore, Lee had only 3,000 men available, and the Walnut Hills had not yet been fortified. However, Sherman's advance stalled in the mud and Rebel obstructions, granting the Confederates precious time to rush reinforcements in by rail and build imposing earthworks and rifle pits. Lee's hastily constructed defenses lay on the bluffs, overlooking a swampy morass known as Chickasaw Bayou that served as a moat for the almost impregnable position. Forests covered much of the Yazoo river bottom, but the southerners had cleared a large field of fire that turned the Walnut Hills into an artilleryman's dream. Although informed of Van Dorn's raid, Sherman did not learn of Grant's actual retreat until after the battle and apparently believed that his 32,000 men could easily overwhelm whatever opposition Pemberton could muster.[29]

Sherman's expedition consisted of four divisions commanded by Brigadier Generals Andrew J. Smith, George W. Morgan, Frederick Steele, and Morgan L. Smith. On December 29, Sherman ordered a frontal assault against the daunting Rebel line in the Battle of Chickasaw Bayou, which by now contained 14,000 men in the brigades of Brigadier Generals Seth Barton, John Gregg, John C. Vaughn, and Edward D. Tracy and a provisional division under Stephen D. Lee with the brigades of Colonels William T. Withers and Allen Thomas. The provisional division contained a number of Trans-Mississippi units from Louisiana and the 2nd Texas Infantry.[30] The Federals had discovered only a few crossings over the bayou, and when Sherman ordered Morgan to begin the assault, he bluntly announced, "We will lose 5000 men before we take Vicksburg, and may as well lose them here as anywhere else."[31] When Colonel John F. De Courcy learned that his brigade would lead the charge, he mournfully remarked, "My poor brigade!"[32] The Union assault began around 11:00 A.M. after an ineffective cannonade and stumbled through the swamp, only to shot to pieces in front of the earthworks. As General Morgan remembered, "All formations were broken; the assaulting forces were jammed together, and, with a yell of desperate determination, they rushed to the assault and were mowed down by a storm of shells, grape, and canister, and minie-balls which swept our front like a hurricane of fire."[33] In an impressive counterattack, the 26th Louisiana along with part of the 17th Louisiana tore into the Union flank, capturing four regimental flags, 331 prisoners, and 500 rifles. Darkness mercifully put an end to the fighting, and that night the weather turned miserable when a cold rain poured down on the exposed Federals. Sherman refused to order any additional assaults and retreated on January 1–2 after suffering 208 killed, 1,005 wounded, and 563 missing, or 1,776 total casualties. Pemberton reported his loss as 63 killed, 134 wounded, and 10 missing, which equaled 207 casualties.[34] Disease from exposure also ravaged the northern ranks. After the withdrawal, Thomas Townsend of the 23rd Wisconsin Infantry wrote that the campaign "came very near proving the ruin of the 23 Regt" because the men spent "five days in a nasty low swamp without our tents and while there it came a drenching Rain wetting us very nicley in consequence of which our Regt is nearly half sick at the present time."[35] After the bloodletting, Sherman wrote to his wife on January 4, 1863, "It will in the end cost us at least ten thousand lives to take Vicksburg," a figure twice as high as his original estimate.[36]

Grant's retreat and Sherman's defeat could not have come at a worse time for the North. The winter of 1863 saw a dramatic decline in Union morale, which plummeted to perhaps its lowest level of the war. The humiliating defeat at Fredericksburg and a near defeat at Stones River, Tennessee, combined with Sherman's bloody fiasco at Chickasaw Bayou and Grant's retreat in North Mississippi, ended the costly year of 1862 with the major Union armies stalemated. At the same time, Grant found himself distracted by political considerations resulting from the lucrative cotton trade within his department. When northern armies penetrated deeply into the Lower South, they gained access to large amounts of southern cotton that had skyrocketed in price due to the blockade. Smuggling and illegal trading began almost immediately, as speculators purchased cotton and resold it in the North for enormous profits. Unable to stop the trade and hoping to entice occupied southerners back into the Union, the Lincoln administration permitted the Treasury Department to issue a small number of trade permits to loyal planters and merchants. President Davis also reluctantly accepted the traffic, as it provided necessities that the Confederate army desperately needed, such as salt, provisions, and money. Despite the attempted regulation, the extensive cotton trade stimulated bribery and corruption among Union officers in the occupied cities, especially New Orleans and Memphis. Northern merchants paid for much of the cotton in gold, which the Confederate government could then exchange abroad for arms, equipment, and other war material transported by blockade runners. Grant and Sherman deplored the trade, as it aided their enemy, and both considered it to be treasonous. Both generals blamed much of the speculation on Jews, of which a number did participate, but Jewish businessmen hardly constituted a majority of those involved.[37] While in command of Memphis in August, Sherman fumed to Secretary of the Treasury Salmon P. Chase that "the Commercial enterprise of the Jews soon discovered that 10 cts. would buy a pound of Cotton behind our Army, that 4 cts. would take it to Boston where they would receive 30 cents in Gold." Sherman complained that the "bait was too tempting and it spread like fire; when here they discovered that Salt, Bacon, powder, fire arms, percussion Caps &c. were worth as much as Gold, and Strange to Say this traffic was not only permitted but encouraged."[38]

On November 9, Grant ordered Major General Stephen Hurlbut at Jackson, Tennessee, to "refuse all permits to come south of Jackson for the present. The Israelites especially should be kept out."[39] On the next day, he further directed that "no Jews are to be permitted to travel on the railroad southward from any point. They may go north and be encouraged in it; but they are such an intolerable nuisance that the department must be purged of them."[40] As the overland campaign stalled and occupation frustrations mounted, Grant's racist rhetoric escalated, especially when his own father arrived with three Jewish traders seeking to use Grant's connections to profit from the controversial commerce. On December 17, Grant complained to Washington that all his attempts to prohibit the illegal flow of goods had failed, that "the Jews seem to be a privileged class that can travel anywhere," and, he added, "If not permitted to buy cotton themselves they will act as agents for some one else, who will be at a military post with a Treasury permit to receive cotton and pay for it in Treasury notes which the Jew will buy up at an agreed rate, paying gold."[41]

That same day, he issued the infamous General Orders No. 11, which dictated that "the Jews, as a class violating every regulation of trade established by the Treasury Department and also department orders, are hereby expelled from the department within twenty-four hours."[42] While many Americans in the nineteenth century shared Grant's anti-Semitism, this appalling display of intolerance remains the most shameful act the general committed during the war. Grant biographer Jean Edward Smith described the order as "one of the most blatant examples of state-sponsored anti-Semitism in American history."[43] General Orders No. 11 provoked outrage from evicted residents and influential Jewish citizens who brought the matter to President Lincoln's attention. Lincoln promptly forced Grant to rescind the despicable order on January 4. The year 1862 had been a turbulent one for Grant. It began with his spectacular victories at Forts Henry and Donelson, and then the Union hero had been nearly removed from command following the Battle of Shiloh. At the end of 1862, Grant found himself confronted with a stalled campaign, a vicious guerilla conflict, an epidemic of smuggling and corruption, and the vain-glorious ambitions of John McClernand. Although Grant had remained with the army and effectively defended his territory from Confederate counteroffensives, the failure of his first campaign against Vicksburg and the issuing of General Orders No. 11 represent Grant's least impressive performance of the war.[44]

On New Year's Day 1863, the Emancipation Proclamation went into effect, forever altering the nature of the war and significantly affecting Union morale. While many northern soldiers supported Lincoln's mea-sure, a substantial number of Federals from the midwestern and Border States opposed the proclamation or considered it an act of desperation that would only inspire the South to continue the war. These men also bitterly rejected the proposed enlistment of African American soldiers into the Union army. The social implications of the controversial decree angered numerous soldiers who blatantly expressed the intense racial bigotry of the era. Darius Hall Dodd of the 83rd Indiana wrote to his mother from Gaines Landing, Mississippi, on January 8, 1863, "Niggers are plenty[.] Every white man almost in the army has a nigger to cook for him & black his boots. Wash his clothes &c."[45] On March 27, a private in the 97th Indiana Infantry, Andrew Bush, confessed to his wife Mary, "The next proclamation that old Abe puts out I wish he could make it so we could shoot all the negroes we could see for I hate them worse every day." Bush candidly declared, "I intend to shoot one every time that I can get the chance to for I don't think that they are human beings."[46] On February 9, Sergeant Cyrus Boyd of the 15th Iowa noted in his diary, "Poor creatures these contrabands. . . . The men in our camp treat them worse than *brutes* and when they come into camp cries of 'Kill him' 'drown him' &c are heard on every hand[.] The prejudice against the race seems stronger than ever." Boyd denounced those who opposed African American regiments and concluded, "I should like to see all such *idiots* put in the *front* and in the *ditches*[.] If any African will stand between me and a rebel *bullet* he is *welcome* to the honor and the *bullet too*."[47]

Lincoln's proclamation hastened the death of the South's peculiar insti-tution, which had been steadily weakening in the areas conquered by the Union army. While a small number of slaves remained loyal to their own-ers, the vast majority left when Federal armies approached. Colonel Man-ning F. Force of the 20th Ohio documented one example while marching with the Army of the Tennessee. Force's men approached one plantation as slaves plowed the fields and decided to seize the planter's mules. As Force explained, "The soldiers like mules, and the negroes gladly unhar-nessed them, and helped the soldiers to mount. I said to one, 'The soldiers are taking your mules.' The quick response was, 'An' dey is welcome to 'em, sar; dey is welcome to 'em." The colonel remembered that the slaves "looked wistfully at the marching column" and soon left the fields to follow the 20th Ohio on its journey. In the midst of the freed slaves, Force observed that "one tall, stern woman strode along, carrying a wooden tray and a crockery pitcher as all her effects, looking straight to the front. Some one asked, 'Auntie, where are you going?' She answered, without looking, 'I don't car' whicher way I go, so as I git away from dis place."[48] The recently freed slaves acted as laborers, cooks, and servants for the Union army and, from 1863 on, as soldiers. Former slaves also became a vital source of Union intelligence, serving as spies and guides for the Army of the Tennessee on Grant's long march to Vicksburg.[49]

The winter of 1863 also saw an increase in the severity of the interaction between Union soldiers and southern civilians. Historians organize Civil War Mississippi society into multiple hierarchical castes, with a small upper class of elite plantation owners dominating the social order. The middle class consisted of professionals and yeomen farmers, followed by poor whites, while free blacks and slaves made up the lowest class. Federal soldiers treated each class differently based on their political loyalty and level of perceived threat. In many cases, large planters and wealthy slave owners fled before advancing Union armies reached their homes, as they characteristically supported secession and often held high positions in either the local, state, or Confederate governments. In many cases, the aristocrat planters relocated in hopes of preserving as much of their livestock, luxury goods, and slaves from northern armies as possible and to escape potential retribution for their efforts to encourage secession. The middle-class yeomen and poor whites supported either side, depending on their personal circumstances and family history, and generally attempted to preserve their property from the destruction of both armies. The poorest class of white civilians, who had the most to lose in the conflict and little to gain regardless of the outcome, usually endeavored to avert trouble with the military authorities and cast their adaptable allegiance to the side that controlled their local homes and appeared to be winning the war. Authentic southern Unionists constituted a small, repressed minority in the region who generally escaped to the North upon secession or quietly concealed their beliefs until Union armies gained control of their area. Most southern Unionists had a northern background or had recently arrived in the United States as a foreign immigrant.[50]

In 1863, Union military policy regarding southern civilians escalated dramatically. At the outbreak of the war, Federal occupation forces hoped to persuade rebellious southerners to return to the Union by enacting a

policy of conciliation that tried to limit property damage and did not inter-
fere with the institution of slavery. Northern commanders based this strategy upon the belief that the war would be brief and that most ordinary
southerners remained loyal but had been coerced into supporting secession
by a malicious "slaveocracy" of wealthy planters. Early in the conflict, most
Union generals, including Grant and Sherman, issued strict orders against
plundering by soldiers and severely punished offenders if caught. Although
it aided in securing Unionist areas in western Virginia and the Border
States, when the war continued on through 1862 and an easy victory
proved elusive, the policy of conciliation failed.[51] As secessionist support
rose after Confederate victories that summer, Federal forces instituted a
stricter treatment of civilians that historians term "pragmatic." During
the pragmatic phase of the war, Union commanders concentrated on
destroying the Confederate military and "viewed civilians as peripheral
to their concerns."[52] As wartime tensions mounted and a brutal guerilla
conflict erupted in occupied territory, Federal armies began to actively liberate slaves, hold entire communities accountable for guerilla activity, and
permit soldiers to forage for supplies from civilians. After the bitter defeats
of late 1862, most of the northern high command understood that stronger
measures were required to destroy the South's ability and will to continue
the war.[53]

In 1863, Grant and the Army of the Tennessee invented a relentless
type of warfare known as "hard war" on the march to Vicksburg. Grant's
men had become experienced foragers after the Holly Springs raid, and
for the men in the ranks, the transition to hard war was an expected but
clear escalation of the pragmatic policy. Hard war has been defined as
"actions against Southern civilians and property made expressly in order
to demoralize Southern civilians and ruin the Confederate economy, particularly its industries and transportation infrastructure," which "involved
the allocation of substantial military resources to accomplish the job."[54]
In the hard war phase, Union commanders concentrated on destroying
the South's ability to wage war by attacking economic, transportation,
industrial, and military targets. Federal armies eliminated any resource that
could be used to maintain Confederate armies, such as factories, railroad
networks, manufacturing centers, telegraphs, livestock, and agricultural
products. Hard war attacked both government and civilian property, but
Union soldiers usually left occupied homes intact after appropriating livestock and provisions. Additional buildings, such as smokehouses and corn-
cribs, would be ransacked and fence rails burned for fuel. Stored cotton
might also be razed, and all slaves would be freed. Frequently, Union soldiers regarded unoccupied residences as the property of rebels who did

not deserve protection and usually plundered and sometimes burned these houses, especially the large mansions of wealthy planters.[55]

Those citizens who attempted to violently resist Federal foraging parties faced swift retribution and, at the least, most often had their homes burned. In the Mississippi River valley, innocent civilians often lost their homes for the actions of local guerillas and Confederate cavalry, and sometimes entire towns suffered. Although, as historian Mark Grimsley notes, Union commanders "usually sought to punish communities in a firm but controlled fashion, the situation was so inherently volatile that it created an upward spiral of violence. . . . When guerillas fired at Union vessels along the western rivers, it became common practice to go ashore and burn the nearest dwellings."[56] After repeated guerilla attacks, Federal soldiers burned Greenville, Mississippi, and Randolph, Tennessee, to the ground, leaving the residents to endure a precarious existence as wartime refugees.[57] In the Civil War, two types of foraging existed for both armies. Authorized foraging included an organized foraging party of soldiers under the direction of officers who often gave receipts for property collected, though typically only those who could prove unquestionable loyalty to the Union qualified for reimbursement. Unauthorized foraging consisted of a small number of soldiers who seized food and other goods without official permission or the observation of officers. Stragglers and deserters conducted much of the unauthorized foraging and usually bore responsibility for the worst outrages against civilians. In practice, officers assigned to authorized foraging parties tried to limit theft of personal property and other excesses, but the actual restraint observed by the soldiers depended upon the caprice and control of the commanding officer. Although formally prohibited, stealing proved simply impossible to stop, as the least restrained elements of both armies took advantage of the lawlessness created by the war to pilfer from the countryside. As Illinois Sergeant Ira Blanchard recalled in his memoirs, by the spring of 1863, "stealing for the mere fun of the thing had become chronic, and helpless women and children suffered much abuse at the hands of the 'hateful Yankees' as they called us."[58] Blanchard admitted that by this time in the war, "Private property was nowhere respected, and it is no wonder that the inhabitants of the South fled in abject terror at the approach of the 'hordes of the North.'"[59] Areas that endured hard war, such as Central Mississippi, witnessed astounding physical destruction and privation.[60]

During the Civil War, documented rapes by soldiers of either army rarely appear in surviving records, even in the most bitterly contested regions. Such crimes most often occurred in areas under occupation rather than during an actual campaign, and convicted rapists usually faced execution. The ever-present threat of battle kept campaign soldiers fully occupied and under strict discipline, leaving little time or opportunity for sexual outrages to be committed. In contrast, when the dissatisfaction of garrison life combined with boredom and alcohol, soldiers with little to do perpetrated more excesses against civilians. And while few reported rapes appear in court-martial records and other primary sources, that does not necessarily prove they did not happen in an era when such controversial subjects were rarely mentioned.[61] One Confederate diarist, Emilie McKinley, inscribed in her journal on May 23, 1863, that Federal soldiers "came and took nearly all of my provisions, still I took it patiently—but now I have to tell you an act, that will make any gentleman blush." At some later time, an unknown hand removed the next two pages of the entry that detailed the dishonorable deed.[62] Another theory argues that the ready availability of prostitutes that followed the armies may have decreased the number of rapes, though this is disputed.[63] As Sergeant Cyrus F. Boyd of the 15th Iowa noted in his diary on February 16, 1863, "Whiskey and sexual vices carry more soldiers off than the *bullet.*"[64]

Hard war devastated morale and eradicated the will to resist. The Union not only shattered the secessionists' capacity to wage war but also eliminated their desire to sustain the conflict. The lack of protection from marauding Federal armies proved the weakness of the Confederate government, and desertions from units raised in the afflicted areas increased dramatically, further draining Rebel armies. Mississippi soldiers who received letters from home detailing deprivation and destitution often left the army to provide for their families. Mississippi units that recorded an increase in desertions learned firsthand the effectiveness of hard war, and later in the war regiments from Georgia and the Carolinas would endure similar attrition. As the Magnolia State became one of the first areas of the Confederacy to suffer hard war, the scorched landscape foreshadowed the ultimate failure of the secessionist dream. Although most Union forces later left Central Mississippi to conquer other portions of the South, the desolation of hard war rendered this region virtually useless to the Confederacy for the rest of the war.[65]

After Sherman's army retreated from Chickasaw Bayou, McClernand finally arrived to assume command of the Mississippi River expedition on January 3. After consulting with Sherman and Porter, McClernand decided to take his newly named Army of the Mississippi up the Arkansas River to capture the Confederate garrison at Arkansas Post. Arkansas Post, the first capital of Arkansas Territory until 1821, lay on a bend in the Arkansas River some 117 miles downriver from Little Rock and 25 miles from the Mississippi River. Some 5,000 Rebels defended the stronghold under the command of Brigadier General Thomas Churchill, and in late December a small force of Louisiana cavalry from Arkansas Post had seized the unarmed Union transport *Blue Wing* on the White River. In order to remove this menace to Union navigation on the inland rivers, Porter ordered nine gunboats to support McClernand's assault force of more than 30,000 men. The defenses of the post consisted of square-shaped Fort Hindman containing two nine-inch and one eight-inch Columbiad cannon, along with four 10-pound Parrotts and four six-pound smoothbore cannon. Fort Hindman had eight-foot-high earthen walls 18 feet thick fronted by an eight-foot-deep moat with a series of rifle pits and earthworks ranging from the fort to Post Bayou on its western flank. Chains connected to piles driven into the river extended halfway into the Arkansas River from the opposite shore, forcing attacking ships to sail directly in front of the fort's guns. Churchill commanded the three brigades of Colonels Robert Garland, James Deshler, and John W. Dunnington. Garland's brigade consisted of the 6th Texas Infantry, the 24th Texas Cavalry (dismounted), the 25th Texas Cavalry (dismounted), Hart's Arkansas battery, and Denson's company of Louisiana cavalry. Deshler's brigade contained the 10th Texas Infantry, the 15th Texas Cavalry (dismounted), the 17th Texas Cavalry (dismounted), the 18th Texas Cavalry (dismounted), and Haldeman's Texas battery. Dunnington's brigade included the defenders of Fort Hindman along with Crawford's Arkansas Battalion, the 19th Arkansas Infantry, a detachment of the 24th Arkansas Infantry, and Nutt's company of Louisiana cavalry. The garrison of Arkansas Post also contained two independent companies of Texas cavalry, while sailors from the Confederate navy served the heavy guns in Fort Hindman. Camp epidemics had severely reduced the ranks, and fewer than 3,000 Rebels remained healthy enough to shoulder a rifle. While a few regiments had been equipped with rifles, most of the dismounted cavalrymen still relied upon shotguns or smoothbore muskets, effective only at close range.[66] When he arrived at Arkansas Post, Captain Gil McKay of the 17th Texas Cavalry accurately described the position as "Ft. Donelson No. 2."[67] On January 9, the Union fleet arrived and announced their presence by firing a few shells into the Confederate works. The next day, McClernand's two corps landed under the protection of Porter's fleet and attempted to flank the Rebel defensive lines. After failing to find a suitable route through the swamp, McClernand decided to attempt a frontal assault on January 11.[68]

Porter's gunboats had probed Fort Hindman's defenses on January 10 and began intermittently shelling Confederate positions early in the morning on January 11. At 1:00 P.M. on January 11, the Union fleet began a general attack that pounded Fort Hindman into ruin and swiftly knocked out all three heavy cannon. Soon thereafter, Federal soldiers began their assault, with most of the fighting being done by Steele's and Andrew J. Smith's divisions. McClernand's men charged through the abatis and into a ferocious fire from artillery, rifles, muskets, and shotguns. The advance stalled, but the overwhelming number of Federals began to wear down the Rebels, and after Porter's gunboats silenced Fort Hindman, the Union navy and land-based artillery began enfilading the Confederate line. Captain Samuel T. Foster of the 24th Texas Cavalry recalled one shell "killing one man and cutting off both legs of his brother. The one that had his legs shot off turned his body about half way to speak to his brother, not knowing that he was dead. As soon as he saw his brother was dead," Foster remembered, "he takes his pistol (a 6 Shooter) puts it to his head and killed himself."[69] Around 5:00 P.M., white flags appeared over the breastworks. Churchill lost 60 killed and perhaps 75 wounded while inflicting 140 killed, 923 wounded, and 29 missing on the attackers, for a total of 1,092 Union casualties. Despite the heavy losses, McClernand reveled in triumph after capturing "4,791 Confederate soldiers, 7 stands of colors, 17 pieces of artillery, 10 gun carriages, 3,000 stands of small arms, 130 swords, 50 colt pistols, 40 cans of powder, 1,650 rounds of shot, 375 shells, 46,000 rounds of small arms ammunition, and 563 animals."[70] The capture of nearly the entire garrison of Arkansas Post provided the Union with their largest single haul of prisoners since the fall of Island No. 10. Holmes lost almost a quarter of his Arkansas army in the battle, along with a mountain of badly needed supplies and equipment. The defeat further weakened Confederate strength in the Trans-Mississippi and ended any real chance of transferring men across the river to Vicksburg. On January 18, Grant took personal command of the expedition, reducing McClernand to commander of the XIII Corps while Sherman continued to lead the XV Corps.[71] Although he initially had doubts about the operation and informed Halleck that McClernand had "gone on a wild goose chase," Grant later admitted that "when the result was understood I regarded it as very important. Five thousand Confederate troops left in the rear might have caused us much trouble and loss of property while navigating the Mississippi."[72]

Upon arrival, Grant transferred Major General James B. McPherson's XVII Corps to join Sherman and McClernand at Milliken's Bend, Young's Point, and other locations across the Mississippi River from Vicksburg. While encamped there, Grant recalled, "The problem then became, how to secure a landing on high ground east of the Mississippi without an apparent retreat. Then commenced a series of experiments to consume time, and to divert the attention of the enemy, of my troops and of the public

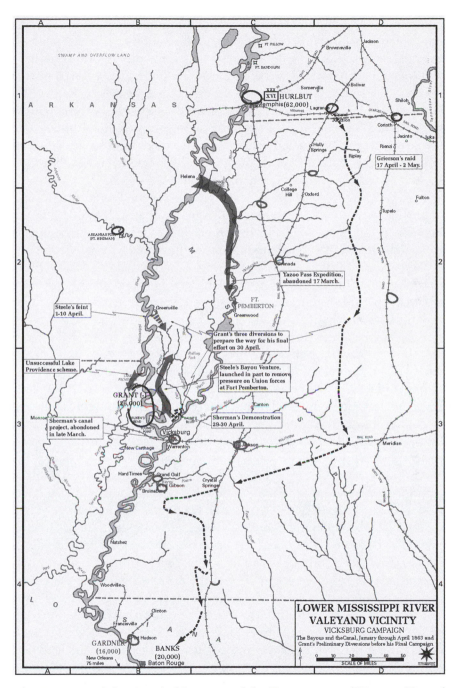

The Bayous and the Canal. (Courtesy of the Department of History, United States Military Academy)

generally."[73] During the winter months, cold weather, heavy rains, and rampaging plagues debilitated the Army of the Tennessee. On February 20, Private Henry Clemons of the 23rd Wisconsin Infantry informed his wife, "I have not been very well for two weeks I have had the shits—that is what we call it here and it is shits and no mistake but I am getting better." He detailed that his unit camped "in A cursed swamp with nothing but the wet ground to sleep on and the water is poison to any one that drinks it . . . they can't keep us here much longer if they do there wont be Enough of us left to swear by." Clemons sadly reported to his hometown, "We have lost 19 men in our company and only three have been killed."[74]

The rising water levels left little dry ground for the Federals to occupy, and while he waited for better campaigning weather in the spring, Grant kept his men occupied with various endeavors to either gain an approach to Vicksburg or find a route circumventing the Rebel bastion. At the end of January, Union engineers restarted work on the canal on De Soto Point that General Williams had begun the previous June and on another canal at Duckport. Although initial efforts appeared promising, the canals failed to function properly, and even if they had, Union ships would still have to sail past Confederate batteries at Warrenton and elsewhere.[75] On January 28, Sherman informed his wife, "Here we are at Vicksburg on the wrong side of the river trying to turn the Mississipi by a ditch, a pure waste of human labor."[76] On February 7, Sherman wrote to Curtis, "Our canal here don't amount to much. It is full of water, but manifests no disposition to change the channel. It is a very small affair, and we can hardly work a barge through it for stumps."[77] At the end of March, Grant gave up on the fruitless venture.[78]

Also in January, Grant began another attempt to bypass Vicksburg by creating a waterway from Lake Providence, Louisiana, to the Red River through a series of bayous and tributaries. For almost two months, McPherson's Corps labored on the project, but the Lake Providence route likewise proved to be futile, and Grant suspended the effort in late March. While soldiers and freed slaves worked on the canals, Grant initiated a new "experiment" with more potential than his first two schemes. On February 2–3, Union engineers breeched a levee at the Yazoo Pass that allowed Porter's gunboats to sail into Moon Lake, from which Union gunboats could then sail into the Coldwater and Tallahatchie Rivers and eventually on to the Yazoo River. From the Yazoo River, Grant's men could land near Haynes' Bluff and approach Vicksburg from the north and east. On February 24, the Yazoo Pass Expedition began when General Brigadier General Leonard Ross led 4,500 men from the XIII Corps accompanied by 10 gunboats under Lieutenant Commander Watson Smith into the flooded channel. Due to the overhanging timber and obstructions felled by retreating Rebels, Smith and Ross advanced slowly on the 700-mile journey, granting Pemberton time to dispatch reinforcements under Major General William W. Loring to oppose the expedition.[79]

Loring's 2,000 men, including the 2nd Texas Infantry and Waul's Texas Legion, quickly built a crude defensive post christened Fort Pemberton, where the Tallahatchie and Yallabusha Rivers unite to form the Yazoo. Confederate engineers constructed Fort Pemberton out of cotton bales covered by earth on a bend in the river channel that could be approached only through a swampy area, and Loring ordered the merchant ship Star of the West scuttled to block Union navigation down the Tallahatchie River. Fort Pemberton lay on ground barely higher than the river but soon mounted eight heavy cannon and substantial earthworks. On three different occasions in March, Smith's gunboats challenged the Confederate defenders of Fort Pemberton, but the stubborn cannoneers repulsed the Union fleet each time.[80] During one of the artillery duels, Loring earned his nickname of "Old Blizzards" when he reportedly shouted, "Give them blizzards, boys! Give them blizzards!"[81] The makeshift bastion did not impress Private Ralph J. Smith of the 2nd Texas Infantry, and the Texan later observed, "This fort was not a brilliant example of military engineering. A shell from a gunboat had exploded a magazine, killing and severely wounding twelve or fifteen men, which occurred soon after our arrival. We always referred to it as a slaughter pen."[82] Soon thereafter, Grant's men opened another breech in the levee opposite Helena, Arkansas, in hopes of flooding Fort Pemberton. The southern outpost survived the deluge, and in early April the Union gunboats steamed back to the Mississippi River, where they had started from in February.[83]

The breaks in the levees on both sides of the river flooded areas of Mississippi and Louisiana, causing extensive property damage and adding further misery to the civilian population. On March 12, Luther H. Cowan wrote to his wife that the breech in the levee for the Lake Providence waterway "will cause hundreds of rich plantations to be deserted by the owners, darkies and all, and destroy millions of dollars worth of property."[84] One eyewitness on the Yazoo Pass Expedition, Lieutenant Henry A. Kircher of the 12th Missouri Infantry, recognized the importance of such economic destruction when he explained to his parents, "I am convinced that we can do much more damage to the South, and thereby bring it to the realization that they were asses and fools to attempt to ruin our country, if our army at the present would concentrate mainly on destroying the Southern plantations and means of production rather than on pressuring them with powder and lead." Kircher and other common soldiers in the Army of the Tennessee created hard war, realized its persuasive effects, and called for its use before higher-ranking officers accepted such practices. As Kircher noted, "Hunger is more powerful than powder and lead, and according to all appearances they would rather stay healthy than see themselves starve."[85]

In mid-March, Grant attempted his last "experiment" to approach Vicksburg, the Steele's Bayou Expedition. On March 12, Porter discovered in a personal scouting mission that water levels had risen enough due to heavy rains and the breeched levee at Yazoo Pass to open a navigable route from the mouth of the Yazoo River into Steele's Bayou and then on through Black Bayou, Deer Creek, and southward through the Rolling Fork and Big Sunflower Rivers back into the Yazoo River, thus bypassing the obstructions at Chickasaw Bayou. After returning to the Yazoo, Porter would be in the rear of Fort Pemberton and able to threaten Confederate fortifications at Haynes' and Drumgould's Bluffs. However, in order for the expedition to succeed, Porter's gunboats would have to travel 130 miles in a roundabout route to through narrow waterways overgrown with timber. On March 14, the ironclads *Mound City, Louisville, Carondelet, Cincinnati,* and *Pittsburgh,* accompanied by four mortars and four tugboats, sailed into Steele's Bayou. The fleet made steady progress until reaching the thick timber of Black Bayou, where Porter's ships battered their way through the trees while sailors cut low-hanging branches that threatened the smokestacks, dropping the occasional snake onboard. Fifty pioneers from Sherman's XV Corps arrived on March 16 aboard the steamer *Diligent* to assist in removing obstructions. When the Confederates discovered Porter's expedition, they began to cut trees to block the gunboats' progress, and the Federal advance slowed to about half a mile per hour while in Deer Creek near the Rolling Fork of the Sunflower River. On March 19–20, Lieutenant Colonel Samuel Ferguson and his small command harassed the Union ships with sniper fire from the banks and attempted an assault on a battery Porter had deployed on ancient Native American burial mounds. Soon, Brigadier General Winfield Featherston's brigade arrived to support Ferguson, and the Rebels began cutting trees in front of and behind the flotilla in an effort to trap the Union fleet. As the situation grew more desperate, Porter appealed to Sherman for rescue by dispatching two couriers. One courier, a freedman well acquainted with the area, carried a message written on tissue paper and wrapped in a tobacco leaf. While waiting for Sherman's response, an anxious Porter began preparations to destroy the gunboats rather than surrender his ships.[86]

Sherman ordered Colonel Giles A. Smith's brigade to race ahead on a night march to save the fleet, and Smith's men arrived late on March 21.

Featherston's Rebels failed to seal the trap, and Sherman himself led more reinforcements to Porter's aid on March 22. Porter's fleet escaped back through the bayous on March 23–25, and the Confederates lost perhaps their best opportunity to capture a substantial portion of the Mississippi Squadron during the Vicksburg campaign. Such a loss of the precious gunboats could have seriously delayed, if not defeated, Grant's efforts to open the Mississippi River to Union navigation. Porter reported a loss of four sailors wounded and one killed in the expedition, and Sherman listed two men killed. Exact Confederate casualties are unknown, but they must have been relatively light.[87] "Thus ended in failure the fourth attempt to get in rear of Vicksburg," stated Grant in his memoirs.[88]

While Grant struggled to gain an approach to attack Vicksburg, Porter and the Union navy continued their efforts to sever the Confederacy's aquatic supply line with the Trans-Mississippi. On February 2, the ram *Queen of the West* ran past the Vicksburg batteries to interdict Rebel traffic on the Mississippi and Red Rivers. For nearly two weeks, the *Queen of the West* effectively obstructed Confederate river transport, destroying four Rebel steamboats and inflicting more than $200,000 in damages. On February 14, the *Queen of the West* attacked Fort Taylor (later renamed Fort De Russy) some 45 miles upstream from the mouth of the Red River. During the engagement, the *Queen of the West* ran aground before being crippled by a Confederate shell, allowing the Rebels to capture a valuable prize. On February 13, Porter followed up on the initial success of the *Queen of the West* when the ironclad *Indianola* successfully steamed past the Vicksburg defenses. The *Indianola* patrolled the rivers until February 24, when a Confederate fleet consisting of the repaired *Queen of the West*, the ram *William H. Webb*, and the gunboat *Dr. Beatty* confronted the Union ironclad some 30 miles downriver from Vicksburg. In a thrilling nighttime battle, the *Queen of the West* and the *William H. Webb* rammed the *Indianola* seven times and captured the Federal warship.[89]

After losing two valuable ships to the Confederates, Porter determined to continue his downriver operations with a far cheaper subterfuge. For a grand total of $8.23, Porter directed carpenters to construct a 300-foot raft on top of a coal barge, complete with dummy smokestacks, casemate, wheelhouses, and one large "Quaker gun" projecting from the bow. The construction crew covered the raft with tar and added two blazing smudge pots to provide smoke for the smokestacks. The refitted coal barge flew a skull-and-crossbones flag from the bow and the U.S. flag from the stern, and painters inscribed on the side of the vessel in three-foot-long letters the slogan "DELUDED PEOPLE CAVE IN." On February 24, the replica gunboat floated past the Vicksburg artillery and eventually ran aground roughly a mile from where a Confederate crew labored on the disabled *Indianola*. Terrified of the phony warship, the Rebels scattered after burning the priceless prize of war. The humiliating ruse had cost the Confederates an excellent chance to interrupt Grant's campaign with a state-of-the-art ironclad. To make matters worse, on the night of March 14, Admiral Farragut managed to steam two ships, the sloop *Hartford* and the gunboat *Albatross*, past the Port Hudson batteries. When reinforced by the ram *Switzerland* from the Union fleet above Vicksburg, the small fleet enabled Farragut to interrupt the vital Trans-Mississippi supply line and establish a naval communications link between Grant's Army of the Tennessee and the Army of the Gulf under Major General Nathaniel P. Banks.[90]

At the end of March 1863, Grant made the fateful decision to risk his army in an amphibious landing in southern Mississippi downriver of Vicksburg in a dramatic attempt to subdue the Rebel fortress. On March 29, Grant ordered McClernand's XIII Corps to lead the way south through the Louisiana swamps, followed by McPherson's XVII Corps while Sherman's XV Corps occupied Pemberton's attention opposite Vicksburg. Drawing upon knowledge gained the year before in North Mississippi, Grant resolved to preserve a standard supply line for ammunition, ordnance, medicinal supplies, salt, coffee, and hardtack while relying on the civilian population of Mississippi to furnish the balance of necessary provisions. Both Sherman and McPherson opposed Grant's audacious strategy. Sherman himself preferred returning the Army of the Tennessee to Memphis, from where it could resume the failed campaign of the previous fall.[91] After delivering his views to Grant, on April 10 the fiery Ohioan wrote to his wife Ellen, "The only true plan was the one we started with. . . . This was our plan at Oxford in December last, is my plan now, and Grant knows it is my opinion."[92]

Still, despite Sherman and McPherson's opposition, Grant continued his preparations to assume to offensive. In order to further distract Pemberton, Grant directed Major General Frederick Steele's division of Sherman's Corps to conduct a reconnaissance in force against the Deer Creek plantations and capture Greenville, Mississippi. Steele's Greenville Expedition provided further experience with the harder war that the Army of the Tennessee would perfect during the upcoming campaign. On April 11, Grant informed Steele, "Rebellion has assumed that shape now that it can only terminate by the complete subjugation of the South or the overthrow of the Government." The Union commander explained, "It is our duty, therefore, to use every means to weaken the enemy, by destroying their means of subsistence, withdrawing their means of cultivating their fields, and in every other way possible."[93] Steele's division left

Milliken's Bend on April 2 and for the next two weeks ransacked deserted plantations, destroyed valuable cotton and 500,000 bushels of corn, seized more than 1,000 livestock, and freed more than 1,000 slaves.[94] Lettie Vick Downs, a women living on Deer Creek, recorded in her journal, "They destroyed every gin and all corn. . . . Four of the negroes left (not as many as I expected to leave). Some little furniture was saved, but the most of it was destroyed."[95] A Union eyewitness, Brevet Major Charles Miller of the 76th Ohio Infantry, reported, "The valley is rich in corn and cotton; immense quantities of the former were found stored in cribs which the army destroyed. It is estimated that a million dollars worth of property was destroyed or carried off by this expedition." Miller reported that his men "marched 'rout step' with all they could carry of the products of the country: pigs, chickens, turkeys and honey every day at the mess board." The Greenville Expedition forced Pemberton to assign a small force under Stephen Dill Lee to obstruct Steele's advance and cost the Vicksburg garrison a mountain of desperately needed supplies. Miller observed that "a great number of mules, horses and cattle were led and driven along, and occasionally an old family carriage was seen in the procession, pulled by a pair of mules and laden with chickens, geese and bacon with 'bummers' riding in grotesque style on the cushioned seats," while "three hundred negroes, men, women, and children, followed the army loaded with bundles of all descriptions."[96] On April 19, Sherman proudly informed Grant, "I think the Deer Creek country has been afflicted enough to make them, in the future, dread the Yankee's visit."[97] Steele's men returned to Milliken's Bend on April 24.

While Steele devastated Deer Creek, Union cavalry further diverted Pemberton's attention away from Grant's maneuvering in Louisiana. In mid-April, Federal forces launched two cavalry raids against Pemberton's northern front. The first, led by Colonel Benjamin Grierson, left La Grange, Tennessee, on April 17. Grierson led 1,700 men south through the heart of Pemberton's department and wrecked the Southern Railroad at Newton's Station on April 24. While Pemberton focused on capturing the raiders, Grierson continued south, cutting telegraph lines, burning bridges, and striking the New Orleans, Jackson, & Great Northern Railroad before reaching Union-occupied Baton Rouge on May 2. At the same time, Rosecrans dispatched a force of 1,500 mule-mounted infantry under Colonel Abel D. Streight to raid through northern Alabama and sever the Western and Atlantic Railroad, which supplied Braxton Bragg's Army of Tennessee. Pursued by Nathan Bedford Forrest's cavalry, Streight's men reached Rome, Georgia, before being forced to surrender on May 3. While Forrest achieved a great victory and captured Streight's entire brigade, the pursuit exhausted his command and kept the "Wizard of the Saddle" from raiding Grant's supply lines at a critical moment in the campaign as he had done the year before. Grierson's raid, perhaps the most famous Union cavalry operation of the war, thoroughly distracted Pemberton and exposed the fatal lack of cavalry in the Department of Mississippi and East Louisiana. In December 1862, General Joseph E. Johnston had transferred three-quarters of Pemberton's mounted forces to Bragg's Army of Tennessee, leaving the Vicksburg commander powerless to respond to Grierson's 475-mile raid and virtually blind to Grant's movements. The concurrent Union raids effectively shielded Grant's preparations for his amphibious operation and further weakened the Confederacy's fragile rail system.[98]

The harsher nature of the war became more apparent as the Army of the Tennessee marched south. On April 19, Captain Bernard Schmerhorn of the 46th Indiana Infantry noted from Dawson's Plantation, Louisiana, "A certain degree of desolation & destruction, necessarily marks the passage of a large army through an enemy country, which here as elsewhere is greatly increased by the carelessness & wauntoness of the troops." Schmerhorn observed, "If the angel of destruction had passed over this region the blight could not have been more complete."[99] The Confederate Army of Vicksburg could do little to halt the devastation. A staff officer for Major General John H. Forney, Major C. Stephens Croom, wrote in his diary on April 23, "At night towards the west, in the neighborhood of the mouth of the Yazoo we saw two large fires, doubtless houses fired by the enemy, who desolate the whole country."[100] A few days later on April 30, Major Maurice K. Simons of the 2nd Texas Infantry recorded repulsing a Federal landing party and declared, "It would have don a sick man good to see the raskells make back for their boats. The 'vandles' they set fire to three Houses while I was watching them. It makes ones blood boil to see the villians thus laying our own country at waste."[101]

By mid-April 1863, Grant had reached the turning point of his career. Although he had achieved great victories, the long, frustrating campaign against Vicksburg had encouraged critics to call for his removal from command while draining the health and morale of his men. For example, as late as April 13, Captain George B. Carter of the 33rd Wisconsin Infantry wrote to his brother, "My opinion of Grant is that he is a thunderous failure and this seems to be the general feeling pervading the army here as far as I can ascertain."[102] On April 20, Grant authored "Special Orders, No. 110," which gave detailed instructions for his subordinate commanders in "the present movement to obtain a foothold on the east bank of the Mississippi River, from which Vicksburg can be approached by practicable roads."[103] To conquer Vicksburg, Grant would undertake one of the boldest gambles of the war. He would conduct an amphibious landing and risk his army by marching deep into enemy territory. If Grant failed, there would be no secure avenue of escape and the Army of the Tennessee would have to fight its way out or surrender. If he succeeded, he would strike a fatal wound to the Confederate States of America. The moment of decision had arrived.

3

∞∞∞

"The road to Vicksburg is open"

By the middle of April 1863, John C. Pemberton had held successfully defended Vicksburg for almost six months. He had rebuilt the Confederate army in Mississippi after the disastrous defeat at Corinth and thwarted five major attempts by Grant to take the city, all while simultaneously battling an array of supply deficiencies, administrative conflicts, and disgruntled citizens. Although he had effectively defended his department, he lacked both the resources and the temperament to seize the initiative and take the offensive. Heavily outnumbered, he had begged both President Davis and General Johnston in vain for more cavalry, guns, manpower, and resources. Now, the Yankees appeared to be everywhere and nowhere. The Greenville Expedition and Sherman's demonstrations against Haynes' Bluff held his attention to Vicksburg, while Grierson's raid caused chaos in his rear, indicating the possibility of a renewed Union offensive in North Mississippi. At the same time, Nathaniel Banks's Army of the Gulf was marching toward Alexandria, Louisiana, threatening a major assault against Port Hudson. Pemberton could only ponder where the next blow would fall. Grant's army may be preparing to attack Vicksburg directly, or it could be redeployed either to northern Mississippi to act in conjunction with the Army of the Cumberland or south to aid Banks's campaign against Port Hudson. The drastic superiority of the Union navy and Pemberton's pitiful lack of cavalry gave Grant the ability to strike almost anywhere before Confederate scouts would recognize the threat, leaving the Pennsylvania Rebel little choice but to play a dangerous waiting game.[1]

Supply problems only worsened with Farragut's interdiction of the Red River on April 1.[2] In his postwar account, Private Ralph J. Smith of the 2nd Texas Infantry remembered that in the spring of 1863, "Provisions became exceedingly scarce while we were stationed at Warrington and continued so until a piece of bacon was looked upon as a treasure to be jealously guarded."[3] While Pemberton attempted to improve chronic food shortages, ordinary Confederates took advantage of the opportunities that nature and local citizens provided. Smith recalled foraging for wild honey and crayfish, a delicacy that "added much to the relish of our corn dodger."[4] Louisiana soldiers also gained a reputation for consuming the ubiquitous "mudbugs." William H. Tunnard of the 3rd Louisiana Infantry explained that in his camp at Snyder's Mills, Mississippi, "Cray-fish soup was no rarity in camp. The Mississippians looked with great amazement and much disgust at the keen relish with which 'them ere Cre-owl Louisianans' devoured this species of food. They could not appreciate such a peculiar taste."[5]

On April 4, Brigadier General John S. Bowen ordered the 1st and 2nd Missouri Infantry regiments from Colonel Francis Cockrell's Missouri brigade across the Mississippi River to Louisiana to support the 15th Louisiana Cavalry Battalion opposing McClernand's march. Bowen, then in command at Grand Gulf, had received reports of Federal activity across the river and sent Cockrell's command to investigate. Cockrell's small force skirmished with the Union advance but could do little to stop the overwhelming blue host.[6] After the war, Corporal Ephraim Anderson of the 2nd Missouri Infantry remembered one incident from this assignment that occurred while raiding Dunbar's plantation to seize an outpost of the 2nd Illinois Cavalry and "about twelve hundred contrabands." After capturing the Illinois pickets, Anderson and his fellow Missourians burst into the plantation house, only to find "a very ludicrous and amusing scene" in a bedroom on the second floor. There, the Rebels encountered "a tall, spare, grave-looking personage, accompanied by a young, full-grown, athletic and very black negress." The incident prompted "prolonged and boisterous merriment" among the Confederates, whose laughter further intensified when Anderson and his companions "discovered that this live and interesting sybarite was the chaplain of a regiment, which our prisoners below fully confirmed."[7] Driven back by Federal reinforcements, the Missourians retreated with their prisoners, including the luckless Illinois chaplain, who now had to practice his ministry in substantially less pleasant surroundings.

After making contact with McClernand's Corps, Cockrell notified Bowen of the suspicious Federal advance. Bowen promptly informed

Pemberton, who wired Richmond on April 9, "Enemy is constantly in motion in all directions. . . . Also reported, but not yet confirmed, movement under McClernand, in large force, by land west of river and southward. Much doubt it."[8] On April 11, Pemberton received a piece of intelligence reporting that 40 transports had been seen steaming north on the Mississippi River to Memphis, soon followed by another fleet of transports and gunboats. While a large number of Federal transports did indeed steam upriver, they were only empty vessels being transferred to support Rosecrans. Thoroughly convinced by Grant's deceptions, both Pemberton and Johnston believed rumors that Grant's army would be redeployed to reinforce Rosecrans and even began preparations to transfer 8,000 men from the Army of Vicksburg to Bragg's Army of Tennessee.[9]

These Confederate delusions were shattered during the night of April 16, 1863, when Admiral Porter commanded a fleet of eight gunboats and three supply transports in a furious race past the Vicksburg defenses. The flotilla consisted of the ironclads *Benton*, *Lafayette*, and *Tuscumbia*; four City-class ironclads, *Louisville*, *Pittsburg*, *Mound City*, and *Carondelet*; and the tinclad ram *General Price*. Porter's run began at 9:15 P.M. and caught Vicksburg's officers in the midst of an ill-timed ball. Still, the Federal fleet soon encountered an intense bombardment from the Rebel batteries. Blazing bonfires illuminated De Soto Point and the riverbank at Vicksburg, providing the Confederate artillerists with the necessary light to fire at the shadowy targets through the smoke. While the defenders did fire more than 500 rounds, with some 70 striking their targets, most of the Union gunboats suffered little damage. In the end, Porter lost one transport, the *Henry Clay*, and one coal barge and suffered 12 wounded. The stunning passage of the Mississippi Squadron forced Bowen to return Cockrell's regiments from Louisiana and persuaded Pemberton to recall the troops already on their way to Bragg's army. On April 22, Porter repeated his earlier feat by successfully rushing six more supply transports past the Vicksburg batteries carrying 600,000 rations for the Army of the Tennessee. This time, Rebel gunners sunk one transport, the *Tigress*, killing two sailors and wounding six. The bold gamble of running the batteries forever cut the desperately needed supply link to the Trans-Mississippi and provided Grant with the boats necessary to cross the Mississippi River at any point he desired south of Vicksburg.[10]

After the Mississippi Squadron survived the fiery passage, Grant decided to use the transports to land his forces at Grand Gulf, Mississippi, 30 miles south of Vicksburg. To keep Pemberton's attention focused on Vicksburg, on April 27, Grant ordered Sherman's XV Corps to demonstrate against the southern citadel while the main army landed downriver. On April 23, a worried Sherman had informed his brother John that "we are actually moving on one of the most hazardous & desperate enterprises that any army ever undertook" and expressed his doubts about Grant's Vicksburg venture.[11] One week later, on April 29, Porter ordered the gunboats to eliminate the twin Confederate forts at Grand Gulf. In six hours, Porter's warships fired more than 2,300 shells at the Rebels, but Bowen had prepared his defenses well, and the defenders held out despite having every cannon but one disabled. The failed operation cost the Union 24 killed and 56 wounded, while Bowen lost three killed and 15 wounded.[12] After the bombardment, Grant boarded Porter's flagship, *Benton*, and later remarked, "The sick of the mangled and dying men which met my eyes as I boarded the ship was sickening."[13] The setback left Grant with no choice but to abandon his attempted landing at Grand Gulf and search for a feasible location farther downriver. On the night of the April 29, Porter ran his flotilla past the damaged Grand Gulf batteries while Grant's columns marched south. That night, a freed African American informed Grant of a potential landing site at Bruinsburg, Mississippi, that contained a suitable road inland to Port Gibson. Grant immediately took advantage of the discovery and issued orders to transport the army across the Mississippi River on the following day.[14]

On April 30, 1863, 24,000 soldiers and 60 cannon of the Army of the Tennessee landed on the Mississippi shore at Bruinsburg without encountering opposition. In his memoirs, Grant remembered that after the landing, he enjoyed "a degree of relief scarcely ever equaled since. Vicksburg was not yet taken it is true, nor were its defenders demoralized by any of our previous moves. I was now in the enemy's country, with a vast river and the stronghold of Vicksburg between me and my base of supplies." "But," he continued, "I was on dry ground on the same side of the river with the enemy. All the campaigns, labors, hardships and exposures from the month of December previous to this time that had been made and endured, were for the accomplishment of this one object."[15] The Federals soon began to push inland, and by the end of the day, McClernand's men had secured the bluffs and stationed pickets 13 miles from shore. After midnight on the morning on May 1, 1863, advance units from Colonel William M. Stone's brigade encountered Confederate pickets and began skirmishing.[16]

Bowen's scouts had observed Union soldiers marching inland, and the Georgia-born Missourian quickly sent this intelligence to Pemberton. Immediately after receiving news of the attack at Grand Gulf on April 29, Pemberton had ordered the brigades of Brigadier Generals Edward D. Tracy and William E. Baldwin to march from Vicksburg and reinforce

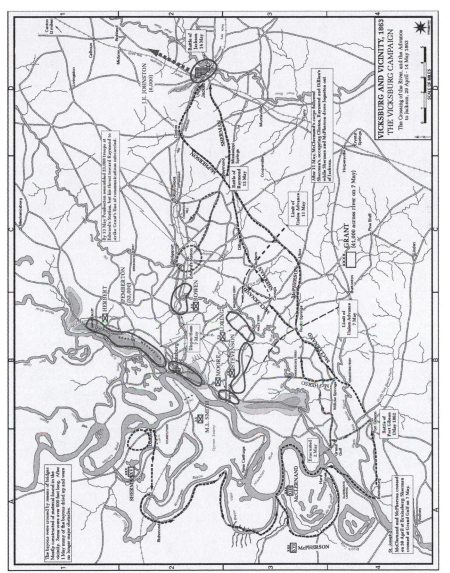

The Vicksburg Campaign, April 29–May 14, 1863. (Courtesy of the Department of History, United States Military Academy)

Bowen's garrison. Tracy's brigade arrived first on April 30, allowing Bowen to deploy two brigades to guard the dual roads leading from Bruinsburg to Port Gibson. Bowen positioned Brigadier General Martin E. Green's brigade to defend the Rodney Road, which consisted of the 15th, 19th, 20th, and 21st Arkansas Infantries, the 1st Arkansas Cavalry Battalion (dismounted), the 12th Arkansas Sharpshooters Battalion, and the 1st and 3rd Missouri Cavalries (dismounted). Bowen reinforced Green's brigade with the 6th Mississippi Infantry and the Pettus Flying Artillery, which brought its strength to roughly 1,000 men. On his right flank, Bowen ordered Brigadier General Edward Tracy's brigade to protect the Bruinsburg Road. Tracy's brigade contained some 1,500 men in the 20th, 23rd, 30th, 31st, and 46th Alabama Infantries. The initial reports collected by Confederate scouts estimated the Federal force to be around 3,000 men, which would indicate another raid similar to Steele's earlier Greenville Expedition.[17]

The terrain in the area around Port Gibson presented Bowen with an excellent defensive position. The environment from the river to the town consisted of a series of ridges and ravines overgrown with timber, brush, and cane. The dense tangles of vegetation seriously hindered Union efforts to maneuver and gave the Confederates a key advantage that would limit the Federals' numerical superiority. In his report, Grant described the Port Gibson battlefield as "the most broken country I ever saw. The whole country is a series of irregular ridges, divided by deep and impassable ravines, grown up with heavy timber, undergrowth, and cane. It was impossible to engage any considerable portion of our forces at any one time."[18] Bowen's two brigades had little chance of successfully resisting against a determined Union attack, but Brigadier General William E. Baldwin's brigade was en route from Vicksburg, and Colonel Francis M. Cockrell's brigade remained in supporting distance at Grand Gulf. Bowen, the best division commander in the Army of Vicksburg, initially estimated his force to contain 8,000 men, but straggling and detachments reduced his command to between 5,000 and 6,000 men and 16 cannon. Bowen's brigades served as Pemberton's "shock troops," but his elite units faced more than three times their number against Grant's 18,000 veterans and 58 pieces of artillery.[19]

In the darkness of the early morning hours of May 1, scattered skirmishing erupted between the advanced elements of the armies, but both sides waited for dawn to fully engage. At 5:30 A.M., McClernand ordered the XIII Corps to attack toward Port Gibson. McClernard divided his force by ordering Brigadier Generals Eugene A. Carr, Alvin P. Hovey, and Andrew J. Smith to march their divisions east along the Rodney Road while Brigadier General Peter J. Osterhaus's division advanced north along the Shaifer Road until it connected with the Bruinsburg Road. Due to the thick undergrowth and uneven landscape, Osterhaus made slow progress against Tracy's Alabamians. Sharp fighting occurred as Osterhaus sent forward substantial skirmish lines, but the Rebels fought stubbornly despite the loss of their brigade commander. Early in the fighting, a Federal bullet struck Tracy in the back of the neck, making the 29-year-old Georgian the first Confederate general to die in the Vicksburg campaign. After Tracy's death, Colonel Isham Garrott assumed command of the brigade as it slowly fell back to a new position along a ridge on the Bruinsburg Road around 10:00 A.M.[20]

Simultaneously along the Rodney Road, overwhelming Federal numbers steadily drove Green's brigade back despite tenacious resistance. Early in the morning, Green requested support from Tracy, who sent the 23rd Alabama Infantry and a section of the Botetourt Virginia Artillery (the only Virginia unit in the Army of Vicksburg) to the Rodney Road. When the Alabamians reached Green's position, Bowen ordered the 23rd Alabama and the 6th Mississippi to counterattack, but the Federals swiftly repulsed the Rebel assault. Bowen soon realized that he was vastly outnumbered, but he determined to fight to hold his position until Baldwin's and Cockrell's brigades reached the battlefield. Shortly after 10:00 A.M., Carr's and Hovey's men surged forward and overwhelmed Green's lone brigade, driving the Rebels back from Foster Ridge. In the charge, McClernand's men captured two cannon of the Botetourt Virginia Artillery, three caissons, three ammunition wagons, 200 prisoners, and the flag of the 15th Arkansas. At that point, Brigadier General William E. Baldwin's brigade arrived to anchor a new defensive line along Irwin's Branch of Willow Creek. Baldwin's brigade contained 1,614 men in the 17th and 31st Louisiana Infantries along with the 4th and 46th Mississippi Infantries. Recognizing that Green's exhausted brigade needed time to rally and reorganize, Bowen ordered Green's men to march to the right flank to support Tracy's brigade on the Bruinsburg Road.[21]

Soon thereafter, Colonel Francis M. Cockrell's Missouri brigade arrived from Grand Gulf, but unfortunately for Bowen, the famous Missouri brigade had only three of its regiments present, as the remainder had been detached elsewhere. When Cockrell's 1,259 men appeared, Bowen directed the 6th Missouri Infantry to the Bruinsburg Road to aid Tracy's hard-pressed brigade and held the 3rd and 5th Missouri in reserve. While McClernand's divisions attacked Baldwin's brigade, Bowen ordered Cockrell's two regiments to counterattack against the Union right flank. The Missourians gave the Rebel Yell and unleashed a savage assault that pushed back the 56th Ohio and 47th Indiana of Colonel James R. Slack's brigade. However, the Missourians soon collided with the 29th Wisconsin and Brigadier General William P. Benton's brigade, supported by 24 cannon from Hovey's division, and the Federals' superior numbers steadily repulsed Cockrell's two regiments.[22] In his diary, Captain George W. Covell of the 3rd Missouri chronicled, " 'Their artillery opened on us with great rapidity, and as soon as we got within range the infantry poured the Minie balls into our ranks as thick and fast as hailstones from a thunder cloud or rain drops in an April shower.' " According to Covell, "'The storm of leaden rain and iron hail which was flying through the air was almost sufficient to obscure the sunlight.' "[23] As Cockrell's men fell back, Bowen rode out to rally the Missourians, and with tears in his eyes the Rebel commander declared, " 'I did not expect that *any* of you would get away, but the charge *had* to be made, or my little army was lost.' "[24] At 1:20 P.M., Bowen wired Pemberton, "We have been engaged in a furious battle ever since daylight; losses very heavy. General Tracy is killed. . . . They outnumber us trebly. There are three divisions against us. . . . The men act nobly, but the odds are overpowering."[25]

At 2:00 P.M., Union reinforcements from Major General John A. Logan's division of McPherson's XVII Corps reached the battlefield from Bruinsburg. Grant sent Brigadier General John E. Smith's brigade to aid Osterhaus's division along the Bruinsburg Road and Brigadier General John D. Stevenson's brigade to reinforce McClernand's Corps on the Rodney Road. Throughout the afternoon, the fighting continued along the Bruinsburg Road as Osterhaus's division assaulted Tracy's and Green's brigades. Desperate to hold their position, the 6th Missouri boldly counterattacked but had to withdraw before being overwhelmed by the numerically superior Federals. In the late afternoon, Grant directed Brigadier General Elias Dennis's brigade of Logan's division to support Osterhaus, who soon forced the Confederates to retire along the Bruinsburg Road. At roughly the same time, Bowen's line along the Irvin Branch of Willow Creek began to collapse due to a lack of ammunition and relentless pressure from McClernand. At 5:30 P.M., Bowen, who had had four horses shot out from under him that day, grudgingly gave the order to retreat. During the night, the Rebels escaped as Grant's fatigued command lacked the strength to pursue. Bowen reported his casualties as 60 killed, 340 wounded, and 387 missing, along with four cannon lost from the Botetourt Virginia Artillery. The Army of the Tennessee suffered 131 killed, 719 wounded, and 25 missing. Through bloody fighting at Port Gibson, Grant won a victory that secured his beachhead on the Mississippi shore downriver from Vicksburg and allowed him to continue his march inland.[26]

As the Battle of Port Gibson ended, Grant's 12-year-old son Fred reached the battlefield from Bruinsburg, where his father had left him earlier. As Grant proudly recalled, "My son accompanied me throughout the campaign and siege, and caused no anxiety either to me or to his mother, who was at home. He looked out for himself and was in every battle of the campaign."[27] Although he had won an important victory, Grant knew that the struggle to capture Vicksburg had only just begun. As there had not been enough wagons ferried across the Mississippi River to haul the ammunition, Grant directed "immediately upon landing that all the vehicles and draft animals, whether horses, mules, or oxen, in the vicinity should be collected and loaded to their capacity with ammunition."[28] Thomas Wise Durham of the 11th Indiana observed, "It was equal to a circus parade in a country town to see this ammunition caravan." According to Durham, the improvised train consisted of "fine family carriages loaded with boxes of ammunition and drawn by an ox team, or an old mule and horse hitched together, rigged with plow harness, shuck collars and rope lines to drive with." Durham reported that "cotton wagons, ox carts and even dog carts—everything that could be found in the country that had wheels, and every kind of animal and harness with which to pull them, were pressed into service. No such sight has ever been seen since old Noah entered the Ark."[29]

On May 2, the Army of the Tennessee captured Port Gibson, which had been abandoned in Bowen's retreat. Residents could only stand by in stunned silence as the triumphant Union army marched through the streets. Sergeant Ira Blanchard of the 20th Illinois noted that as he "passed through the main street of the city, men, women and children filled the walks or gazed anxiously from the upper story windows, as though a monster show had come to town."[30] Private William Wiley of the 77th Illinois Infantry recorded that after the Union army entered Port Gibson, "The boys looted the town going through the stores and taking whatever suited them best."[31] One eyewitness, Florison D. Pitts of the Chicago Mercantile Battery, chronicled in his diary that Grant's army "occupied Port Gibson at 9 o'clock. . . . Boys jerked every thing they wanted from the stores."[32] Outside of the town at Colonel Benjamin Humphrey's plantation, the Federals also seized a Confederate commissary depot with 8,000 pounds of bacon left behind in the hasty retreat.[33]

Grant's rapid advance forced Bowen to evacuate Grand Gulf on the night of May 2, and the Union navy secured the crucial river landing the following day. The Confederate retreat enabled Grant to use Grand Gulf as a supply base to continue the transportation of men and supplies across the Mississippi River, including Sherman's XV Corps.[34] Grant described the state of the campaign on May 3 when he wrote to Sherman, "The enemy is badly beaten, greatly demoralized, and exhausted of ammunition. The road to Vicksburg is open. All we want now are men, ammunition, and hard bread. We can subsist our horses on the country, and obtain considerable supplies for our troops."[35]

Sherman's XV Corps swiftly marched from their camps opposite Vicksburg and crossed the Mississippi River at Grand Gulf on May 6–7. After the war, Charles A. Wilson of the 76th Ohio described the route through the swamps by recalling, "This bayou was fairly teeming with alligators. Our road skirted the bayou and these ugly creatures were crawling everywhere, many of them on the roadway, and were run over by the artillery and baggage wagons." Wilson further noted that "they were all sizes from a foot or so long to quite formidable dimensions, but did not appear to be at all dangerous or vicious, and created no disturbance."[36] Sherman drove his men to reinforce Grant as soon as possible. Indianan Thomas Wise Durham remembered that as the XV Corps crossed the Mississippi River, "All this time Sherman was standing by the gang plank, making the air blue with his cursing the men for not moving faster. As a 'cusser' he was the finest artist at the business that you could imagine."[37] Once Sherman landed in Mississippi, the Army of the Tennessee contained some 44,000 experienced and hard-fighting soldiers.[38]

From May 1 to May 17, the decisive period of the campaign, logistics represented the Achilles' heel of Army of the Tennessee. Until Grant reached the environs of Vicksburg and secured a consistent supply line from the U.S. Navy along the Mississippi River, the entire army would be forced to rely on a tenuous supply chain that could provide only essential ammunition and basic rations. The fighting at Port Gibson had cost Grant a day and alerted Pemberton to the Union invasion. On May 3, Grant rode to Grand Gulf and established communications with his superiors. That day, Grant learned that Banks would not arrive at Port Hudson in time to support the Army of the Tennessee in its current operations. Knowing that his opponent would not surrender Vicksburg without additional bloodshed, Grant decided not to dispatch McClernand's Corps to aid Banks and instead to drive his army into the heart of the state to sever the Southern Railroad of Mississippi that supplied Vicksburg.[39] As he explained in his memoirs, "I therefore determined to move independently of Banks, cut loose from my base, destroy the rebel force in rear of Vicksburg and invest or capture the city."[40]

Grant's decision to march his army into the interior of Mississippi with a limited supply chain ranks as one of the boldest gambles of the entire war. Grant determined this course of action on his own initiative without awaiting for permission from General in Chief Halleck, whom he knew would never approve of such a dangerous maneuver. Indeed, even Sherman advised Grant not to pursue this endeavor and instead recommended waiting until sufficient supplies could be stockpiled in a supply base at Grand Gulf before continuing the campaign. Grant responded that he did not "calculate upon the possibility of supplying the army with full rations from Grand Gulf. I know it will be impossible without constructing additional roads. What I do expect is to get up what rations of hard bread, coffee and salt we can, and make the country furnish the balance."[41] That would be quite a daunting enterprise. Historian Warren Grabau notes that at the time, "A Union infantry division of 6,000 men required a minimum of 18,000 pounds of food per day. Double that weight to include the containers, and it follows that twelve wagons per day, with cargoes devoted entirely to food, were required just to feed the troops a minimum ration."[42]

Throughout the first weeks of May, the Army of the Tennessee rampaged through the Magnolia state in a rapid campaign that historians have described as a "Blitzkrieg through Mississippi," relying on small farms and plantations for all provisions aside from the basic rations of coffee and hard tack.[43] Luckily for Grant's men, the interior of the state had not endured intense campaigning during the early years of the war and provided a veritable feast for the invading Federals. On May 6, Sherman wrote to his wife from Grand Gulf, "The Planters never dreamed of our Coming. They had planted vast fields of corn & vegetables, and we find old corn, and some beef cattle. It is folly to suppose the enemy to be suffering for food—They have plenty of Beef and corn."[44] Grant asserted in his memoirs that "beef, mutton, poultry and forage were found in abundance. Quite a quantity of bacon and molasses were also secured from the country, but bread and coffee could not be obtained in quantity sufficient for all the men." In order to produce a sufficient quantity of bread, Grant directed that grindstones at occupied plantations be operated, and "these were kept running while we were stopping, day and night, and when we were marching, during the night, at all plantations covered by the troops."[45]

The organized foraging expeditions continued to be sent out throughout the campaign regardless of weather, terrain, or armed opposition. War correspondent Sylvanus Cadwallader of the *Chicago Times* testified that "army wagons by scores and hundreds were sent out daily from ten to fifteen miles, escorted by infantry details sufficient to protect them from any sudden foray by Confederate Cavalry." The reporter detailed that the wagons "returned at nightfall groaning under the weight of impressed supplies, and increased by the addition to the train of every vehicle, no matter what its description, that could bear the weight of a sack of grain, pieces of salt meat, or pails full of butter, eggs, honey or vegetables."[46] A few days after landing in Mississippi, Sherman informed his wife on May 9 from Hankinson's Ferry, "We are short of wagons and provisions, but in this starving country we find an abundance of corn, hogs, cattle sheep and Poultry. Men who came in advance have drawn but 2 days rations in 10, and are fat."[47] Pemberton's meager cavalry, already scattered by multiple Union raids, could offer little resistance to the foraging parties or the ammunition trains. "With a moderate cavalry force at my disposal," Pemberton argued in his report, "I am firmly convinced that the Federal Army ... would have been unable to maintain its communications with the Mississippi River, and that the attempt to reach Jackson and Vicksburg ... would have been as signally defeated in May, 1863, as a like attempt ... in December, 1862."[48]

The foraging expeditions and Union occupations of plantations had devastating economic consequences for the owners. From May 3 through May 7, Logan's division of the XVII Corps camped at the Bagnell plantation on the Big Black River. After the war, the estate applied for restitution as Unionists to the Southern Claims Commission. The claim, titled "Amount of Stock & Property Consumed & taken off by Gen. U.S. Grant's Army," alleged the loss of 95 cotton bales either burned or seized and the seizure of 15 mules, two horses, 40 head of sheep, 15 milk cows, 10 work oxen, 25 calves, 100 hogs, one mule wagon, four sets of wagon gears, 3,800 bushels of corn, 4,000 pounds of bacon and hams, five tons of fodder, 30,000 feet of lumber used in the construction of tent shelters, and 8,000 fence rails burned for fuel. In total, the ill-fated planter calculated the damage to equal $29,855, which utilized the 1863 price of cotton, then exceptionally high due to the conflict.[49]

The claim does not contain the loss of slave labor, which would have increased the estimated damage by tens of thousands of dollars. The Bagnell plantation likely had a large number of slaves who may have been transported elsewhere by their owners before Logan's division arrived or became emancipated upon occupation. The account also does not list any burned buildings or stolen personal property, which reveals that the owners probably remained in the home during the ordeal. Abandoned plantations experienced greater destruction as Union soldiers typically plundered and often burned unoccupied residences. Although Logan's division stayed at the plantation for only five days, the extensive loss of labor, equipment, and livestock would have rendered the property useless for Confederate agricultural production until the end of the war.[50]

The loss of livestock proved particularly devastating to the state's civilian population. Sylvanus Cadwallader stated that "horses, mules and cattle were brought in by droves of hundreds. I frequently saw horses, cattle and mules of all ages and condition; milch cows and calves; sheep, goats and lambs; turkeys, geese, ducks and chickens, driven together in one drove."[51] Contrary to popular belief, Grant's men did not limit their foraging to the homes of secessionists only. The decision to rely upon the countryside for rations affected the fortunes of Unionists and African Americans as well. In Claiborne County, for example, 11 white Unionists and eight African Americans applied for and obtained reimbursement from the Southern Claims Commission for damages inflicted in the Vicksburg campaign. Several others, including at least four African Americans, filed claims that did not receive compensation. Even if the commission's agents established the applicant's loyalty and approved the claim, the claimant often had to settle for far less than the amount requested. One free African American in Claiborne County, Rosetta L. Newsom, filed a claim for $2,441.00 for seized livestock and food. After being investigated, the commission agents acknowledged, "When the Army in May '63 crossed the Mississippi at Port Gibson & Grand Gulf they were obliged to take all they could for subsistence.—But it is also plain, that much of this taking was lawless—mere depredations." Ultimately, the commission awarded Newsom $389.00.[52] As Cadwallader affirmed, "The country was much richer in food products than we had expected to find it. If owners could establish their loyalty they were given regular vouchers for everything taken—if not, not."[53]

The Vicksburg campaign pioneered the use of hard war against the southern home front in ways that Mississippi civilians could never have imagined before. As Grant's army marched inland, it consumed or destroyed valuable resources that the Confederate army desperately needed to survive. The loss of livestock and crops ensured that little would be left to support the rebellion in this area even if Grant's invasion ended in defeat. As the march continued, each horse seized, each cow slaughtered, and each bushel of corn commandeered would be one less that Pemberton could utilize to supply his army. Although little genuine fighting had taken place thus far in the campaign, Grant's army had weakened the South's will and ability to continue the war more by economic warfare than by actual combat. Union armies had foraged and appropriated supplies before in previous campaigns, but the march to Vicksburg drastically exceeded all prior raids and expeditions in its amount of logistical consumption and economic devastation. The campaign also taught an entire army of Federal soldiers the value of hard war techniques in suppressing southern resistance, which they would later use in Georgia and the Carolinas with brutal effectiveness in 1864 and 1865.

Grant's determination to largely sustain his army from foraging expeditions generated anxiety from a few Union soldiers. Osborn Oldroyd of the 20th Ohio Infantry admitted, "My fear is that they may cut our supply train, and then we should be in a bad fix. Should that happen and they get us real hungry, I am afraid short work would be made of taking Vicksburg."[54] In order to provide the needed provisions in addition to those provided from Grand Gulf, Grant had to advance his army at a swift pace before Pemberton could unite his forces to oppose the invasion.[55] As the continued foraging expeditions rapidly depleted food supplies in the immediate area, the Federals had to continue to maneuver farther into the state. On May 3, McClernand explained this situation to Grant when he wrote, "My corps will be out of rations to-morrow. . . . I ask that you will cause rations to be sent out immediately. . . . Lieutenant-Colonel [Wesford] Taggart is behind, collecting what articles of subsistence he can, but the troops in advance left scarcely anything."[56]

The foraging expeditions forced Union soldiers to interact with southern civilians more than ever before, but in some cases the attempted contact ended in comical misfortune. Sergeant Ira Blanchard recalled that early in the campaign, his unit had embarked on a night march when "one of our boys saw something rolled up in a blanket in the corner of the fence. Wishing to have a little fun, he dodged out of the ranks and giving the bundle a kick exclaimed, 'Hello, old fellow! Where did you get your whiskey?' " In a moment of shock and terror, another Federal soldier "shied up and said 'Look out, that's General Sherman!' " Although Blanchard did not report Sherman's reaction to this rude awakening, one can assume that the general let loose a torrent of fury. Before Sherman could locate the perpetrator, Blanchard explained, "The soldier flew back to the ranks in an instant, and was careful how he kicked the next man before he knew who he was."[57]

On May 1, as Bowen's division battled against Grant's beachhead at Port Gibson, Pemberton transferred his headquarters from Jackson to Vicksburg and began to unite his widely dispersed command into an army capable of challenging the Army of the Tennessee. That same day, General Johnston telegraphed Pemberton, "If Grant's army lands on this side of the river, the safety of Mississippi depends on beating it. For that object you should unite your whole force."[58] Pemberton agreed and even appealed to President Davis to evacuate the Confederate garrison at Port Hudson in order to concentrate as many soldiers as possible. Davis ultimately rejected this request and answered, "To hold both Vicksburg and Port Hudson is necessary to a connection with Trans-Mississippi."[59] To prepare for the possibility of siege, Pemberton ordered the meat ration in

Vicksburg reduced and directed that provisions and ammunition be stored inside the city. While Pemberton organized the Army of Vicksburg north of the Big Black River, a precious 10 days elapsed without serious combat erupting between the two armies. Although Johnston had been notified of Grant's landing and of the fighting at Port Gibson on May 1, he made no immediate effort to travel to Mississippi and assume overall command, which he could have as commander of the Department of the West. Nor did he make any effort to promptly order significant reinforcements from Bragg's Army of Tennessee to be transferred to Vicksburg, aside from 4,000 cavalry sent to operate in northern Mississippi.[60] Finally, on May 9, Confederate Secretary of War James A. Seddon ordered the haughty Virginian to "proceed at once to Mississippi and take chief command of the forces there, giving to those in the field, as far as practicable, the encouragement and benefit of your personal direction."[61] Johnston began traveling to Jackson, but the journey would take several days, and by the time he arrived, the Confederate cause in Mississippi would be in a severe crisis.[62]

On May 7, Grant began advancing his three corps to the northeast in an effort to break the Southern Railroad of Mississippi, which connected Vicksburg with Jackson and had been damaged in Grierson's raid. McClernand's XIII Corps marched on Grant's left adjacent to the Big Black River with Sherman's XV Corps in the center and McPherson's XVII Corps on the Union right flank. As the Army of the Tennessee prepared to cross Fourteenmile Creek, on May 11, Grant instructed McPherson to secure Raymond, the county seat of Hinds County. Grant directed his subordinate to "use your utmost exertions to secure all the subsistence stores you that may be there, as well as in the vicinity. We must fight the enemy before our rations fail, and we are equally bound to make our rations last as long as possible." As Grant explained to McPherson, "Upon one occasion you made two days' rations last seven. We may have to do the same thing again."[63]

On May 12, McPherson and two divisions of the XVII Corps reached the outskirts of Raymond and stumbled into Confederate Brigadier General John Gregg's 3,000-man brigade lurking in thick woods behind Fourteenmile Creek.[64] Aware of Grant's advance on the railroad, Pemberton had prepared the Army of Vicksburg for an attack along the Big Black River. On May 11, the Pennsylvanian instructed Gregg to march his brigade from Jackson to Raymond with orders to attack the Union army in the flank or rear if Grant approached the Big Black River. Gregg, an Alabama native and prewar resident of Fairfield, Texas, recruited the 7th Texas Infantry at the outbreak of the war and had commanded the regiment in its first engagement at Fort Donelson. After being exchanged, Gregg received a promotion to brigadier general and the command of a brigade in Pemberton's department. Gregg's brigade, which consisted of the 3rd, 10th, 30th, 41st, and 50th Tennessee Infantries; the 1st Tennessee Infantry Battalion; and the 7th Texas Infantry, reached the town on the 11th unaware that McPherson's entire corps was on its way to Raymond. On May 12, Gregg's scouts warned him of the approach of a Union column, which they grossly underestimated to contain 2,500 to 3,000 men. To meet the threat, Gregg deployed his brigade in the woods between the Utica and Lower Gallatin Roads supported by three guns from Captain Hiram Bledsoe's Missouri Battery. At 10:00 A.M., a brisk firefight erupted as the Federals discovered the Rebel skirmish line. Believing that he faced only a single Union brigade, Gregg decided to launch a daring attack upon the Union center and right flank.[65]

Due to the thick timber and growing smoke clouds, McPherson could not determine how many Confederates lay behind Fourteenmile Creek, so he deployed the brigades of Brigadier Generals Elias S. Dennis and John E. Smith from Logan's division before continuing the advance. Once Brigadier General Marcellus Crocker's division arrived, McPherson would have more than 10,000 men and 22 cannon to oppose Gregg's lone brigade. Around noon, the 7th Texas, now under the command of Colonel Hiram Granbury, initiated the echelon assault on the Union center and charged through the unprepared and isolated 23rd Indiana. However, the regiment soon collided with intense resistance from several adjacent units from Logan's division.[66] One northern soldier facing the Lone Star onslaught, Lieutenant Henry Otis Dwight of the 20th Ohio, recalled that his men used the bank of Fourteenmile Creek as a trench, and "we dropped on the ground right there and gave those Texans all the bullets we could cram into our Enfields, until our guns were hot enough to sizzle. They gray line paused, staggered back like a ship in collision which trembles in every timber from the shock."[67] Despite the storm of lead, the Texans maintained the advance. "Then they too gave us volley after volley, always working up toward us, breasting our fire until they had come within twenty, or even fifteen paces. In one part of the line some of them came nearer than that and had to be poked back with the bayonets," narrated Dwight.[68] Major Khleber Miller Van Zandt of the 7th Texas Infantry later recalled, "We advanced to meet the enemy, expecting not more than two regiments. Much to our astonishment, we ran into McPherson's Corps, and there followed the most disastrous battle in which I ever took part. In an hour's fighting, more than 50 per cent of our men were killed or wounded."[69]

The 3rd Tennessee continued the assault, and the two Confederate regiments slammed into Logan's division. Sergeant Osborn Oldroyd from Dennis's brigade recorded in his diary, "The regiment to the right of us was giving way, but just as the line was wavering and about to be hopelessly broken, Logan dashed up, and with the shriek of an eagle turned them back to their places, which they regained and held."[70] However, when the next three regiments of Gregg's brigade advanced into an open field and found themselves confronted by an enormous number of Union soldiers, they wisely fell back rather than engage in a suicidal frontal assault. While the Confederate attack initially enjoyed some success, at 1:30 P.M., the reinforced Federals began to overwhelm Gregg's men and eventually drove the stubborn Rebels back in a disorganized withdrawal. As the rest of the Confederate line began to crumble in the face of vastly superior numbers, Gregg ordered his exhausted brigade to retreat shortly after 4:00 P.M. Although the Union won the battle, the 7th Texas had proven its courage and removed the stain of its surrender at Fort Donelson by losing a staggering 158 casualties out of 306 engaged in some two hours of fierce fighting at Raymond.[71] McPherson's Corps won a victory in the Battle of Raymond at a cost of 68 killed, 341 wounded, and 37 missing, while Gregg's brigade lost 73 killed, 252 wounded, and 190 missing. Although overshadowed by the larger battles of the war, survivor Ira Blanchard observed that "seldom in any engagement was the loss greater in proportion to the numbers engaged than on that bloody field at Raymond." Blanchard detailed that he had "passed over the field soon after the firing had ceased, and the dead were strewn thickly over a space of about ten acres; behind every tree, in every hollow, or behind every log some poor fellow had crawled away and died."[72] To add insult to the injury of defeat, the townspeople of Raymond had to witness the triumphant Federals consume the victory feast they had prepared for Gregg's Confederates.[73] Osborn Oldroyd sardonically wrote, "The citizens had prepared a good dinner for the rebels on their return from victory, but, as they actually returned from defeat they were in too much of a hurry to enjoy it."[74]

The Battle of Raymond convinced Grant to alter his strategy to conquer Vicksburg. Instead of directly marching against the Southern Railroad, Sherman and McPherson's Corps would now attack the vital industrial and transportation center of Jackson, while McClernand's men confronted Pemberton and the Army of Vicksburg. The advance against the capital city of Mississippi placed the Army of the Tennessee between Pemberton's main army and the growing Confederate force then assembling in Jackson. Thus far in the campaign, Grant had thoroughly outgeneraled Pemberton, and after May 13, the Confederate army in Central Mississippi would be fatally divided. The Army of the Tennessee now lay between two Confederate armies, greatly inhibiting their communications and providing Grant with a key strategic position. But Pemberton and his soldiers remained defiant, anxiously awaiting a climactic battle against the Union invader. The next 10 days would witness the most intense fighting of the entire campaign and decide the ultimate fate of Vicksburg.[75]

4

⤙⤚⤛

"Time is all-important"

On May 13, as Gregg's brigade fell back to Jackson, General Johnston reached the capital of Mississippi and assumed command of all Confederate units defending the city.[1] At 8:40 P.M., Johnston wrote a dispatch to Pemberton, who had moved his headquarters to Bovina, and urged an attack on the Army of the Tennessee at Clinton. Johnston declared to his subordinate that "it is important to re-establish communications, that you may be reinforced. If practicable, come up in his rear [Sherman's] at once. . . . The troops here could co-operate. All the strength you can quickly assemble should be brought. Time is all-important."[2] Nonetheless, despite the fact that reinforcements from across the Confederacy were en route to Jackson and would arrive soon, bringing his total strength to around 12,000, Johnston quickly concluded that a defense of Jackson would be futile and wired to Confederate Secretary of War James A. Seddon, "I am too late."[3] Jackson had been partially fortified, and a vigorous defense could have possibly hindered Grant long enough to allow Pemberton a chance to cooperate with Johnston. Historian William C. Davis argues that "if Johnston had left for Mississippi two weeks earlier, he could have effected a junction with Pemberton" and that "if, on his own authority as commander of the Western division, he had taken a division or more with him, instead of a mere brigade, Johnston might have been able to cut his way through to his subordinate even as late as he did move."[4] Once he did arrive, the Virginia general refused to risk a large-scale battle and instead ordered Jackson to be evacuated early on

May 14. Johnston ordered his men to retreat to the northeast to Canton, in the opposite direction from Pemberton and any chance of uniting the two Confederate armies.[5]

Certainly, by this point in the campaign, a delay of even a few days represented a serious threat to the Army of the Tennessee. Deep in enemy territory, with a fragile supply line that extended all the way back to the Mississippi River, Grant faced a distinct possibility of being cut off. While the countryside would provide enough provisions to sustain his army temporarily, no further supplies of ammunition could be collected if the Confederates cut the Union lifeline. In addition, the foraging demands of both armies would quickly exhaust food supplies in the area, leaving the Union army little choice but to starve or surrender. Logistics represented Grant's greatest weakness during the campaign, and while his correspondence displays little fear of either Confederate commander, it does indicate a serious concern for supplying the army.[6]

In the 1860 census, Jackson had reported a population 3,191, but the demands of war had significantly altered the Mississippi state capital. Jackson, a major industrial and transportation nucleus, had experienced rapid growth from wartime production.[7] The city possessed the state arsenal, several vital factories and machine-shops, and contained the junction of the New Orleans, Jackson, and Great Northern Railroad, which ran north to south and connected with the Mississippi Central Railroad at Canton, with the Southern Railroad of Mississippi, which ran east to west and connected Vicksburg with Selma, Alabama. The loss of Jackson would devastate the Confederate cause in the western theater both politically and strategically, and it clearly contained enough value to justify a major battle. Nonetheless, Johnston refused to risk an engagement to save the capital of Mississippi. It was an ill omen that foretold Johnston's future conduct during the campaign and his evident disregard for Vicksburg itself. The fall of Jackson introduced a new intensity of destruction in the campaign and resulted in the first major urban demolition of the war in the western theater.[8]

Within Jackson, *New York Tribune* war correspondent Junius Henri Browne viewed the increasing panic with delight. Brown and a small group of fellow reporters had been captured in a reckless attempt to run past the Vicksburg batteries on May 3, and from his captivity in the capital city, the journalist recorded that at "the street corners were knots of excited men, discussing the prospects of the future with more feeling than logic. To us, who had long been careful observers, it was evident they were at a loss what to do; and you can imagine we rather enjoyed the trepidation of the Rebels."[9] Governor John J. Pettus hastily transferred the state government to Enterprise, Mississippi, and several Jacksonians followed the governor's example by fleeing from the threatened city.[10] Browne reported that he witnessed "a number of vehicles of various kinds loaded with household furniture, and men, women, children, and black servants, all greatly excited, moving rapidly out of town."[11]

However, not all Jacksonians dreaded the approach of the Yankees. Browne asserted, "A panic of the most decided kind existed among all classes of society; but we had no difficulty in perceiving that the negroes of both sexes, young and old, enjoyed the quandary of their masters and mistresses." Although the mayor urged residents to defend their city, little civilian resistance occurred aside from those few who joined the Mississippi State Troops. Browne derisively noted that, "If the citizens were flying to arms, they must have concealed them somewhere in the country, and have been making haste in that direction to recover them. They were certainly leaving town by all possible routes, and by every obtainable means of conveyance."[12] Thomas Frank Gailor, then a six-year-old fleeing the city with his parents, later recalled that "the shells burst like fire-rockets over the city. Many houses were on fire. It was a gorgeous spectacle. I can see now our old Negro servant dodging behind the lamp-posts every time a shell burst." Gailor further detailed, "I recall the terror-stricken flight of thousands of women and children as we streamed along the roads that hot day, with everything we could carry. I had two suits of clothes on, and mother was wearing her furs—for we did not know whether the house would escape the fire."[13]

On May 14, Sherman's and McPherson's Corps drove back the Confederate rear guard in the brief Battle of Jackson and entered the city in triumph. The Army of the Tennessee seized the valuable resources of Jackson at a cost of 42 killed, 251 wounded, and seven missing, while Johnston's casualties are estimated to have been roughly 845. In addition, Grant's men captured 17 cannon and a large amount of supplies the Confederacy could ill afford to lose.[14] Johnston's defense of Jackson had lasted less than 24 hours and surrendered one of the most important cities in the state after little more than a skirmish. Knowing that his entire army would be needed to attack Vicksburg, Grant promptly decided to destroy Jackson's industrial and transportation resources instead of depleting his force by garrisoning the city. Grant provided a foretaste of the future when he ordered Sherman and the XV Corps to demolish Jackson's war-making potential. Grant recalled after the war that "Sherman was to remain in Jackson until he destroyed that place as a railroad centre, and manufacturing city of military supplies. He did the work most effectually."[15] On May 14, Grant detailed two divisions from Sherman's Corps to guard

Jackson and "collect stores and forage, and collect all public property of the enemy. ... You will direct ... therefore, to commence immediately the effectual destruction of the river railroad bridge and the road as far east as practicable, as well as north and south."[16]

The capture of Jackson changed Sherman's military career forever. While the fiery Ohioan had burned small river towns before as retaliation for partisan attacks on Union shipping, Sherman had criticized the devastation inflicted by Federal soldiers in previous campaigns and had little confidence in Grant's proposal to provision the Army of the Tennessee from the countryside. No major damage had occurred in the fall of other large southern cities, such as New Orleans and Nashville. However, the destruction of Jackson's manufacturing facilities and transportation infrastructure proved to Sherman the value of the torch, and he would use similar methods after the fall of other southern cities, such as Atlanta, Georgia, and Columbia, South Carolina. Likewise, Grant's extensive use of foraging foreshadowed Sherman's use of such methods in his March to the Sea the following year. The first Union occupation of Jackson would be the first significant instance of hard war in the western theater.

During the occupation, Grant and Sherman visited one particular textile factory owned by Joshua and Thomas Green and stood by as employees, generally young women, worked at looms making cloth labeled " C.S.A."[17] The generals watched in silence until, as Grant remembered, "I told Sherman I thought they had done work enough. The operatives were told they could leave and take with them what cloth they could carry. In a few minutes cotton and factory were in a blaze."[18] After the war, when Grant was president of the United States, one of the owners visited Washington to lobby Congress for restitution on the grounds that the factory had been private, not public, property and asked the president for a statement supporting their claim. Grant refused.

That night, Grant slept in the same room in the Bowman House Hotel that Johnston had used during his brief stay in Jackson. As the Union commander organized his forces to march west toward Vicksburg, he had little time to spare for the protection of private property within the city.[19] Correspondent Cadwallader recalled, "Many calls were made upon him by citizens asking for guards to protect their private property, some of which perhaps were granted, but by far the greater number were left to the tender mercies of Confederate friends."[20] These "Confederate friends" had aided Grant's mission before he entered Jackson by burning commissary stores, cotton, and railroad cars that could not be evacuated in time. When the Army of the Tennessee entered Jackson, fires were already blazing in parts of the city. To make matters worse for residents, officials at the Mississippi

State Penitentiary unwisely released the inmates when Grant threatened the city, and the convicts only added to the mayhem by plundering throughout the town.[21]

Sherman's men quickly reduced the industrial resources of Jackson to ruins. Cadwallader declared that "foundries, machine-shops, warehouses, factories, arsenals and public stores were fired as fast as flames could be kindled. Many citizens fled at our approach, abandoning houses, stores, and all their personal property, without so much as locking their doors."[22] The Federals also burned the stored cotton that had escaped destruction at the hands of Johnston's retreating army. Charles Dana testified that "I remained with Sherman to see the work of destruction. I remember now nothing that I saw except the burning of vast quantities of cotton packed in bales, and that I was greatly astonished to see how slowly it burned."[23]

While the Federals began their work of destruction, a state of anarchy existed, allowing a mob of newly freed slaves, Confederate deserters, released convicts, lower-class whites, and Union soldiers to pillage freely before order could be restored. Cadwallader could only stand by and watch while "negroes, poor whites—and it must be admitted—some stragglers and bummers from the ranks of the Union army" ransacked and "carried off thousands of dollars worth of property from houses, homes, shops and stores, until some excuse was given for the charge of 'northern vandalism,' which was afterwards made by the South." The war reporter detailed, "The streets were filled with people, white and black, who were carrying away all the stolen goods they could stagger under, without the slightest attempt at concealment, and without let or hindrance from citizens or soldiers."[24] The sacking of Jackson continued through the night, and it would not be until the evening of May 15 that Sherman reestablished order under martial law.

One Union soldier in Jackson, Sergeant Ira Blanchard, later affirmed, "The place was sacked by the cavalry and many of the public buildings burned, and the army under Johnson completely routed."[25] Charles A. Wilson, a Federal eyewitness, recalled, "What grieved me most I think was to see the sugar warehouses with their tiers upon tiers of sugar hogsheads, going up in fire and smoke. I loved sugar—it had always been a luxury with me." During the chaos, Wilson secured "eight or nine canteens of it, hung to my shoulders, as we marched out of the city. But my endurance proved not equal to my zeal for sugar. One by one the canteens had to go as the straps cut into my shoulder." Grant's men discovered a considerable amount of tobacco in Jackson, and Wilson chronicled that "an immense amount of plug tobacco was brought out by the soldiers, their hankering for the weed evidently on the same scale as mine for sugar.

I think enough was left strewed over the ground at our first camp to thatch a good-sized village."[26] During the Confederate retreat, Johnston's men burned the Pearl River railroad bridge, and the Union army destroyed the railroad tracks that left the city at least three miles out in all directions.[27] Sherman wrote in his official report that "I estimate the destruction of the [rail]roads 4 miles east of Jackson, 3 south, 3 north, and 10 west."[28] The XV Corps laid the rails on top of burning ties and twisted the track beyond repair to create a useless mass of metal that the men called "Sherman's neckties."[29]

Sometime during the looting, Federal soldiers stumbled upon stocks of alcohol, stimulating the pandemonium. In a letter to his father on May 22, Adjutant Edward Stanfield of the 48th Indiana admitted that "the boys lived high that afternoon. Plenty of tobacco, corn meal & pea nuts to say nothing of whiskey (a very poor article by the way)."[30] Similarly, Private George M. Lucas of the 11th Missouri Infantry recorded the drunken landscape on May 15 when he wrote, "Bivouacked in the Public Square at Jackson, Miss. All is confusion and tumult. The confiscated whiskey is suffering severely and three fourths of the men are drunk[.] Deliver me from another such a place as this."[31] The supplies of cheap whiskey lasted through the night for those who choose to imbibe. On May 16, the 4th Iowa Cavalry received orders to impose martial law and restore military discipline. Private Jacob Gantz inscribed in his diary that day that "this morning we left jackson. about left the town on fire we had a hard time getting the drunk men out. a great many was left because they was drunk. they could not walk well."[32] The bacchanalia gave the XV Corps quite a reputation within the Army of the Tennessee. On June 17, Lieutenant Henry Kircher of the 12th Missouri Infantry wrote his mother that "in Jackson, all of Sherman's corps masqueraded and got drunk and played the fool."[33]

Sherman's men did not spare the state library from their fury of vandalism either. Charles Dana Miller wrote that on May 16 he "visited the Mississippi State Library where the soldiers were helping themselves to books apparently without objections being made by General Sherman. I secured a few small volumes such as I could carry conveniently, but saw a good many expensive works I would have liked, could I have obtained transportation."[34] For bored soldiers who had little leisure activities to help break the monotony of camp life, books were a precious commodity. While marching to Jackson, Osborn Oldroyd observed that "the boys frequently bring in reading matter with their forage. Almost anything in print is better than nothing. A novel was brought in to-day, and as soon as it was caught sight of a score or more had engaged in turn the reading of it."[35]

The Federals lost control of the fires set in Jackson, and soon flames spread to the residential areas. After Grant captured the city on May 14, Private Greenman added to his diary, "Some one started a fire just at dark, and the City is burning, and although every effort is being made to put out the fire it is spreading, and it looks as though the whole City will be destroyed."[36] Osborn Oldroyd recorded that "some of the boys went down into the city to view our new possession. It seems ablaze, but I trust only public property is being destroyed, or such as might aid and comfort the enemy here-after."[37] One retreating Rebel in Johnston's army recalled, "Throughout the silent watches of the night, the twinkling stars looked down upon the merciless conflagration kindled by the enemy. Much of Jackson was laid in ashes."[38] Once Grant's men abandoned Jackson, the Confederates found the city's industrial capacity reduced to smoldering fires and piles of ashes. On June 2, Lieutenant Rufus W. Cater of the 19th Louisiana Infantry noted in a letter to his cousin, "I could see from where I stood the rubbish and ashes of buildings that had been demolished by the brutal and fiendish foe—Among these were the Bank and the state penitentiary."[39] While Grant's men stayed in Jackson for only 36 hours, Governor John Jones Pettus estimated the Federals inflicted $10 million worth of damage. With manufacturing facilities and railroads reduced to rubble, the city of Jackson would be of little benefit to the Confederacy for the rest of the war.[40]

On May 15, Sherman began organizing the XV Corps to leave Jackson the following day to reinforce the rest of the Army of the Tennessee. Sherman ordered Brigadier General Joseph A. Mower to "push the work of destruction, especially of types, presses, sugar, and everything public not needed by us. The work should be all done by 10 a.m. to-morrow." Sherman instructed Mower to "be sure to destroy all tents by burning them in a pile to the rear of the State-house to-morrow about noon. You may release all prisoners (citizens) whom we don't want to carry along; some now, others just as you start." Sherman concluded his message by advising his subordinate, "You must work at night, if necessary, to destroy what might be useful to an enemy."[41]

That same day, John Merrilees of Battery E, 1st Illinois Light Artillery, wrote in his diary, "Details have been at work all day, collecting all government property and destroying it, throwing the ammunition into the Pearl River, and burning everything else. Great quantities of stuff were found, little or nothing having been got away." The soldiers destroyed more than Confederate government property, as the artilleryman added, "Enormous quantities of sugar and tobacco were stored all over town, which the men made free with. The town all day was a scene of wildest confusion, plundering going on universally among the stores, which the guards made very feeble efforts to prevent." Some soldiers also robbed from private homes. Merrilees asserted that "by night everything valuable of government property had been destroyed, but private property was still being pillaged by the men. Stores and private houses were gutted, buildings fired, and the terrible scene of uproar and violence prevailing everywhere."[42]

Sometime later on May 15, Sherman learned of the plundering and wrote to Mower, "It is represented to me that the provost-marshal is giving license to soldiers to take the contents of stores, taking things not necessary or useful. This, if true, is wrong." Sherman instead insisted upon restraint and commanded that "only such articles should be taken as are necessary to the subsistence of troops, and the private rights of citizens should be respected." The red-bearded general demanded, "Please give the matter your attention. The feeling of pillage and booty will injure the morals of the troops, and bring disgrace on our cause. Take every possible precaution against fires at the time of our leaving to-morrow."[43] However, surviving accounts indicate that Mower did not fully restore discipline until sometime that evening when Union cavalry finally established order. John Merrilees recorded that "this state of things went on till 11 o.c. at night, when the 4th Iowa Cavalry were ordered to clear the streets and arrest every man without a Brigadier's pass; which they at once proceeded to do and with good success, charging up and down with drawn sabres."[44]

Both Grant and McPherson left Jackson on May 15, and Sherman's two divisions completed their work of destruction and began to march westward the next day. Sherman remembered that just as he began to leave, "a very fat man came to see me, to inquire if his hotel, a large frame-building near the depot, were doomed to be burned." Sherman replied that he "had no intention to burn it, or any other house, except the machine-shops, and such buildings as could easily be converted to hostile uses." Sherman noted that "he professed to a law-abiding Union man, and I remember to have said that this fact was manifest from the sign of his hotel, which was the 'Confederate Hotel:' the sign 'United States' being faintly painted out, and 'Confederate' painted over it!" Sherman admitted that "I had not the least purpose, however, of burning it, but, just as we were leaving town, it burst into flames and was burned to the ground."[45] While Sherman never discovered the perpetrators of the fire, Brevet Major Charles Dana Miller confessed that his company "found a hotel here called the 'Confederate House' as the large sign indicated on its front. This had been painted over the words 'United States House.' The boys concluded that it had better close up business under its new title and accordingly applied the torch."[46]

During the Vicksburg campaign, abandoned homes typically suffered more than occupied residences. Those Jacksonians who had fled from the city generally lost more than those who stayed behind to protect their private property. John Merrilees described meeting a "Mrs. Freeman" on May 16 who had escaped from Jackson before the battle and "returned last night, and is in a terrible state of mind to find it gutted from top to bottom: all the wealth of dry goods and finery of every description, with which it was filled, disappeared, the wrecks littering the floor a foot or two deep." Merrilees observed that Freeman's houseguest, "Miss Lucy Gwin" seemed to be "in deep tribulation over the loss of her new bonnet, splendid velvet cloak, bracelets, earrings, and Lord only knows what not; all of which she says, the miserable Yankees have got." Gwin did not hide her disappointment at Johnston's failure to defend the city. Merrilees wrote, "The rebel authorities also came in for a share of her fiery indignation. 'It is getting to be a pretty state of things, when a few miserable Black Republicans can come and take the capital of the State,' says she." Nonetheless, the young rebel still supported the Confederacy, and Merrilees documented that "she took great consolation though, in letting us know that we wouldn't be here long: that the terrible General Joseph Johnston would soon be back, and then—not one of us would get out of Mississippi alive."[47]

Shocked at the wreckage of private homes, Merrilees admitted, "It is hard to see such wholesale plundering without feeling sorry for the sufferers." Due to the Freemans' strong support for secession, the Union artilleryman resolved, "Still, the misfortunes of war could not have fallen where there would be less reason to regret them than in this case . . . they couldn't very well play Union, and even lacked impudence to ask redress of Sherman, or a guard." Despite the fact that the Freeman women now occupied the home, Union soldiers took revenge upon the prominent Confederate family. While Merrilees readied his men to march west from Jackson, he finished his entry by observing, "Freeman's house on fire— some of our men's work I am afraid."[48]

Two days later, one of the most interesting men in the South at that time arrived in Jackson. British observer Arthur Fremantle visited the Mississippi capital on May 18 during his three-month tour throughout the Confederacy and recorded in his famed diary, "I saw the ruins of the Roman Catholic church, the priest's house, and the principal hotel, which were still smoking, together with many other buildings which could in no way be identified with the Confederate government. The whole town was a miserable wreck, and presented a deplorable aspect." Fremantle displayed genuine compassion for the plight of civilians and noted, "Nothing could exceed the intense hatred and fury with which its excited citizens speak of the outrages they have undergone—of their desire for a bloody revenge, and of their hope that the Black Flag might be raised." After viewing the destruction in Jackson, Fremantle affirmed that "during the short space of thirty-six hours, in which General Grant occupied the city, his troops had wantonly pillaged nearly all the private houses. They had gutted all the stores, and destroyed what they could not carry away."[49]

One Jacksonian whom Fremantle described guarded his home and faced down a crowd of looters by sitting on his veranda with a loaded double-barreled shotgun. When the mob threatened the property, the man raised his shotgun at the group and asserted, "No man can die more than once, and I shall never be more ready to die than I am now. There is nothing to prevent your going into this house, except that I shall kill the first two of you who move with this gun. Now then, gentlemen, walk in."[50] The spoils-seeking multitude retreated empty-handed and left the home untouched.

Many other residents were not so fortunate in preserving their possessions. Fremantle recalled encountering an old despondent planter, "mounted on a miserable animal which had been left him by the enemy as not being worth taking away." Fremantle narrated that "the small remains of this poor old man's sense had been shattered by the Yankees a few days ago. They cleaned him completely out, taking his horses, mules, cows, and pigs, and stealing his clothes and anything they wanted, destroying what they could not carry away."[51] Although the residents of Jackson called for revenge, the city would be of little use to the Confederacy for the remainder of the war. Indeed, Grant's campaign created thousands of war refugees and improvised citizens that state and local authorities could not provide for, and this only further weakened Confederate resolve and resources.

While the destruction in Jackson stunned residents, the damage inflicted in the brief occupation left most of the city intact. Grant's army torched property related to the war effort, such as arsenals, "the government foundry, a gun-carriage foundry, the railroad depot, and the state penitentiary building that housed a cotton-processing operation," but spared the Governor's Mansion and the Mississippi state capitol.[52] War reporter Sylvanus Cadwallader wrote in his account, "On our occupation of Jackson in May, pains were taken to leave all private, and much of the public property of the place uninjured. No buildings were burned by us that did not contain Confederate property or were in some way in the use of the Confederate government. Many even of these escaped."[53] Although Union soldiers did deliberately burn a few houses and some others blazed when fires got out of control, most residential houses remained intact. When the Federals returned to Jackson later in the war, the devastation would be even greater.

While Grant focused his attention on capturing and subduing Jackson, Pemberton had concentrated the Army of Vicksburg near Edwards Station. Pemberton had united most of his outlying units to confront the Union invader, but he marched east with only three of his five divisions, under Major Generals Carter L. Stevenson and William W. Loring and Brigadier General John S. Bowen. Pemberton left the divisions of Major Generals John H. Forney and Martin L. Smith to defend Vicksburg, though there was no major threat to the city other than Grant's Army of the Tennessee. While the three divisions contained reliable veterans, especially Bowen's command, the army's high command had little confidence in the Pennsylvania-born Pemberton. Loring in particular had already proven himself to be untrustworthy in carrying out his orders, and if any division should have remained in Vicksburg, it should have been his. Loring, who had lost an arm while fighting in the Mexican War, had little loyalty or respect for his commanding general. Pemberton's three divisions contained some 23,000 men, which meant that they would be outnumbered roughly three to two in any major engagement with Grant's army.[54]

For the first time in his career, Pemberton would be commanding an army in a major battle. Naturally cautious, Pemberton preferred to remain behind a defensive line along the Big Black River, roughly 12 miles from Vicksburg. This strategy had worked perfectly some five months before in the Battle of Chickasaw Bayou and would have left Pemberton's men much closer to the two divisions left in Vicksburg. However, Pemberton deferred to the wishes of his division commanders, who sought to confront Grant's army east of the Big Black River. The Army of Vicksburg had remained in static garrisons for most of Pemberton's tenure of command and was not accustomed to the physical demands of lengthy marches. The ensuing straggling further weakened the already outnumbered Army of Vicksburg.[55]

On the morning of May 14, Pemberton received a copy of Johnston's order sent from Jackson on the previous day ordering him to march to Clinton and unite the two Confederate armies. A five- to six-hour ride separated the two armies by courier, and it would take time for Pemberton's forces to march the 19 miles from Edwards Station to Clinton.[56] Pemberton himself opposed the edict and observed to one of his staff officers that "such a movement will be suicidal."[57] However, ignoring his own orders to Pemberton, Johnston instead directed his command to march away from the Army of Vicksburg after the evacuation of Jackson toward Canton, making any attempted junction impossible. To make matters worse, Johnston had sent three separate couriers to carry a copy of the message to Pemberton to increase the chances of one making it through. One of those couriers happened to be a Union spy who promptly shared this vital intelligence with McPherson, who then informed Grant. Forewarned that Pemberton planned to march east to unite with Johnston, Grant began moving his army to block the advance of the Army of Vicksburg.[58]

After receiving the ill-considered order on May 14, Pemberton immediately responded with the declaration, "I move at once with whole available force," but he correctly warned Johnston that "the men have been marching several days, are much fatigued, and I fear will straggle very much. In directing this move, I do not think you fully comprehend the position that Vicksburg will be left in, but I comply at once with your order."[59] Pemberton initially ordered the army to march to Clinton, leaving behind some 9,000 men to guard the Big Black River Bridge and protect Vicksburg. However, the Confederate commander had his doubts about the operation and convened a council of war with all general officers present with the army. After reading aloud Johnston's dispatch, the Pennsylvanian asked for the council's opinions. Pemberton wrote in his official report that "a majority of the officers present expressed themselves favorable to the movement indicated by General Johnston," but others, including Loring and Stevenson, argued instead that the army should march to the south in hopes of interrupting Grant's supply lines.[60] Once this was accomplished, Grant would then be forced to attack the Army of Vicksburg in a defensive position of their choice. Although the plan had some merit, it would be out of character for Grant to passively watch his opponent to cut his supply lines and then idly wait for the Confederate army to prepare a defensive position without striking at either Pemberton or Vicksburg itself. Pemberton's abysmal lack of cavalry continued to affect army intelligence, and even at this point, he had only two cavalry regiments accompanying the army, which had little idea where Grant's army was located or where it was headed. While Pemberton wisely opposed the risky plan and favored remaining behind the Big Black River, he reluctantly agreed to the scheme against his own better judgment. In one moment of indecision, Pemberton squandered whatever respect he still maintained amongst the officers of the Army of Vicksburg and left his subordinates, particularly Loring, with an inflated sense of their own tactical judgment. The consequences would be disastrous for the Confederacy.[61]

After adopting the council's recommendation, Pemberton notified Johnston that the Army of Vicksburg would now be marching southeastward on the Raymond-Edwards Road and the Turkey Creek Road to Dillon's plantation rather than Clinton. On May 15, while Sherman devastated Jackson, Pemberton's three divisions began the advance, but delays in distributing rations and ammunition postponed the movement until 1:00 P.M. Recent storms had transformed the roads into muddy quagmires and washed away the bridge over a flooded Bakers Creek, which halted the entire army until scouts discovered another intact bridge. Pemberton then decided to return to the Jackson Road to cross the creek and then turn south on the Ratliff Road, which intersected with the Raymond-Edwards Road. Again, a lack of cavalry scouting had hampered Pemberton's knowledge of the terrain on which the army was to maneuver. The supply problems from the morning and the lack of intelligence regarding the terrain and location of the enemy reflected the army's inexperience with maneuver warfare and served as a poor forecast for the upcoming battle that Pemberton expected to fight. That night, the army rested along the Ratliff Road with Loring's men in the lead, followed by Bowen's two brigades, while Stevenson's large division and the army's wagon train camped near the vital crossroads of the Jackson Road, the Middle Road, and the Ratliff Road. The roads intersected about 700 yards south of Champion Hill, which ascended to 140 feet above the local terrain and dominated the area. Bowen's division did not arrive until after midnight, and Stevenson's brigades did not reach the area until 3:00 A.M. Aside from posting a few pickets, Pemberton did little during the night to prepare his tired army for a possible battle in the morning.[62]

While Pemberton's advance blindly staggered forth, Grant organized some 32,000 well-rested men to confront the Army of Vicksburg. The Army of the Tennessee had been victorious thus far in the campaign, but after taking Jackson the Federals began to feel hunger for the first time since their landing in Mississippi. As Sergeant Ira Blanchard of the 20th Illinois Infantry remembered, "Our rations had now given out and there was no hope of obtaining more until we could open communications with the fleet above Vicksburg, and to do this would require much hard fighting." The area between Jackson and Vicksburg had already been heavily foraged by Pemberton's army, leaving little for Grant's men to subsist on. Blanchard reported that his regiment "had been moved so rapidly that we had little opportunity to forage off the country, and it had been run

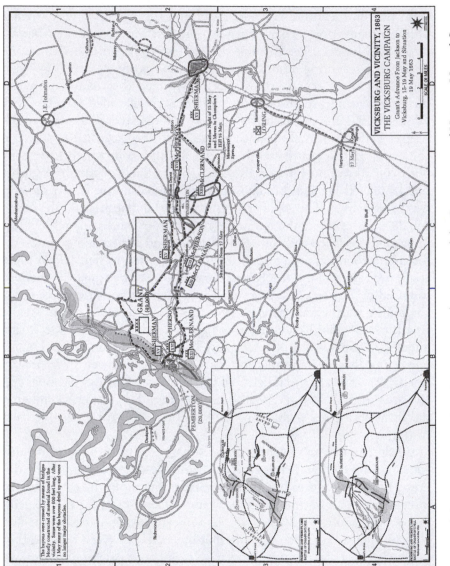

The Vicksburg Campaign, May 15–19, 1863. (Courtesy of the Department of History, United States Military Academy)

over so much by the Southern Army there was little left." The Army of the Tennessee could not survive long under such conditions, and if Grant did not fight his way back to the Mississippi River, his men would have to either starve or surrender. The march to Vicksburg would be a race against time, and the men in the ranks knew that they would have to break through Pemberton's army to survive. As Blanchard recalled, "For two days we fasted and 'twas no use now to holler 'Bread or blood' for the officers could not furnish the bread, but the blood we were getting."[63]

About 5:00 A.M. on May 16, Federal soldiers captured two employees of the Southern Railroad of Mississippi who reported (with astonishing accuracy) the location of Pemberton's army and estimated its size to be roughly 25,000. From his headquarters in Clinton, Grant swiftly ordered seven divisions to march westward and defeat the Confederate offensive while Sherman's remaining two divisions completed their work of destruction in Jackson. To the north, two divisions under Major General John A. Logan and Brigadier General Marcellus M. Crocker from the XVII Corps marched on the Jackson Road along with Brigadier General Alvin P. Hovey's division from McClernand's XIII Corps. McClernand himself accompanied the divisions of Brigadier Generals Peter Osterhaus and Eugene A. Carr on the Middle Road. To the south, McClernand's remaining division under Brigadier General Andrew J. Smith advanced along the Raymond Road followed by Major General Frank P. Blair Jr.'s division from Sherman's XV Corps. Grant rode with McPherson on the Jackson Road but gave firm orders to his subordinates not to bring on a general engagement until the army was concentrated. Around 6:30 A.M., Grant's cavalry scouts discovered and engaged pickets from Pemberton's inadequate cavalry screen.[64]

At roughly the same time, as Pemberton and Colonel Wirt Adams discussed the tactical situation, a courier arrived and handed the Confederate commander another dispatch from Johnston. The Virginian had been infuriated when he received Pemberton's message stating that he would not obey the order directing the Army of Vicksburg to march to Clinton. In the new message, Johnston reiterated his previous orders and informed Pemberton, "Our being compelled to leave Jackson makes your plan impracticable. The only mode by which we can unite is by your moving directly to Clinton, informing me, that we may move to that point with about 6,000 troops. ... Let me hear from you immediately."[65] However, while Johnston apparently expected Pemberton to march immediately to Clinton directly into the midst of Grant's Army of the Tennessee after receiving this directive, he did not order his own forces to march to a possible junction and instead continued his retreat toward Canton.

As Pemberton's chief engineer, Major Samuel H. Lockett, observed after the war, "Pemberton moved from Edward's depot in obedience to a dispatch from General Johnston, ordering him to attack in the rear a force which he supposed General Johnston was going to engage in front. Instead of this, he encountered Grant's victorious army returning ... from the capture of Jackson."[66]

Although Colonel Wirt Adams had just reported contact with Federal cavalry, Pemberton resolved to obey Johnston's decree and issued orders for a countermarch. The Confederate commander gathered his senior officers at the Ellison house around 8:00 A.M. and informed them of the new plan. While the stunned subordinates stared in disbelief, Pemberton directed the army's wagon train at the rear of the column to return to Edwards Station in order to reach Clinton by marching to the north around Grant's army. The train consisted of some 400 wagons with worn-out teams, and it would take several hours for the wagons to be turned around and to clear the road for the rest of the Army of Vicksburg. As the sounds of thundering cannon opened upon Confederate pickets, Loring suggested that the army should immediately form a battle line. Still intending to obey Johnston's orders, Pemberton deployed his three divisions in a battle line three miles long to delay any Union advance and allow the army to retreat back to Edwards Station. Loring's 6,500-man division, containing the brigades of Brigadier Generals Abraham Buford, Winfield S. Featherston, and Lloyd Tilghman, guarded the Confederate right flank along the Raymond Road. Bowen's steadfast division held the Confederate center with 4,800 men in two brigades commanded by Colonel Francis Cockrell and Brigadier General Martin E. Green. Stevenson's division contained 11,700 men in the brigades of Brigadier Generals Seth Barton, Stephen D. Lee, Alfred Cumming, and Colonel Alexander W. Reynolds. Upon learning of the countermarch, Stevenson instructed Reynolds's brigade of Tennesseans and Marylanders to protect the wagon train, leaving some 9,000 men to secure the Rebel left flank along the vital crossroads south of Champion Hill. If Grant's men captured the crossroads and blocked Pemberton's escape route along the Jackson Road to the bridge over Bakers Creek, the Army of Vicksburg would be trapped and destroyed.[67]

Contact first occurred on the Confederate right, where Loring and Bowen occupied a strong position along a ridge behind Jackson Creek with a clear field of fire. However, the strongest Union column lurked beyond the Rebel left flank along the Jackson Road. Incredibly, Pemberton had no idea that three of Grant's divisions menaced his left flank until Stephen D. Lee astutely ordered a reconnaissance that discovered Hovey's division approaching from the north. Lee, who had been reassigned to assume command of Tracy's Alabama brigade after its commander died at Port Gibson, rushed his men to deploy along the cleared crest of Champion Hill around 9:15 A.M. By that point, Federal skirmishers were already probing along both the Middle and Jackson Roads. Realizing the serious danger that threatened the very survival of the Army of Vicksburg, Lee informed Stevenson of the peril and pleaded for reinforcements to secure the Confederate left flank.[68]

Grant, riding with McPherson on the Jackson Road, did not want to initiate a general engagement until each wing of his army had reached the battlefield. Around 10:00 A.M., Grant arrived and assessed the situation. He remembered in his memoirs, "Champion's Hill, where Pemberton had chosen his position to receive us, whether taken by accident or design, was well selected. It is one of the highest points in that section, and commanded all the ground in range."[69] Despite the strong position, Grant realized that he had the tactical advantage and ordered an immediate attack. Hovey's division had already engaged the Rebels, and reinforced by Logan's division, the Federal assault began at 10:30 A.M. Stevenson stretched his lines to counter the Union advance and ordered the 34th, 36th, and 39th Georgia Infantry regiments from Cumming's brigade to reinforce Lee's right, while his other brigade of Georgians under Seth Barton moved from the crossroads to secure Lee's left flank. Only two regiments from Cumming's brigade, the 56th and 57th Georgia, remained behind to guard the crossroads. In his report, Stevenson described his new line as "single, irregular, divided, and without reserves." The Rebel general also admitted that "under the supposition that the army was to move forward in pursuance of the instructions given in the morning, this ground was not reconnoitered with a view to taking up a position for battle until we were on the move facing the enemy."[70]

More than 10,000 Union soldiers charged into the Rebels on Champion Hill. At first, Stevenson's men held their ground, but soon the Confederate line began to crumble in the face of the overwhelming blue onslaught. Hovey's men broke through Stevenson's division on Champion Hill, capturing several cannon and driving the Confederates back from the crucial crossroads in disorder. Pemberton had been aware of the Union attack on his left flank, but the Pennsylvanian had been absorbed by the Union columns on the Middle and Raymond Roads and had not ordered reinforcements to his threatened left. Instead, Pemberton had been attempting to initiate an attack of his own with his other two divisions, but this offensive failed to materialize when Loring informed Pemberton that the Union position appeared too formidable to assault. Around

2:00 P.M., Stevenson urgently requested that reinforcements be sent to the left flank, but the Federals drove his men from the hill before they could arrive. Pemberton, who was at his headquarters at the Roberts house on the Ratliff Road, at last realized the danger confronting the Army of Vicksburg and immediately ordered Bowen to march to the crossroads.[71]

At first, Pemberton directed Bowen to send only one brigade to reinforce Stevenson, but as the crisis intensified, he soon ordered Bowen's entire division to advance at a run. Although both Bowen and Loring had encountered Union columns, neither division had thus far been involved in major fighting. Loring redeployed Buford's and Featherston's brigades to cover the area previously occupied by Bowen's division while Tilghman's brigade remained behind to guard the Raymond Road. Due to the rough terrain and confusion of battle, the Union commands had become disorganized and ill prepared for a counterattack.[72] As Cockrell's Missourians passed the Champion House, Corporal Ephraim Anderson recalled witnessing a "novel appearance on the battle-field," for at that moment "in the yard was a group of ladies, who cheered the men on, and were singing 'Dixie.'"[73] Inspired by the ladies, Bowen's two elite brigades stormed into the Federals on Champion Hill in one of the most celebrated charges of the war. Years later, Anderson remembered seeing Colonel Francis Cockrell using one hand to hold "the reins and a large magnolia flower, while with the other he waved his sword, and gave the order to charge."[74] At 2:30 P.M., Bowen's division of Missourians and Arkansans swept through the crossroads and recaptured the crest of Champion Hill.[75]

For a few precious moments, it looked as through Pemberton might snatch victory from the jaws of defeat. In his account, Ephraim Anderson asserted that "the battle here raged fearfully—one unbroken, deafening roar of musketry was all that could be heard. The opposing lines were so much in the woods and so contiguous, that artillery could not be used." The Missourian declared that the "ground was fought over three times, and, as the wave of battle rolled to and fro, the scene became bloody and terrific—the actors self-reliant and determined; 'do or die,' seemed to be the feeling of our men, and right manfully and nobly did they stand up to their work."[76] In his report, Pemberton stated that Bowen's two brigades "under their gallant leaders, charged the enemy, and for the time turned the tide of battle in our favor, again displaying the heroic courage which this veteran division has made conspicuous on so many stricken fields."[77]

However, Confederate success was fleeting. Although Bowen's men fought desperately and drove the Federals back three-quarters of a mile, Grant prevented a total breakthrough by ordering Crocker's division to enter the fight along with 16 cannon in a massed battery. Hovey's men began to rally and return to the battle, while Bowen's brigades depleted their strength and ammunition. Desperately, Pemberton ordered Buford's and Featherston's brigades from Loring's division to reinforce Bowen, but "Old Blizzards," either intentionally or unintentionally, led his command down the wrong road. Precious time elapsed while Pemberton's staff frantically searched for the overdue brigades. Loring had been openly critical of Pemberton throughout the campaign, and his conduct during the day displayed little inclination to participate in the battle that decided Vicksburg's fate. Ultimately, only the rallied remnants of Stevenson's division aided Bowen's division. As Bowen's men fought furiously to hold their position, McClernand finally unleashed Osterhaus's and Carr's division along the Middle Road. Earlier in the day, Grant had ordered McClernand's column to attack along the Middle Road, but the political general had delayed his assault until after Bowen's counterattack. Strangely, Grant's other column along the Raymond Road failed to seriously engage Loring's division at any time during the day. Faced with the imminent threat of being cut off from the rest of the army, Bowen reluctantly gave the order to withdraw.[78]

Around 4:00 P.M., the remnants of Stevenson's and Bowen's shattered brigades routed. When Loring's men finally appeared, they encountered the fleeing remains of two Confederate divisions and the broken dreams of John C. Pemberton's military career. Loring's men hastily formed a battle line and prepared to advance, but before the assault began, Loring received an order from Pemberton to cancel the attack and cover the army's retreat. In his report, Pemberton bitterly protested, "Had the movement in support of the left been promptly made when first ordered, it is not improbable that I might have maintained my position, and it is possible the enemy might have been driven back," although, he admitted, Grant's "vastly superior and constantly increasing numbers would have rendered it necessary to withdraw during the night to save my communications with Vicksburg."[79] With the Federals controlling the Jackson Road, the Army of Vicksburg had no escape route over Bakers Creek. Fortunately, early in the day, Pemberton had directed his chief engineer, Major Samuel Lockett, to supervise the repair of the damaged bridge on the Raymond Road. The pioneer company had finished the bridge around 2:00 P.M., and by then Bakers Creek had subsided to the point that it was now fordable. Pemberton's retreating army streamed across Bakers Creek while Tilghman's brigade served as the rear guard along the Raymond Road. During the closing moments of the battle, Tilghman died instantly when an artillery shell struck his body, nearly cutting him in two.[80]

After Stevenson's division crossed Bakers Creek, what was left of Bowen's two brigades protected the Raymond Road bridge while Loring's division covered the retreat. However, Federal soldiers soon appeared on Bowen's left flank after crossing Bakers Creek on the Jackson Road. Realizing that his command lacked the strength to engage in further combat, Bowen withdrew his division after sending a message to Loring informing him of his decision. Pemberton and what remained of his army hurriedly evacuated Edwards Station that night and marched for the fortifications at the Big Black River. Loring briefly considered fighting his way across the creek, but the Union position on the west bank meant that his division could be trapped if Grant's pursuit force attacked his rear. In desperation, "Old Blizzards" decided to abandon the rest of the army and retreat to the southwest in hopes of finding a new route to the Big Black River. After stumbling through the darkness, Loring observed the blazing fires of Confederate supplies at Edwards Station and concluded that Grant now blocked any possible rendezvous with Pemberton. Instead, Loring resolved to attempt to unite with Johnston's army, thus fulfilling the initial order that had ultimately led to the Confederate disaster at Champion Hill. On May 19, Loring's men safely reached Johnston's force at Jackson, but the division had had to abandon all of its artillery and much of its equipment along the way.[81]

After the fighting ceased, Grant quickly organized a pursuit that occupied Edwards Station around 8:00 P.M. By the end of the day, the Army of the Tennessee had inflicted a devastating defeat on their enemy and had won the largest and most significant battle of the Vicksburg campaign. The Army of Vicksburg suffered 381 killed, 1,018 wounded, and 2,441 missing, which totaled 3,840 casualties. Most of the Confederate losses occurred in Stevenson's and Bowen's divisions, as Loring's three brigades saw only limited action. The Army of the Tennessee reported 410 killed, 1,844 wounded, and 187 missing, which amounted to 2,441 casualties. The Jackson Road column, which essentially fought and won the battle largely on its own, accounted for almost all of the Union dead and wounded. In addition, the Army of Vicksburg lost a large amount of valuable supplies and equipment, including 27 cannon. Although pleased with the victory, Grant realized that McClernand's delays allowed Pemberton's army to escape.[82] After the war, Grant complained, "Had McClernand come up with reasonable promptness, or had I known the ground as I did afterwards, I cannot see how Pemberton could have escaped with any organized force."[83]

After the battle, Union Sergeant Ira Blanchard wrote that he and his comrades "began to feel the pangs of hunger again, as we had had nothing scarcely for the last two days." As Blanchard wandered over the battlefield looking for something to eat, he "picked out a clean looking 'Reb' who had been shot down, and whose carcass lay stretched at full length on the grass, sat down beside him, and from his well filled haversack of corn bread and beef, made a sumptuous meal." After eating, Blanchard examined the dead man's clothing and discovered a copy of the New Testament, in which he read Romans 12:20: " 'If thine enemy hunger, give him to eat; if he thirst, give him to drink.' " Blanchard observed, "The poor fellow was now obeying the spirit and letter of that command; now, if never before in all his life. Little did that man think when he was so carefully preparing that haversack with 3 days rations, that a 'blue-bellied yankee' would devour the contents thereof."[84]

The next morning, Grant's forces continued their pursuit and shortly after sunrise encountered Pemberton's defenses along the Big Black River Bridge, only 12 miles from Vicksburg. Pemberton, unaware of Loring's decision to march to Johnston's army, still held a defensive beachhead on the east bank of the river in the hopes that his missing division would arrive before Grant's army. The Confederate fortifications ran across a horseshoe bend in the river and consisted of breastworks protected by an abatis of felled trees behind a 400-yard killing zone. Bowen commanded the beachhead, defended on the flanks by his two battered brigades and in the center by Brigadier General John C. Vaughn's Tennessee brigade from Smith's division, which had yet to be engaged in battle during the campaign. Vaughn's brigade had been reinforced by the 4th Mississippi Infantry from Brigadier General William E. Baldwin's brigade. The mile-long Rebel line contained some 4,000 men and 18 cannon, and Pemberton had such confidence that it would hold that he feared that Grant would attempt to cross the river at one of the nearby fords to flank the position rather than risk a frontal assault. The mile-long railroad bridge had been planked to allow the crossing of wagons and artillery, and, in addition, the steamer *Dot* had been converted into a makeshift pontoon bridge to allow a second avenue of retreat across the river in case the Federals broke through. Bowen's orders were to hold until Loring crossed, at which point the bridge and steamer would be burned.[85]

McClernand's Corps, minus Hovey's worn-out division, led the Federal march. Morale was high in the ranks after the victory at Champion Hill. That day, Ohioan Osborn Oldroyd wrote in his diary, "We have not known defeat since we left Fort Donelson, and we propose to keep our good record up. We have seen hard times on some hotly contested fields, but mean to have nothing but victory, if possible, on our banner."[86] Upon arrival, McClernand quickly deployed the divisions of Carr, Ostherhaus, and A. J. Smith and began an artillery duel with the Rebels. On the Union right, Brigadier General Michael Lawler moved his brigade forward to cover a depression close to the Confederate defenses. Around 9:00 A.M., Lawler's entire brigade charged forward and struck the Rebel line held by Vaughn and Green. Vaughn's regiments had been raised in the predominantly Unionist area of East Tennessee, and many of the men had been drafted against their will into the Confederate army. Perhaps for this reason, Vaughn's men broke and fled after some three minutes of resistance. McClernand's other brigades soon joined the charge, attacking Bowen's brigades in both front and flank. The Confederate line suddenly disintegrated, and thousands of southerners surrendered or ran to the rear over the bridges. Many of those who could not reach the bridges attempted to swim the Big Black, and a few drowned in the attempted escape.[87] Ephraim Anderson later narrated that his company's lieutenant "stripped himself to his shirt and drawers, and landed safely on the opposite bank, without any other clothing; in crossing, he lost a beautiful sword, presented to him by the company. The lieutenant travelled in his scant apparel for some distance, until at a house near the road he obtained clothes."[88]

In the midst of the chaos, Major Samuel Lockett gave the order to burn the bridges after the last Confederates crossed. Lockett's action gave time for a stunned Pemberton to withdraw what was left of his army into Vicksburg.[89] In his report, Pemberton lamented that "a strong position, with an ample force of infantry and artillery to hold it, was shamefully abandoned almost without resistance. The troops occupying the center did not do their duty."[90] Confederate casualties are unknown for the Battle of the Big Black River Bridge, but the Army of Vicksburg lost 1,751 men taken prisoner and 18 cannon captured. Federal casualties amounted to 39 Union soldiers killed, 237 wounded, and three missing.[91] As Major Samuel Lockett stated after the war, "The affair of Big Black bridge was one which an ex-Confederate participant naturally dislikes to record."[92] That night, Lockett rode with a downcast Pemberton back to Vicksburg. According to Lockett, the commanding general turned to him and said, "Just thirty years ago I began my military career by receiving my appointment to a cadetship at the U.S. Military Academy, and to-day—the same date—that career is ended in disaster and disgrace."[93]

That same day, a conference of the Confederacy's high command ended nearly 1,000 miles away in the Confederate White House in Richmond, Virginia. At the meeting, Jefferson Davis, General Robert E. Lee, and the Confederate cabinet debated what to do about the crisis in Mississippi. After four days of deliberation, the conference determined not to send reinforcements from the Army of Northern Virginia to Mississippi but instead to grant permission for Lee to lead an invasion of the North in hopes of winning a decisive battle in the eastern theater. Lee, who had fought and won the Battle of Chancellorsville in early May as Grant advanced into Central Mississippi, felt that such an offensive held greater strategic potential for the Confederacy than successfully defending Vicksburg.[94] Also, transferring a division from Lee's army to reinforce Johnston would do little to improve the latter's cautious nature, and as historians Scott Bowden and Bill Ward argue, the "tedious process—which would require a minimum of 14 different rail lines and transfers from Richmond, Virginia, to Jackson, Mississippi—would have consumed three weeks under the most favorable circumstances."[95] As a result, Lee's army would march north to Gettysburg that summer while Davis attempted to reinforce Vicksburg from less threatened areas of the Confederacy.[96]

For the rest of May 17, Pemberton's defeated army retreated past shocked civilians alongside the road to Vicksburg. One eyewitness, Mary Loughborough, recalled that mounted men and army wagons were "rattling down the street—going rapidly one way, and then returning, seemingly, without aim or purpose: now and then a worn and dusty soldier would be seen passing with his blanket and canteen; soon, straggler after straggler came by, then groups of soldiers worn and dusty with the long march." When Loughborough and other observers fearfully asked the cause of the retreat, the defeated Confederates answered, " 'We are whipped; and the Federals are after us.' " After suffering defeat at Champion's Hill and the Big Black River Bridge, the once proud Army of Vicksburg had lost all confidence in their commander, and morale had collapsed. Reflecting upon the panicked and disorganized columns, Loughborough declared, "Where these weary and wornout men were going, we could not tell. I think they did not know themselves."[97]

Behind Pemberton's army trailed a growing procession of southern refugees seeking the shelter of Fortress Vicksburg. One of the families, the Lords, consisted of Reverend Dr. William Wilberforce Lord; his wife Margaret; their children Eliza (known to her family as Lida), Sarah, William Jr., and Louisa; and their household servants. Reverend Lord had first come to Vicksburg in 1853 to serve as the rector of Christ Episcopal Church. Although a native New Yorker, when the war began, Reverend Lord continued to tend his flock and even served temporarily as the chaplain of the 1st Mississippi Light Artillery.[98] After the war, William Lord Jr. affirmed, "My father, though a Northern man by birth, had spent the greater part of his young manhood in ministering to the people of the South" and "felt spiritually wedded to them as the people of his adoption, and morally obliged to remain with them in the time of their most urgent necessity and direst trouble."[99] Years later, Lida Lord recalled the sight of Pemberton's retreating army and wrote, "Strange as it seems now, we were in a tremendous hurry to follow them." Continuing her narration, she observed, "I don't believe the people of the North could ever be made to comprehend what an awful bugaboo their armies were to the women and children of the South—unless some few upon the borders still remember their own horror of the 'rebels.' "[100]

The previous year, Reverend Lord had evacuated his family from Vicksburg to the Flowers's plantation for safety during the naval siege of Vicksburg. The Lord family returned when the Federal fleet withdrew but later had to flee to Flemens Granger's plantation, named Oakland, after the Army of the Tennessee landed at Bruinsburg.[101] Upon learning of Pemberton's retreat from the Big Black River, the Lord family and their servants hastily collected a few possessions and journeyed to Vicksburg, where Lida Lord witnessed "thousands of camp-fires" in the night, "so closely blended in a gloom of haze and smoke that we literally seemed to be within the hollow center of a great star-sprinkled sphere." Lida declared that it "was a beautiful, even wonderful sight, but we did not linger to admire it, for behind us on the dark road to Bovina crept closer and closer the awful shadow of—Grant."[102]

After the Union victory at the Battle of the Big Black River Bridge, Grant immediately began organizing a pursuit of Pemberton and the Army of Vicksburg. While Grant had been deploying his divisions before the Federal attack, a staff officer from Banks arrived with an order from Halleck directing Grant to withdraw to Grand Gulf and combine forces with Banks's advance on Port Hudson. The order had been written on May 11 and was clearly out of date. Realizing that the current situation required immediate action, Grant ignored the order and proceeded to win the Battle of the Big Black River Bridge. After the victory, Grant began preparations for the final march to Vicksburg. Since the Confederates destroyed the two bridges over the river, Grant's men had to appropriate construction material from the surrounding plantations to build three makeshift bridges.[103] Journalist Sylvanus Cadwallader reported that the building "was done by tearing down the dwelling houses, barns, stables and cotton gins nearest at hand, and flooring the cotton bale and timber floats which were bound together and anchored in the river."[104]

At the rear of the Army of the Tennessee marched Sherman's XV Corps, which had completed their work of destruction in Jackson. While passing through the town of Bolton, Sherman stopped to have a drink of water from a well. As the red-bearded general sat on his horse, he noticed a book lying on the ground. After examining the text, Sherman realized that he had in his possession Jefferson Davis's personal copy of the U.S. Constitution. Apparently, the unique artifact had been obtained by Union soldiers who plundered the Davis plantation. Soon thereafter, one of Sherman's staff officers led a group of soldiers to the plantation of the Confederate president's older brother, Joseph Davis. The soldiers visited Joseph Davis and seized two of his carriage horses.[105]

The logistical situation continued to be the greatest threat to Grant's army. If the Army of the Tennessee could not reach the Mississippi River and establish contact with the Union navy, the supply of provisions would quickly be exhausted. Charles Dana Miller recalled, "The troops were short of rations and many went hungry. The country was bare of supplies after two armies had passed over it. It was very difficult especially for the officers to obtain food, and in some instances they paid fifty cents apiece for crackers."[106] Soldiers of the 31st Illinois Infantry later remembered, "Not more than five days' rations had been issued to the army since May 1st, and everything along the line of march from water mill to farm house had been eaten." The area along the march to Vicksburg had been stripped to the point where "everything that grunted, squaked, gobbled, or cackled had found its way into the mess pan, or had been stewed in the camp kettle, or roasted on a ramrod, for the soldier must eat before he can march or fight." The men in the ranks knew that they had to fight or starve, as "the country had been stripped from Port Gibson to Jackson, and thence to the Mississippi; hence, all felt a yearning for Haines Bluff where supplies from the Mississippi and the Yazoo would now be brought."[107] On May 17, Osborn Oldroyd recorded in his diary, "We are fighting hard for our *grub*, since we have nothing left but flour, and slapjacks lie too heavy on a soldier's stomach."[108] Likewise, Sergeant Flavius J. Thackara of the 95th Ohio Infantry documented on May 18, "We have scarcely anything to eat, nothing at all for supper and no prospect of any breakfast. If we don't succeed in getting Vicksburg we are in a bad fix."[109]

Finally, on the afternoon of May 18, Grant's men reached their long-sought-after prize of Vicksburg, thus ending one of the most successful offensives in the entire war.[110] During the past few weeks, from May 1 to May 18, the Army of the Tennessee had marched more than 200 miles, won five engagements with the enemy, occupied and devastated the capital city of Jackson, inflicted nearly 8,000 casualties, captured 27 heavy cannon and 61 lighter guns, destroyed miles of invaluable railroad tracks, divided the opposing Confederate forces, and trapped Pemberton's entire army in Vicksburg.[111] That day, as Sherman and Grant inspected the Confederate defenses along Walnut Hills, where Sherman had endured a bitter defeat the previous December at Chickasaw Bluffs, Sherman admitted to his friend, "Until this moment, I never thought your expedition a success; I never could see the end clearly till now. But this is a campaign; this is a success if we never take the town."[112]

5

---◦◦◦◦---

"Vicksburg or hell!"

Immediately after the Battle of the Big Black River Bridge, Pemberton rode back to Vicksburg to make final preparations for an inescapable assault and siege. On May 18, Pemberton received orders from Johnston that warned, "If, therefore, you are invested in Vicksburg, you must ultimately surrender. Under such circumstances, instead of losing both troops and place, we must, if possible, save the troops. If it is not too late, evacuate Vicksburg and its dependencies, and march to the northeast."[1] Once again, Pemberton convened a council of war and asked for their opinion of Johnston's directive. The senior officers of the Army of Vicksburg concluded that "it was impossible to withdraw the army from this position with such *morale* and material as to be of further service to the Confederacy."[2] While the council met, Grant's artillery began firing on the Confederate defenses, and word arrived that the Federals were rapidly completing their investment. On May 7, Pemberton had received direct orders from President Davis to hold Vicksburg and Port Hudson.[3] Realizing that little hope existed for a successful retreat, Pemberton chose to obey his commander in chief and informed Johnston that he had "decided to hold Vicksburg as long as is possible, with the firm hope that the Government may yet be able to assist me in keeping this obstruction to the enemy's free navigation of the Mississippi River. I still conceive it to be the most important point in the Confederacy."[4]

Upon arrival, Pemberton recalled his detached forces and directed that as many provisions as possible be transported into Vicksburg. Rebel soldiers in the trenches worked furiously to prepare their positions for the inevitable Federal attack. As Texan Ralph J. Smith remembered, "Preparations were made to meet the charge which was momentarily expected. Ammunition was issued more freely than rations. Company officers laid aside their swords and took up muskets." However, not every officer rushed to take up the musket. Smith noted that "many of our third Lieutenants discovered sudden demands for their services as cooks at headquarters or other detached duties far from the maddening crowd in blue. We conferred the title of 'dog robbers' on these cooks."[5]

On the night of May 18, the Army of the Tennessee began surrounding Vicksburg. Sherman's XV Corps held the Union right, while McPherson's XVII Corps occupied the center and McClernand's XIII Corps secured the left flank. Before the Federals blocked the roads, Pemberton directed the noncombatants in the city to evacuate. Only a handful of residents obeyed the order, as most chose the hazards of siege over than the uncertainty of life under Union occupation.[6] Mary Loughborough, a St. Louis lady whose husband served in the Army of Vicksburg, explained the civilians' dilemma when she asked rhetorically, "Where can we go? Here we are among friends—we are welcome, and we feel in safety. Let us at least share the fate of those we love so much."[7] Although the residents risked starvation, injury, and possible death, many hesitated to become refugees in the anarchy of a war zone. Women particularly feared for their safety in such chaotic conditions. As Loughborough observed, "If we leave, we cannot tell to what we may be exposed—even now, probably, the Federal army occupy Jackson; if we go into the country, we are liable at any time to be surrounded by them; and to whom can we apply for protection from the soldiery?" Most of the civilians believed, as did Loughborough, that "we must stay, come what will."[8]

Although the Army of Vicksburg had nearly collapsed after the battles of Champion Hill and the Big Black River Bridge, the garrison slowly began to regain cohesion after deploying behind the city's elaborate defenses. Pemberton assigned Martin Luther Smith's division to hold the Confederate left, followed by John H. Forney's fresh division in the center, while Stevenson's weakened brigades defended the right flank, where little fighting was expected. Smith, a native New Yorker, had migrated to the South at age 22 and married into a Georgia family. Like Pemberton, when the war erupted, Smith chose to serve his adopted region rather than return to the North.[9] In reserve, Pemberton held Bowen's division and Waul's Texas Legion as a mobile force ready to reinforce any threatened position. Chief Engineer Lockett had anchored both flanks of the fortifications on the Mississippi River and designed nine major strongpoints connected by trenches to guard the main entries into the city. On the left, Smith's division manned Fort Hill, which protected the River Road, and the trenches that ran to the Stockade Redan, which guarded the Graveyard Road (a redan is a triangular-shaped fort whose apex extends from a defensive line). Forney's brigades manned the Stockade Redan and the 3rd Louisiana Redan, along with the Great Redoubt, built to defend the Jackson Road (a redoubt is an earthwork with multiple sides extending from the main defensive line), and the 2nd Texas Lunette, which controlled the Baldwin's Ferry Road (a lunette is a crescent-shaped fortification projecting from the main defensive line). Stevenson's men occupied the Railroad Redoubt, built to safeguard the Southern Railroad of Mississippi; the Square Fort (later renamed Fort Garrott); the Salient Work, which commanded the Hall's Ferry Road; and the South Fort, which secured the Warrenton Road. An abatis of felled trees and telegraph wire obstructed the approaches to most of the strongpoints, almost all of which lay behind a ditch that ranged from 6 to 10 feet deep. When the Confederate field pieces had been mounted, a total of 102 cannon stood ready to unleash a firestorm into the face of any Federal attack. Behind the earthworks stood some 31,000 tenacious Rebels determined to make Grant pay dearly for any attempt to enter Vicksburg.[10]

The defending Confederates burned all structures that obstructed their line of fire in front of the fortifications. On May 19, Emma Balfour wrote in her diary, "Last night we saw a grand and awful spectacle. The darkness was lit up by burning houses all along our lines. They were burnt that our firing would not be obstructed. It was sad to see."[11] One structure between the lines that survived the torch became a landmark of the battlefield. The white-painted home of New Hampshire–born James Shirley escaped destruction when Union forces killed a Confederate soldier attempting to burn the house. Although the Shirley family owned slaves, they had earned the censure of their neighbors by remaining loyal to the Union and had nearly lost one son to a lynch mob for his refusal to serve in the Confederate army. When the Army of the Tennessee surrounded Vicksburg, the Shirley family became trapped in the resulting cross fire and took shelter in the corner of their chimney for three days. After placing a white sheet on a broom handle and displaying it on the front porch, Federal soldiers relocated the family to one of the famous caves constructed during the siege.[12]

Victorious thus far in the campaign, Grant believed that a swift assault might conquer the city before Pemberton could restore the fighting ability of the Army of Vicksburg. Well aware that the Confederacy would undoubtedly reinforce Johnston in an attempt to save the garrison, Grant hoped to end the campaign before any further Rebels could arrive and threaten his army from the rear. To take advantage of this fleeting prospect, Grant ordered an attack by all of his corps on May 19. However, only Sherman's XV Corps had reached a position to attempt an assault, while McPherson's and McClernand's divisions had yet to fully deploy.[13] That morning, Captain Gabriel Killgore of the 17th Louisiana Infantry in Baldwin's brigade wrote in his diary, "The day promises to be a bloody one— decisive can I not say? of the fate of this nation and having an important bearing on the destinies of the World."[14] Federal artillery unleashed a massive bombardment at 9:00 A.M., but the shelling did little to weaken the defenses. When the cannonade ceased at 2:00 P.M., Sherman's men charged into the killing zone in front of the Stockade Redan along the northeastern section of the fortifications. The redan had walls almost 20 feet thick and nearly 17 feet high, and the approach to the stronghold could be enfiladed on both flanks by Confederates from other positions. The Federals, despite taking appalling casualties, managed to reach the ditch in front of the redan but lacked ladders that would enable them to climb into the fortifications. Sherman's men paid dearly for their commander's lack of reconnaissance as they lay trapped in the shelter of the ditch while Rebels from the brigades of Brigadier Generals William Baldwin, Francis Shoup, and Louis T. Hébert, reinforced by Cockrell's brigade from Bowen's division, inundated the bluecoats with minié balls, canister rounds, and artillery shells with short fuses rolled down as improvised grenades.[15]

In the Union center, the regulars of the 1st Battalion of the 13th U.S. Infantry in Colonel Giles A. Smith's brigade advanced against the Stockade Redan under the command of Captain Edward Washington, a grandnephew of George Washington. Washington fell mortally wounded in the charge, but his men persevered through the maelstrom and became the first Federal unit to plant their colors on the slopes of the Confederate earthworks. After the battle, an examination located 56 bullet holes in the regimental flag, while the national color had been hit 18 times. Both flagstaffs had been struck by projectiles, and a total of 17 color-bearers became casualties in the battalion. The regulars lost 71 killed and wounded out of 250 men in the assault on May 19, a loss of 43 percent. In honor of their bravery, General Sherman ordered that the unit inscribe "First at Vicksburg" upon their flag. "First at Vicksburg" remains the motto of the 13th U.S. Infantry to this day.

As the Federal attack stalled, Sherman's men had no choice but to take cover and wait for darkness to cover their retreat. The survivors struggled for hours under the unforgiving southern sun and the deadly rifle fire of the defenders. To the left of the regulars, the 55th Illinois in Colonel Thomas Kilby Smith's brigade found themselves pinned down with only a few rounds remaining in their cartridge boxes. Four soldiers volunteered to risk death by running back for a resupply of ammunition. Three of the men died in the attempt, but Orion P. Howe, a wounded 14-year-old musician, survived the gauntlet and informed Sherman that his comrades urgently needed cartridges. The regiment soon received their ammunition, and in 1896, Howe received the Medal of Honor for his valor that day.[16]

Despite the heroic sacrifice of Sherman's men, the May 19 assault failed miserably. The poorly planned operation cost Grant 157 killed, 777 wounded, eight missing, and two battle flags captured, while Confederate losses amounted to only around 200. The bloody fiasco also had the inadvertent effect of restoring confidence within Pemberton's dispirited command.[17] Lida Lord described this dramatic conversion when she recalled, "Then began the morale reconstruction of our army. Men who had been gloomy, depressed, and distrustful now cheerfully and bravely looked the future in the face. After that day's victory but one spirit seemed to animate the whole army, the determination never to give up."[18]

After reaching Vicksburg, Grant finally established a secure supply line with the U.S. Navy. While Grant examined the Union position, his men boldly notified their commander of their lack of bread. Grant explained in his memoirs, "I remember that in passing around to the left of the line on the 21st, a soldier, recognizing me, said in a rather low voice, but yet so that I heard him, 'Hard tack.' In a moment the cry was taken up all along the line, 'Hard tack! Hard tack!' "[19] Grant reassured his soldiers that fresh rations were on the way and confirmed in his account that "by the night of the 21st all the troops had full rations issued to them. The bread and coffee were highly appreciated."[20] For the first time since landing in Mississippi, the Army of the Tennessee was fully supplied.

Realizing that it would be impossible for one corps attacking alone to breach the Confederate lines, Grant decided to attempt an all-out assault with all three corps. With a well-fed army and more intelligence on the Rebel fortifications, he ordered that a second attack be attempted across almost the entire defensive line. The Ohioan informed his men that "if prosecuted with vigor, it is confidently believed this course will carry Vicksburg in a very short time, and with much less loss than would be sustained by delay. Every day's delay enables the enemy to strengthen his defenses and increases his chance for receiving aid from outside."[21]

Two exceptional units from the Lone Star State, Waul's Texas Legion and the 2nd Texas Infantry, waited for the enormous Federal assault within the trenches. The 2nd Texas Infantry, assigned to Brigadier

General John C. Moore's brigade, had earned a reputation as a highly drilled and hard-fighting regiment after almost two years of bloody service. Slightly over a year before, the regiment had ferociously attacked Grant and the Army of the Tennessee at the Battle of Shiloh, and the previous October at the Battle of Corinth it had suffered horrendous casualties spearheading a desperate assault on Federal fortifications at Battery Robinette. Waul's Texas Legion, the only authentic legion raised in Texas during the Civil War, manned the lines in Stevenson's division. The Legion had originally contained cavalry, artillery, and infantry units, but authorities transferred the cavalry companies and artillery battery to other commands before the Vicksburg campaign. While the Texans had seen little action thus far in the campaign, both units would prove their courage during the long and bitter siege.[22]

While Waul's Texas Legion remained in reserve, the 2nd Texas Infantry defended a critical section of the Vicksburg defenses, the aptly named 2nd Texas Lunette. The Lunette contained a six-foot-high parapet and commanded a ridge fronted by a ditch that descended to a depth of six feet. Engineers constructed the fort with earthen walls 14 feet thick, armed it with two cannon, and created a second line of rifle pits behind the stronghold in case of a Union breakthrough. Due to size limitations, the Lunette could contain only four companies of the regiment at a time, while the remaining companies defended rifle pits on each flank. The left flank of the fort re-fused back to cover the open roadbed of the Baldwin Ferry Road, which was also exposed to fire from defensive works north of the road some 100 yards away.[23]

At dawn on May 22, Union lines erupted in a four-hour-long bombardment to support the attack. The cannonade destroyed several embrasures for cannon in the earthworks but otherwise did little damage to the defenders. At 10:00 A.M., the bombardment ceased, and all three corps of the Army of the Tennessee surged forward against the "Gibraltar of the Confederacy."[24] The massive battle frightened the civilians within the town, many of whom left the shelter of their caves to observe the fighting. Emma Balfour recorded in her diary that "we were all so interested in the result of the general attack which was then made all around the lines that no one thought of personal danger. That was a glorious day for us."[25]

On the Union right, the XV Corps again aimed for the Stockade Redan, this time advancing in a narrow column covered by rifle and artillery fire. A group of 150 volunteers whom Sherman called the "forlorn hope" led the assault, carrying ladders, planks, and bundles of cane to enable Federal soldiers to enter the earthworks. The "forlorn hope" reached their objective, but the Union columns could not overcome the storm of Confederate

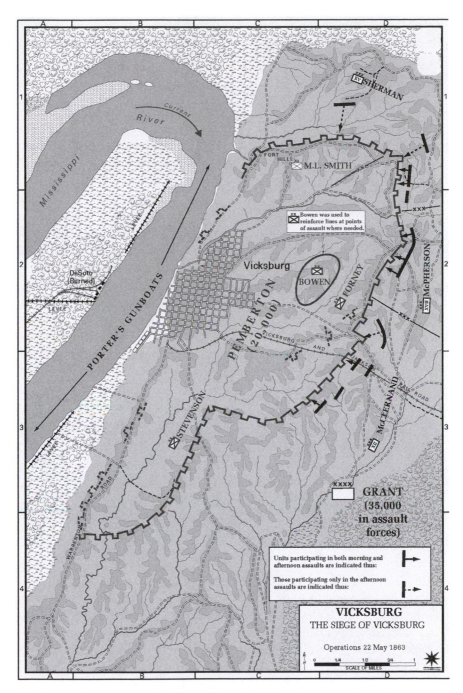

The Second Assault on Vicksburg, May 22, 1863. (Courtesy of the Department of History, United States Military Academy)

lead that filled the ditches with dead bodies. Sherman recalled in his memoirs that "as our troops came in fair view, the enemy rose behind their parapet and poured a furious fire upon our lines; and, for about two hours, we had a severe and bloody battle, but at every point we were repulsed."[26] Despite the failure, 78 members of the "forlorn hope" won the Medal of Honor for their courage that day.[27]

In the Union center, the XVII Corps assaulted the 3rd Louisiana Redan and the Great Redoubt. Sergeant Osborn Oldroyd recorded in his diary that before the charge, his comrades in the 20th Ohio "were busy divesting themselves of watches, rings, pictures and other keepsakes, which were being placed in the custody of the cooks, who were not expected to go into action." After watching the soldiers deposit their personal effects to the care of noncombatants, Oldroyd observed, "I never saw such a scene before, nor do I ever want to see it again. . . . Not a bit of sadness or fear appears in the talk or the faces of the boys, but they thought it timely and proper to dispose of what they had accordingly." The XVII Corps fought bravely, but McPherson's attacks met the same fate as Sherman's. Oldroyd recalled that "those who climbed to the top of the fort met cold steel, and, when at length it was found impossible to enter the fort that way, the command was given to fall back, which was done under a perfect hail of lead from the enemy."[28] Inside the Great Redoubt, Mary Todd Lincoln's half brother, Captain David Todd, led his company in the 21st Louisiana against the armed forces of his brother-in-law, President Abraham Lincoln. Many of Todd's comrades in the Great Redoubt had emigrated from Ireland to New Orleans before the war, and during the battle, these Irishmen shot down their fellow Irish immigrants serving in the Union's 7th Missouri Infantry who fought under a green flag decorated with a golden harp.[29]

On the Union left, McClernand's Corps attacked the southern portion of the defenses, concentrating on the 2nd Texas Lunette, the Railroad Redoubt, and the Square Fort. At 10:00 A.M., Brigadier General William P. Benton's brigade, closely followed by Brigadier General Stephen G. Burbridge's brigade, rushed forward from their positions opposite the Lunette into the open killing zone, carrying scaling ladders and shouting "Vicksburg or hell!" The Lunette exploded with murderous fire from the Texans, cutting the charging blue line to pieces and forcing the surviving Federals to seek cover in the ditch fronting the fort. The 2nd Texas had prepared for battle by arming with their issued rifles along with five to six smoothbore muskets per man loaded with deadly buck-and-ball rounds for close-quarters fighting. This additional firepower ravaged the Union ranks.[30] After the war, Texan Ralph J. Smith remembered, "The shocks were terrible and for a while it looked as though we would be overpowered and trampled under foot by mere force of numbers. However after several bloody and devastating charges the boys in blue concluded the[y] had enough for the once and withdrew in disorder."[31] Amazingly, the color-bearer of the 99th Illinois, Corporal Thomas J. Higgins, dashed through the onslaught to the walls of Lunette unhurt, inspiring many of the defenders to cry out, "Don't shoot him. He is too brave; capture him alive." The Texans permitted Higgins to enter the fort, who climbed over the parapet to be captured, flag and all, by Corporal Charles Evans. Thirty-five years later, Higgins earned the Medal of Honor for this remarkable act of courage.[32]

Beneath the fort, McClernand's men engaged in close and bitter combat, firing at the Texans above, who rained lit cannonballs down as improvised hand grenades. One cannon in the Lunette exploded, killing and wounding several Confederates, and the remaining serviceable cannon within the Lunette fired round after round of canister into the struggling blue mass at point-blank range until Federal gunfire rendered it inoperable. Sparks from the intense musket fire ignited cotton bales used to strengthen the defensive works, filling the fort with dense clouds of smoke. In the midst of the chaos, Union soldiers of the Chicago Mercantile Battery and 23rd Wisconsin Infantry hauled a six-pounder cannon to within 30 feet of the Lunette and blasted their own canister rounds at the 2nd Texas. Nonetheless, the attack stalled as Union casualties mounted, and when Confederate reinforcements arrived from Brigadier General Martin Green's brigade, any hope of a Federal breakthrough at the 2nd Texas Lunette ended.[33]

Five hundred yards to the southwest lay the Railroad Redoubt, a defensive work that protected the entrance of the Southern Railroad of Mississippi into Vicksburg. In order to secure the railroad cut that created a 20-foot-deep gap into the ridge, the redoubt extended far in front of the main line of works, earning it the nickname of the "Horn Work" from defending Confederates. Rebel soldiers had created a second line of rifle pits behind the Railroad Redoubt and removed all trees and obstructions in front of both works, leaving an extended and exposed killing field of some 400 yards.[34] The preparatory bombardment severely damaged the Railroad Redoubt, breaching the walls and disabling the fort's three cannon. When McClernand's assault began, soldiers from Brigadier General Michael Lawler's brigade and Colonel William Landrum's brigade were able to evict the 30th Alabama from the fort in brutal combat. Waul's Texas Legion, in reserve behind the Redoubt in the second line of rifle pits, opened a merciless fire that prevented any further expansion of the Union penetration.[35]

The fighting at the Railroad Redoubt resulted in a stalemate, while the Union attacks on the 2nd Texas Lunette and Square Fort failed miserably. McClernand, lacking reserves to exploit the partial breakthrough, sent a note to Grant inaccurately proclaiming that his men had captured the Railroad Redoubt. The political general requested reinforcements and encouraged Grant to renew the assaults all along the line.[36] According to Sherman, Grant read the note and remarked, "I don't believe a word of it."[37] Nonetheless, Grant conceded to McClernand's demands and ordered the assaults to be resumed. Both Sherman and McPherson renewed their attacks, which accomplished nothing more than to add more northern corpses in front of Confederate breastworks. In his sector, Sherman committed a division under Brigadier General James Tuttle led by Brigadier General Joseph Mower's brigade.[38] Before going forward, Sherman asked Mower, "General Mower, can you carry those works?" Well aware of the strength of the Stockade Redan, Mower could only answer, "I can try." Sherman replied, "Then do it."[39] Mower's brigade contained the 8th Wisconsin, who carried their mascot, a bald eagle named "Old Abe," into battle tethered to a perch. Old Abe survived the assault, and his image now adorns the emblem of the 101st Airborne Division. Tuttle's men surged toward the Stockade Redan and suffered the same bloody fate as the rest of the XV Corps.[40] Surveying the fruitless slaughter, Sherman remarked to Tuttle, "This is murder; order those men back."[41]

At 5:30 P.M., Stephen D. Lee observed Union reinforcements approaching the Railroad Redoubt and quickly ordered Waul's Legion to expel the Federals from that position. Lieutenant Colonel E. W. Pettus of the 46th Alabama Infantry led a volunteer squad of 30 Texans and three Alabamians in a dramatic bayonet charge that recaptured the redoubt and captured three officers, 33 enlisted men, and the flag of the 77th Illinois. After securing the fort, one soldier of the Legion proposed to declare Pettus an honorary Texan in recognition of his valor, which immediately went to a vote.[42] As Pettus later recalled, "I was unanimously elected a Texan—the greatest honor I have ever received, although I have had many beyond my deserving."[43] The Railroad Redoubt assault was the only element of the May 22 attack that penetrated Confederate lines, and had McClernand utilized his corps more effectively, he would have had reserves standing by to exploit any breakthroughs rather than having to waste precious hours appealing to Grant for help. Waul's Texas Legion, with help from McClernand's mismanagement, sealed the breach and ended any chance of success for Grant's assault.[44]

In the May 22 assault, the Army of the Tennessee lost 502 killed, 2,550 wounded, and 147 missing. Exact Confederate casualties are unknown but most likely did not exceed 500 men.[45] In front of the 2nd Texas Lunette, the assaulting Union regiments reported 111 killed, 535 wounded, and 11 missing, which represented nearly one-fifth of the 3,199 Union casualties. Soldiers of the 2nd Texas captured some 200 Federal Enfield rifles discarded during the battle, which supplied even more firepower to the defenders.[46] Immediately after the firing ended, Pemberton's men began repairing the damage inflicted on the earthworks and swiftly restored the defensive line. In his report, Grant admitted, "The assault was gallant in the extreme on the part of the troops, but the enemy's position was too strong, both naturally and artificially, to be taken in that way."[47] After the war, Sherman asserted, "I have since seen the position at Sevastopol, and without hesitation I declare that at Vicksburg to have been the more difficult of the two."[48] The bloody slaughter of the assaults persuaded Grant that the impressive Vicksburg fortifications could not be stormed without an enormous sacrifice of life. Unshaken by his failure to conquer the Confederate stronghold, Grant determined to starve the southerners into surrendering. In his memoirs, Grant explained, "I now determined upon a regular siege—to 'outcamp the enemy,' as it were, and to incur no more losses. . . . As long as we could hold our position the enemy was limited in supplies of food, men and munitions of war to what they had on hand. These could not last always."[49] On May 23, the day following the defeat, Grant wrote to Admiral Porter, "There is no doubt of the fall of this place ultimately, but how long it will take is a matter of doubt. I intend to lose no more men, but to force the enemy from one position to another without exposing my troops."[50]

For two days, the wounded and dying Union soldiers from the May 22 assault lingered exposed on the battlefield under the merciless Mississippi sun. The screams of agony and the stench of decomposing bodies made duty in the trenches unbearable. For unknown reasons, Grant refused to propose a truce to collect the wounded, and finally, on May 25, Pemberton had to write to his enemy asking "in the name of humanity" for "a cessation of hostilities for two hours and a half, that you may be enabled to remove your dead and dying men."[51] Grant accepted the proposal, and at 6:00 P.M., firing ceased as soldiers from both armies united to complete the grisly task. The few wounded still alive received medical treatment while burial parties gathered the dead. Some of the men killed in battle could not be collected due to the uneven terrain. Union Sergeant Ira Blanchard reported, "Many had fallen so near the works that their bodies could not be got at; were never buried; their bones were found after the surrender where they fell."[52] During the truce, Union and Confederate soldiers socialized, shared newspapers, and traded goods. Major Maurice K. Simons of the 2nd Texas Infantry wrote in his journal that "it looked really strang to see those of both sides walking up & shaking hands & drinking togeather (the latter always having to come from the Yankees as our men are not supplied with much of it)." Simons noted that the Texans mocked their enemies by asking "why 'they don't come in Town'" and "when are you coming to see us again & pointing to the dead Yankees (that were lay-ing in great numbers round & in front of our fort. . . . These friends of yours deddint make the trip."[53] As Ohioan Osborn Oldroyd described the episode, "Here a group of four played cards—two Yanks and two Rebs. There, others were jumping, while everywhere blue and gray mingled in conversation over the scenes which had transpired since our visit to the neighborhood."[54] The brief truce also allowed family members separated by war to reunite. Missourian Ephraim Anderson remembered, "I saw a young soldier of our command meet a brother, on half-way ground, from the Federal lines, where they met upon a log and conversed until the armi-stice was over."[55] After the cease-fire expired, the men returned to their trenches, and the siege continued.

Immediately after the failed assaults, the Army of the Tennessee began siege operations by constructing fortified positions opposing the Confederate line. From various locations in the earthworks, Union engi-neers also began digging 13 zigzag approaches toward the Rebel defenses in preparation for a possible third assault on Vicksburg. Every day, a fatigue party of Federal soldiers would dig the roughly six-foot-deep and eight-foot-wide approach trenches closer to Pemberton's fortifications. Large round bundles of earth wrapped in cane and vine, known as sap rollers, provided protection from small-arms fire. In front of the earthworks occu-pied by Major General John A. Logan's division, 20 cotton bales mounted on a railroad flatcar shielded the soldiers laboring in the trench known as Logan's Approach. When Pemberton's artillery attempted to shell the sap rollers, massed Union batteries would immediately respond to silence the Confederate cannon. Southern soldiers repeatedly endeavored to set the sap rollers on fire, even using improvised flaming arrows, but Grant's approaches continued to advance relentlessly toward the stronghold throughout late May and early June.[56]

On May 27, Porter unleashed his gunboats upon the river defense bat-teries after hearing false reports that Pemberton had transferred most of his heavy artillery to the defensive line opposite the Army of the Tennes-see. At 8:00 A.M., the ironclads *Benton*, *Mound City*, and *Carondelet*, along with the ram *General Price*, attacked Confederate defenses in the South Fort and Battery Barnes. Shortly thereafter, the ironclad *Cincinnati* steamed south around De Soto Point to engage the northernmost river batteries. After a spirited engagement, the Rebel cannoneers sank *Cincinnati* in three fathoms of water, leaving part of the chimneys and casemate visible above water. *Cincinnati* lost five killed, 14 wounded, and 15 missing in the battle, and six members of her crew earned the Medal of Honor for their actions that day. The victory helped revive morale among soldiers and civilians in Vicksburg and greatly embarrassed Porter, who resolved to raise and repair the vessel as soon as possible.[57] Sergeant William Tunnard of the 3rd Louisiana Infantry wrote in his account of the siege that "this combat was witnessed by hundreds of ladies, who ascended on the summits of the most prominent hills in Vicksburg. There were loud cheers, the waving of handkerchiefs, amid general exultation, as the vessel went down." As Tunnard asserted, "Many despondent soldiers gained renewed courage from the example thus given them by the heroic women of the Hill City."[58] Although Pemberton's men twice attempted to destroy the Union gunboat, both efforts failed. After the siege ended, Porter finally salvaged his ironclad, which ultimately rejoined the fleet and served until the end of the war.[59]

Throughout late May and early June, the siege became a monotonous routine of physical toil interrupted by shelling and sniper fire. Both sides employed sharpshooters to harass the enemy, but Union snipers proved to be especially effective.[60] On May 21, Major Maurice Simons wrote in his journal, "The yankes have closed their lines around our works and their sharp shooters are continually poring a shower of minney balls into or rather at our brest works which renders it quite harrardas. Yes almost certain death for any one to look over the parripet."[61] The most famous Federal sharpshooter of the siege, Lieutenant Henry "Coonskin" Foster of the 23rd Indiana Infantry, used his rifle to support his comrades working on Logan's Approach. Foster earned his nickname early in the siege by appropriating a coonskin cap from the Shirley House and wearing it while on duty. Adorned with his fur headpiece, Foster became so successful as a sniper that he and his fellow soldiers eventually constructed a column out of railroad ties near Battery Hickenlooper known as "Coonskin's Tower." Confederate artillery attempted to destroy the sniper's nest, but Union counter battery fire forced the Rebels to abandon the attempt. During the siege, Coonskin's Tower became an important observation post for Union officers, and even General Grant used the platform to observe Confederate positions. On one visit, Grant barely escaped with his life when a southern soldier found the general in his sights and issued a challenge to take cover before he fired. The tower eventually became so popular among Union sightseers that Foster began charging 25 cents for admission.[62]

Union snipers also killed the most celebrated animal in Pemberton's army, a camel known as "Old Douglas." In 1856, then Secretary of War Jefferson Davis attempted an experiment to test the value of using camels to supply distant military outposts in the Southwest desert. The camels succeeded in their mission and proved to be readily adaptable to the rough terrain and harsh climate, but the approach of the sectional crisis ended any attempt to continue the use of camels in the U.S. Army. One of the surviving animals from the expedition, Old Douglas, had somehow been transported to Mississippi, where he became the mascot of the 43rd Mississippi Infantry. Old Douglas carried the baggage of the regiment through the Iuka and Corinth campaigns and faithfully served the Mississippians until his death at Vicksburg. It is thought that hungry members of the regiment devoured the fallen camel during the siege and that victorious Federal soldiers later made souvenirs from his bones. Today, Old Douglas is honored with his own tombstone in the Soldiers' Rest Confederate Cemetery in Vicksburg.[63]

Throughout the long siege, Vicksburg endured a continuous bombardment from both land and naval artillery. Eventually, the Army of the Tennessee alone massed 220 cannon that fired day and night, stopping only when the artillery crews ate their meals.[64] On June 11, McClernand issued orders that give a good example of the usual daily bombardment, directing that "the 20, 24, and 30 pounder batteries will fire eight guns per hour from each battery, commencing at 6 a.m. and ceasing at 6 p.m. The other batteries will fire five guns per hour, commencing and ceasing fire at the same hours." McClernand instructed his cannoneers to "direct their fire in such a manner as to prevent the enemy from mounting additional guns or erecting additional works, if practicable, and also to throw as many projectiles into the enemy's intrenchments and camps as possible."[65] Porter's gunboats also targeted Vicksburg, blasting the Confederates with massive 13-inch mortars that fired 220-pound projectiles. The immense shells left enormous craters 15 feet deep that awed participants from both sides.[66] The constant barrage terrified the civilian population in Vicksburg and amazed Federal eye-witnesses. After observing the nighttime cannonades, James K. Newton of the 14th Wisconsin Infantry admitted that "at such times I can distinctly hear the shells crash through the houses. Indeed some of the boys went so far as to say they could hear the screams of the women and children[,] but their *ears must have been better than mine.*"[67] Osborn Oldroyd chronicled in his diary that "the inhabitants are now living in caves dug out of the sides of the hills. Alas! For the women, children and aged in the city, for they must suffer, indeed, and should the siege continue several months, many deaths from sickness as well as from our shells, must occur."[68]

The Lord family discovered the dangers of Union shells while preparing their dinner one evening soon after the siege began when "a bombshell burst in the very center of that pretty dining-room" just moments before they sat down to eat. The missile struck their residence, "blowing out the roof and one side, crushing the well-spread tea-table like an egg-shell, and making a great yawning hole in the floor, into which disappeared supper, china, furniture, and the safe containing our entire stock of butter and eggs." Fortunately, the family survived unhurt, and, as Lida Lord detailed, "At first we were too much stunned to realize what an escape we had made. I think I speak only the literal truth in saying that one minute later we should have been seated about that table, now a mass of charred splinters at the bottom of that smoking gulf."[69]

Union forces had periodically bombarded Vicksburg ever since Farragut's naval siege in the summer of 1862, and by the spring of 1863, numerous bomb shelters honeycombed the hills throughout the town. In early May as the Army of the Tennessee marched through Mississippi toward Vicksburg, the new trade of cave production exploded.[70] Mary Loughborough noted that "caves were the fashion—the rage—over besieged Vicksburg. Negroes, who understood their business, hired themselves out to dig them, at from thirty to fifty dollars, according to the size."[71] The cave shelters ranged in size and design, and some of the most impressive included comforts from home, such as furniture, decorations, and servants. Mrs. Loughborough reported that she resided in "an excavation made into the earth, and branching six feet from the entrance, forming a cave in the shape of a T. In one of the wings my bed fitted; the other I used as a kind of dressing room."[72] After the war, Ephraim Anderson recalled that "these holes, or underground houses, were of considerable extent, and frequently had several rooms in them, which were provided with beds and furniture—often carpeted—and were, for the time, the principal abodes of many of the inhabitants."[73] Amazingly, at least two children were born in the caves during the siege, one of whom was appropriately named William Siege Green.[74]

The Lord family first took refuge in a large cave that "consisted of five short passages running parallel into the hill, connected by another crossing them at right angles, all about five feet wide, and high enough for a man to stand upright. In this nest of caves were eight families, with children and servants." Lida Lord stated that her family's section of the shelter housed "three white adults and four children, with our maid Minnie and cook Chloe and Chloe's two little girls."[75] Cave-ins remained a continual fear throughout the siege, and most of the shelters had several entrances to allow an alternative exit if one opening became blocked. One night Lucy McRae, a small child residing in the Lord's shelter, almost died when "a shell came down on top of the hill, buried itself about six feet in the earth, and exploded." McRae wrote that she had just lain down to sleep when an explosion "caused a large mass of earth to slide from the side of the arch-way in a solid piece, catching me under it. Dr. Lord, whose leg was caught and held by it, gave the alarm that a child was buried." Immediately, her mother dashed to save her daughter and soon freed Lucy with aid from other civilians in the shelter. After being rescued, McRae remembered that "the blood was gushing from my nose, eyes, ears, and mouth. A physician who was then in the cave was called, and said there was no bones broken, but he could not then tell what my internal injuries were."[76] Confined into the close quarters of the caves, the citizens of Vicksburg had no choice but to rely upon each other to survive perils no one could have imagined before the war. William Lord Jr. observed that "a common danger abolished the unwritten law of caste. The families of planters, overseers, slave-dealers, tradespeople, and professional men dwelt side by side, in peace if not in harmony."[77] The civilians trapped in the siege had no other security from Grant's bombardment than the damp, dark, depressing, and dangerous caves. When Brigadier General Stephen D. Lee asked Vicksburg socialite Emma Balfour if she had moved her family to a "rat-hole," Balfour recorded, "I told him it seems to me that we were all caught in a rat-hole."[78]

After the near cave-in, the Lord family acquired a more secure dugout in a less exposed area. Lida proudly proclaimed that "it was the coziest cave in Vicksburg, and the pride of our hearts from that day until the fatal Fourth of July." She remembered it containing "an open walk, with a parapet six feet high cut into the hillside. In one wall of this was a low and narrow opening overhung by creeping vines and shaded by papaw-trees. This was our side door." Lida also noted that the new shelter "ran about twenty feet underground, and communicated at right angles with a wing which opened on the front of the hill, giving us a free circulation of air. At the door was an arbor of branches, in which, on a pine table, we dined when the shelling permitted." As a result of the limited size and air circulation in the cave, the Lord family and their servants cooked their meals outside of the entrance. She affirmed that adjacent to the cave lay "a dug-out fire-place and an open-air kitchen, with table, pans, etc. In the wall of the cave were a small closet for provisions, and some niches for candles, books, and flowers." Like most civilians in Vicksburg, the Lords remained outside when the bombardment abated and used the cave only to escape nearby shelling. Lida reported, "Our cave was strongly boarded at the entrances, and we had procured some mattresses which made comfortable beds. For a time we slept in the tent, and only used the cave for a shelter."[79]

Within the beleaguered fortress, the unending barrage drove civilians and combatants to the limits of endurance. On May 24, Surgeon Benjamin D. Lay of the City Hospital in Vicksburg wrote to his commanders, "It becomes my painful duty to notify Lieutenant-General Pemberton that the enemy have for three days past been shelling my hospitals, and to-day their fire is becoming very accurate. My different houses have been struck twenty-one times. I have had 6 wounded men re-wounded." The scarcity of medical supplies and continual cannonade resulted in the deaths of many wounded soldiers who would have most likely survived their wounds. Lay forlornly informed headquarters that "men in their condition, whose nerves are already shattered by wounds, bear this very badly, and I shall have great mortality among my amputations and serious operations." Well aware of the circumstances, the doctor knew that Pemberton could do little to alleviate the suffering. Lay wrote, "The wounds we are having are generally of a very grave character ... being from serious, severe, dangerous, to mortal—some 26 of the last. I do not know that you can help me in this matter; but feel it my duty to notify you of these facts."[80]

Another physician in Vicksburg, Dr. Joseph Dill Alison, wrote in his diary on June 10 that "our situation now becoming desperate. No place of safety, if you stand still there is danger from the pieces of shell that fill the air, and if you move the danger becomes greater. The whole town is enfiladed." Dr. Alison also chronicled the tragic torment of injured soldiers in Vicksburg, noting that "the wounded are killed in the hospitals, Surgeons wounded while attending to their duties. Two days since Major Hoadley was killed in Camp twenty feet of where I was dressing a wound. ... Night is almost as bad as day. The air is filled with missles of destruction."[81] After experiencing the horror of siege warfare firsthand, Alison asserted, "I have read of besieged cities and the suffering of the inhabitants, but always thought the picture too highly painted. But now I have witnessed one and can believe all that is written on the subject." At the end of his entry, Alison concluded, "Rations though short, are still enough, and we have good water most of the time, so do not as yet suffer on that source. But the stench from dead mules and horses (killed by shell) is intolerable."[82]

On June 27, Sherman indicated a probable cause for the shelling of hospitals when he wrote in a letter to his wife, "The enemy in Vicksburg in my judgment shows no abatement of vigorous resistance or short food—with

every house in sight of our lines marked with the Hospital Flag—Orange
Yellow. We cant show a hand or cap above our rifle pits without attracting
a volley."[83] Grant's men may have assumed that the Confederates in
Vicksburg used hospital flags to shield stores of badly needed supplies and
disregarded the emblem. More likely, as historian Peter F. Walker
observed, since "there were almost one hundred of them in the
city ... they would have been difficult to miss."[84] While the targeting of
hospitals may have been accidental, it is certain that Union artillery fire
had deadly consequences for Confederate wounded in Vicksburg.

Diarist Emma Balfour proclaimed in her account that "every shell from
the machines as they came rushing down like some infernal demon,
seemed to me to be coming exactly on me, and I had looked at them so
long that I can see them just as plainly with my eyes shut as with them
open." On May 24, she recorded that a "child [possibly Lucy McRae] was
buried in the wall by a piece of shell, *pinned* to it," and that in one infirmary
where the "wounded had just undergone operations, a shell exploded and
six men had to have limbs amputated. Some of them that had been taken
off at the ankle had to be taken off to the thigh—and one who had lost
one arm had to have the other taken off." The anguish of the continual
barrage became apparent when she declared, "It is horrible and the worst
of it is—we cannot help it."[85]

Another woman in Vicksburg, Mary Loughborough, wrote in her narrative, "But this was unexpected—guns throwing shells from the battle field
directly at the entrance of our caves. Really, was there to be no mental rest
for the women of Vicksburg?"[86] Some of the civilians in town suffered
physically as well as mentally during the siege. Lida Lord reported that
she had heard that "a mother, rushing to save her child from a bursting
shell, had her arm taken off by a fragment. Another mother had her baby
killed on her breast." Lida also testified that "my own little brother,
stooping to pick up a Minie ball, barely escaped being cut in two before
our eyes, a Parrott shell passing over his back so close that it scorched his
jacket." In the end, Lord admitted, "There were many other narrow
escapes and some frightful casualties; but, taking the siege as a whole, there
was among the citizens a surprisingly small loss of life."[87] Likewise, William
Lord Jr. affirmed that "while comparatively few non-combatants
were killed, all lived in a state of terror."[88] Emilie McKinley, a northern
woman from Pennsylvanian who moved to Mississippi before the war
to work as a teacher in Mount Alban, Mississippi, seven miles east of
Vicksburg, noted in her diary on July 12, "Dr. Coffee says he amputated
several limbs for ladies in town struck by shells."[89] While sources differ
and the numbers may have been higher, it is accepted that the Union

bombardment killed at least three civilians and wounded 12 during the siege of Vicksburg.[90]

While the Army of the Tennessee strangled the life out of Vicksburg, Grant began gathering reinforcements to prevent Johnston's Army of Relief from lifting the siege. On May 31, Grant informed Major General Nathaniel P. Banks, the commander of the Army of the Gulf then besieging the Confederate stronghold at Port Hudson, "Vicksburg is the vital point. Our situation is for the first time during the entire Western campaign what it should be. . . . All I want now are men."[91] Grant's blockade greatly hampered Pemberton's communications with Johnston and left the Pennsylvanian little choice but to play a desperate waiting game. In order to protect his rear from Johnston, Grant began constructing a defensive line and dispatching raiding parties into the countryside to seize provisions and supplies needed for any relief expedition. On June 8, Grant wired Halleck, "I will make a waste of all the country I can between the two rivers. I am fortifying Haynes' Bluff, and will defend the line from here to that point at all hazards."[92]

Grant's operations provided further opportunities for Union soldiers to refine their hard war against southern civilians. One woman, Ida Barlow Trotter, remembered after the war, "Our home was surrounded by Yankee's both day and night, as the head-quarters of Gen. Grant were only about a mile from our home. We were utterly in their power and in a constant state of uneasiness for fear we would be killed." During the campaign, a group of Federals arrived at Trotter's home and inquired if any Confederate soldiers remained in the area. Her father replied truthfully that he knew of no southern forces nearby. Shortly thereafter, the Union detachment encountered a Rebel ambush along the road, and in response the Federal soldiers set fire to the house. Trotter recalled "that they at once put the torch to our home and told my father that if he was on the premises at sun-down they would hang him. Leaving our home a mass of smouldering ashes, we went bare headed with nothing except what we had on."[93]

The Union soldiers foraged the farm for food and took "all the provisions they could find, all the stock and fowls and the gardens, orchards and growing fields had been turned into pastures for their horses." With no other option, Trotter's family had to obtain nourishment from Grant's army. Trotter recorded that "we drew our rations just like the soldiers did (and awful living it was to) fat pickled pork, hard tack so old it had bugs in it, a little flour and coffee." Although unappetizing and embarrassing, Trotter's family survived on the barely edible rations. She recounted that her grandmother "soaked the hard tack in water over night to soften it, then fried it in the grease that came out of the meat and drank the coffee without sugar."[94]

Without a home of their own, Trotter's family moved to her grandparent's house. There, she explained, "My grand mother had hid every thing in the house and store rooms that she could possibly hide, and curious were the places in which she secreted them. She had a few shingles taken from the roof, and had many things put in on the ceiling." Trotter reported that "she had all the silver and jewelry buried, in boxes under the house and to keep some meat where we could get it to eat, she put two mattresses on a bed and placed a layer of bacon, hams between them." After securing a source of meat, Trotter's grandmother "had my aunt, a Mrs. Hall ... feign sickness" and instructed Ida to "take the great pea-fowl fly brush used in the dinning room and keep the flies from off the make believe patient—who spent her time patiently reading novels."[95] Lettie Vick Downs, another Mississippi civilian, vented her fury in her diary when she wrote, "The Yankees ripped up my carpets and used them for saddle blankets; took one chair off and threw my dining-room table into the house while it was on fire. Yankees have all of Deer Creek negroes except 4 or 5 old ones."[96]

Some Union soldiers blatantly engaged in plundering southern estates for valuables and typically collected information on buried possessions from freed slaves, who would often disclose the location of their master's treasure. During the campaign, Emilie McKinley chronicled in her diary that numerous Federal soldiers pillaged the Batchelor plantation where she lived. On May 18, the day that the siege of Vicksburg began, Emilie detailed that many groups of Federal soldiers visited the plantation. After examining the house for weapons, she noted that "the first question they asked was, 'Where are the horses?'" The loss of badly needed food and recurring dishonor of having her personal effects searched prompted McKinley to rhetorically ask, "Can the people in the North know or conceive what we suffer? We are tried beyond endurance, and suffer more than we can tell. We will be obliged to coin words to express our utter detestation of the hated." Although her brother served as a Union soldier, McKinley raged, "Can I ever visit the North again, with my present feelings, unnatural as they may be? I cannot ever go there again. I will not, my blood boils as I write, I can hardly write."[97]

A few days later on May 21, McKinley fumed, "The wretches have desecrated our beautiful church at Bovina. They have cut the organ pipes; they gave the prayer books to the negroes. ... How can anyone dare to desecrate the House of God. I wonder they were not afraid that their hands would be palsied in the attempt." In addition to vandalizing churches, the Federals perpetually searched for buried valuables. On May 23, McKinley recorded that "there were some men here today who were determined to find silver in the garden. One fellow with a gun went trampling all over it, knocking his gun down. He said his gun had something in it to find where something was buried." The Union patrols continued, and on June 14, she added, "The Yanks have found all of Mrs. Lane's silver, also Mrs. Sexton's and her jewelry, all buried. Took Mrs. Frank Gibson's dead son's clothing, which she had kept for years." In the chaos of war, one southern woman utilized her own resourcefulness to preserve her property. On May 29, McKinley noted that "Mrs. Booth had gone to Gen. McClernand to get protection. He told her he could not protect her as she had two sons fighting against the U.S. She went home and wrote one [an order for protection] for herself. She drives the Yanks off with it."[98]

Other southern women used more traditional methods to attain security in the anarchic countryside. On May 31, McKinley acknowledged such means when she furiously inscribed, "Mrs. Folkes has scraped up a relationship with Col. Hammond on Gen. Sherman's staff. She had his Ambrotype. . . . A Yankee also made her a present of a gingham dress, one he had stolen. Imagine, she had it on when we met her!" The continued pilfering and lack of an effective response from the Confederate military motivated McKinley to seethe in her journal, "I pray God will visit these devils with punishments equal to those they are inflicting on us." She angrily asserted, "I would call down curses on their heads. I wish we had guerillas so that these men could not so securely tramp around. I would willingly see my house burnt (if I had one) rather than see the wretches so secure from harm."[99]

One southern refugee, Tryphena B. Fox, lost her home and relocated with her family to the Woodburne plantation on the Big Black River. Fox, a native northerner like Emilie McKinley, suffered equally as much from the occupation as natural-born Mississippians. On July 3, she wrote to her mother in Pittsfield, Massachusetts, that the refugees at the plantation had "drawn no rations from the northern army but we shall be obliged to do so soon. Many of the negroes have left, the corn & meat were taken the first week the Yankees came in here & they are driving off cattle & sheep & killing the hogs every day." In addition to the lost livestock and provisions, Fox protested that "the garden is a perfect waste & nothing is left but a few green apples & the flowers & weeds. We are not allowed to pass outside the pickets to gather berries."[100]

Four families then resided on the plantation due to the conflict, further draining the declining supply of food. An anguished Fox wrote, "The cows are yet left to us, but may be taken any day & I cannot but shudder to think—how are these nine children to be fed then—they are all under six years of age." Fox lamented in her letter that "older people can get along with a piece of dry corn-bread, but the little ones will soon suffer from diarrhea & dysentery. Oh! Mother! You Northern people know nothing of the horrors of war & may you be spared what I have suffered during the last year."[101] Max Kuner, a Bavarian immigrant living in Vicksburg, left his home in the city before the siege to take shelter at a friend's plantation in the countryside. After the war, Kuner admitted that when his supply of food dwindled during the campaign, "Finally I was reduced to riding into the Federal camp, and asking for supplies. 'Hey! What you coming here for, Johnny Reb?' would tease the soldiers. 'For something to eat,' I would reply bravely; and it was the honest, even if humiliating, truth."[102] Undoubtedly, the severe hunger and malnutrition resulted in greater disease and death among civilians, particularly when an epidemic of measles swept through besieged Vicksburg, but the exact number of victims will never be known.[103]

The situation inside the beleaguered city grew more desperate with each passing day. By June, Pemberton had reduced his soldier's daily meat ration by one-half, and some hungry Rebels supplemented their diet by stealing vegetables from local gardens and raiding army storehouses. Commissary officers also distributed "pea bread" to the Army of Vicksburg, which became the most remembered and hated cuisine consumed by Confederate soldiers during the siege. "Pea bread," baked from ground cow peas, served as an absolutely unpalatable alternate for cornbread.[104] Louisianan W. H. Tunnard recalled, "This food was very unhealthy, as it was almost impossible to thoroughly bake the mixture so that both pea flour and meal would be fit for consumption."[105] Missourian Ephraim Anderson wrote sardonically, "There was a good supply of this pea in the commissariat at Vicksburg, and the idea grew out of the fertile brain of some official, that, if reduced to the form of meal, it would make an admirable substitute for bread. Sagacious and prolific genius!" Anderson complained, "Perhaps he never swallowed a particle of it . . . the nature of it was such, that it never got done, and the longer it was cooked, the harder it became on the outside" while "at the same time, it grew relatively softer on the inside, and, upon breaking it, you were sure to find raw pea-meal in the centre." The inedible mixture infuriated cooks and soldiers who "protested that it had been on the fire two good hours, but it was all to no purpose; yet, on the outside it was so hard, that one might have knocked down a full-grown steer with a chunk of it."[106]

Soon illnesses such as malaria and dysentery appeared among the besieged, and ultimately Vicksburg's own newspaper, the *Daily Citizen*, began printing its issues on wallpaper.[107] Mary Loughborough reported, "Some families had light bread made in large quantities, and subsisted on it with milk (provided their cows were not killed from one milking time to another), without any more cooking, until called on to replenish." Loughborough admitted that while "most of us lived on corn bread and bacon, served three times a day, the only luxury of the meal consisting in its warmth, I had some flour, frequently had some hard, tough biscuit made from it, there being no soda or yeast to be procured."[108] As the heat increased in June, the southern sun substantially reduced the potable water within the city, forcing Confederate soldiers to dig wells.[109] Lida Lord revealed the circumstances faced by many when she wrote, "We had to buy water by the bucketful and serve it out in rations, so that we realized what thirst meant, and were often hungry. ... We tasted a mule-steak once, but did not like it; it was very dry and tough."[110]

In addition to shelling, sickness, and starvation, Vicksburg's residents faced further perils. Lida Lord declared that "we were almost eaten up by mosquitos, and were in hourly dread of snakes. The vines and thickets were full of them, and a large rattlesnake was found one morning under a mattress on which some of us had slept all night."[111] Life in the confined, claustrophobic caves left few resources for cleanliness and personal hygiene. Margaret Lord confessed in her diary on June 1, "I have not been undressed now for nearly two weeks and we all live on the plainest food— but we are all to learn (as) a child willing to endure far more than yield to the enemy—the children bear themselves like little heroes."[112] In spite of the privation, Lida Lord affirmed, "Our greatest misery was the suspense and inaction. The worst sufferers during a battle are the non-combatants. The victors and victims suffer afterward."[113]

As provisions diminished and "the gaunt skeleton of starvation commenced to appear," Confederate soldiers initiated their own foraging expeditions inside Vicksburg for food, and this led to many episodes of pilfering. For example, one party of soldiers from the 3rd Louisiana Infantry evaded Union shells to gather cabbage from a local garden, while a pair of Missouri soldiers dodged guard dogs and minié balls in a futile quest for chickens.[114] After the war, William H. Tunnard admitted that "such incidents are, perhaps, not very flattering to the morality of the regiment, and will serve to explain how the 'boys,' at times, had an abundance, while their less venturesome and wondering comrades of the Mississippi regiments suffered the pangs of extreme hunger."[115] Traders and store owners in Vicksburg had acquired an infamous reputation for hoarding food and taking advantage of the siege to extort immense profits. Few residents had any sympathy for the merchants when a fire erupted on the night of June 1 that devastated an entire block of downtown mercantiles. Historian Peter F. Walker observed, "The gutted block contained several of the city's grocery stores, owned by merchants suspected and accused of profiteering, and it was common knowledge that the fire was set by persons who were incensed by the merchants' speculation on food."[116]

Soon observers on both sides joked that General Pemberton had been replaced by "General Starvation." While the Confederate garrison lived on reduced rations, Federal soldiers feasted on the bounty of the Mississippi countryside.[117] In his memoirs, Grant reported that several prominent northerners who visited the army at Vicksburg would "bring a dozen or two of poultry" to improve the morale of the men. As Grant observed laconically, "They did not know how little the gift would be appreciated. Many of the soldiers had lived so much on chickens, ducks and turkeys without bread during the march, that the sight of poultry, if they could get bacon, almost took away their appetite. But the intention was good."[118]

To those trapped in Vicksburg, prayer became the only solace obtainable in the midst of continuous shelling and a seemingly never-ending siege. Lida Lord remembered that "service was held daily in the Episcopal church, and was always well attended by citizens, ladies, and soldiers off duty. No one seemed to be deterred by fear of casualties, though the church was pretty badly riddled by fragments of shell and cannon-balls. However," she added, "it was struck only once during prayers, and then there was no great excitement or damage." Miraculously, Reverend Lord and his parishioners avoided serious harm, and Lida confirmed that "before the siege ended a great deal of the beautiful ivy that had covered it for years had been torn, scorched, and killed, and every pane of glass was broken; but no drop of blood ever stained its sacred floor." Lida poignantly recalled, "That daily church service was very impressive. The responses were often drowned by the rattle of musketry and the roar of bombs. ... Many of the women were in deepest black; for Bull Run and Manassas, Fort Donelson and Chickasaw Bayou, had already desolated Mississippi homes."[119] William Lord Jr. recorded that his father stated that "there never were more devout or attentive auditors" in all his years as a minister than that "assemblage of power-grimed and often blood-stained soldiery" during the siege of Vicksburg.[120] Union cannon showed no mercy to the Catholic congregation in Vicksburg either. W. H. Tunnard chronicled that after one Mass when the "congregation was emerging from the building, the Argus-eyed enemy across the river discovered the unusual number of people in the streets, and instantly opened on them with a Parrott gun. ... Several persons were struck by fragments of shells, but, fortunately, no one killed." After enduring such experiences, the Louisianan bitterly declared that "such an unheard-of, ruthless and barbarous method of warfare as training a battery of rifled cannon upon an assembly of unarmed men and worshipping women, is unparalleled in the annals of history."[121]

In spite of the sincere faith of the defenders, the siege continued on into the month of June with no end in sight. In the midst of a brutal southern summer and incessant bombardment, the Army of Vicksburg fought on, desperately trusting that their comrades in General Johnston's Army of Relief and the Trans-Mississippi Department would rescue the besieged fortress. Pemberton and his men could only wait and pray that help would arrive in time.

Major General Ulysses S. Grant, commander of the Army of the Tennessee. (Library of Congress, Prints & Photographs Division)

Major General William T. Sherman, commander of the XV Corps and Grant's most trusted subordinate. (Library of Congress)

Lieutenant General John C. Pemberton, the ill-fated commander of the Army of Vicksburg. (Library of Congress)

General Joseph E. Johnston, Pemberton's superior and commander of the Army of Relief. (Library of Congress)

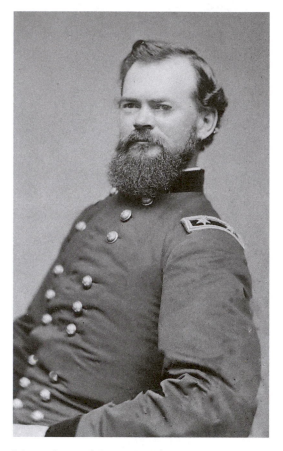

Major General James McPherson, commander of the XVII Corps. (Library of Congress)

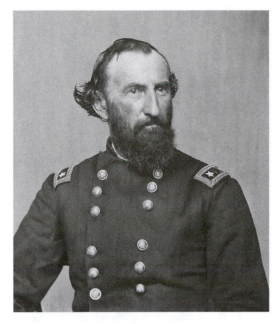

Major General John McClernand, the ambitious commander of the XIII Corps who sought to replace Ulysses S. Grant. (Library of Congress)

Admiral David Dixon Porter, commander of the Mississippi Squadron. (Library of Congress)

Major General John S. Bowen, Pemberton's most reliable division commander.
(Library of Congress)

Brigadier General John Gregg, commander of
Confederate forces in the Battle of Raymond.
(Library of Congress)

Major General Martin L. Smith, a New York native whose division defended the northeastern flank of Confederate defenses during the Siege of Vicksburg. (Library of Congress)

Major General John H. Forney commanded the division that defended the center of the Confederate defenses during the Siege of Vicksburg. (Library of Congress)

Major General Carter L. Stevenson, whose division met disaster at the Battle of Champion Hill. (Library of Congress)

Illustration of the surrender interview between Grant and Pemberton, July 3, 1863. (Library of Congress)

The Shirley House is visible in this photograph of bomb shelters constructed by Logan's division. (Library of Congress)

Fighting in the crater created after the explosion of the mine under the Third Louisiana Redan on June 25, 1863. (Library of Congress)

The Texas Monument at Vicksburg National Military Park. (Library of Congress)

6

"The most valuable conquest of the war"

While Grant's army steadily tightened its death grip upon Vicksburg throughout the early summer of 1863, the Confederate Army of the Trans-Mississippi under Lieutenant General Edmund Kirby Smith urgently endeavored to relieve the besieged citadel. In response to demands from Richmond that commanders west of the Mississippi River in "Kirby Smithdom" attempt to save Vicksburg, Smith dispatched two forces to attack Union supply bases along the western bank of the Mississippi River in Louisiana and Arkansas.[1] While most defenders looked to Johnston's Army of Relief for rescue, the Confederate counteroffensive in the Trans-Mississippi would be the only serious southern attempt to aid Pemberton's trapped Army of Vicksburg.[2]

Smith, who had assumed command of the Trans-Mississippi Department only on March 1, 1863, confronted General Nathaniel P. Banks's Army of the Gulf advancing northward against Alexandria. Banks began his offensive on April 11 and quickly compelled Confederate Major General Richard Taylor's 3,000-man army to retreat to the northwest across Louisiana. Banks captured Alexandria on May 7, effectively occupying Taylor's force and deterring the Army of the Trans-Mississippi from threatening Grant's amphibious landing at Bruinsburg on April 30. During the operation, Banks utilized the same brutally effective methods Grant used in Mississippi to deprive the Confederate army of badly needed supplies throughout the countryside.[3] Historians William L. Shea and Terrence J. Winschel observe, "The soldiers of the Army of the Gulf consumed or destroyed huge amounts of food and forage and confiscated much-needed boats, wagons, and draft animals. Banks, like Grant before him, discovered that certain bountiful areas of the Confederacy were capable of supporting an army on the march." Conditions in Louisiana paralleled the situation in Mississippi. Shea and Winschel confirm that throughout the expedition, "foraging degenerated into vandalism, and the fertile Bayou Teche country was devastated. The Federals liberated about six thousand slaves, many of whom joined in the orgy of destruction."[4]

The Union advance created another successful distraction that prevented Confederate forces in the Trans-Mississippi from uniting against Grant's army and achieved significant results in depleting the southern supply base. Shea and Winschel state that "Banks devastated a large swath of Louisiana and gobbled up or destroyed immense amounts of food that otherwise would have gone to Confederate forces."[5] Banks initially hoped to combine his forces with McPherson's Corps from Army of the Tennessee after capturing Alexandria, but Grant's amphibious invasion of Mississippi made a junction of the two Union armies impossible. Instead, Banks ultimately decided to dispatch his army to the east and attack the Confederate fortress at Port Hudson, Louisiana. In mid-May, Banks began transporting the Army of the Gulf across the Mississippi River and reached Port Hudson on May 22, the very day that Grant hurled his legions against Vicksburg. The New York–born Confederate commander of the garrison, Major General Franklin Gardner, had graduated from West Point in 1843, the same year as Ulysses S. Grant. Similar to his superior Pemberton, Gardner had married into an elite southern family and resigned his commission in 1861 to join the Confederacy. Gardner had been forced to dispatch thousands of men to reinforce Pemberton before Banks arrived and could muster only three brigades comprised of 5,765 men from Alabama, Arkansas, Mississippi, Tennessee, and Louisiana to defend the forts. The garrison of Port Hudson contained only 14 heavy guns and 40 light cannon, but the uneven terrain and elaborate defenses proved to be as formidable as those at Vicksburg. Banks, commanding more than 25,000 men in four divisions, decided to assault Port Hudson in hopes of achieving a swift victory before seasonal diseases could ravage his ranks.[6]

Despite the long odds, Gardner resolved to hold out as long as possible. As the Army of the Gulf surrounded the stronghold, Gardner proclaimed, "The enemy are coming, but mark you, many a one will get to h——l before he does to Port Hudson."[7] Gardner's men worked frantically to strengthen the defenses, taking full advantage of Banks's repeated delays. At 6:00 A.M. on May 27, Banks finally unleashed his divisions in a disorganized and inept attempt to storm the Confederate defenses. Had the

Union attacks been properly coordinated, they would have likely succeeded due to overwhelming numerical superiority. Instead, Gardner's men defeated a series of futile, piecemeal assaults across the defensive line.[8] One Confederate defender, Private Edward Young McMorries of the First Alabama Infantry, recalled that after the assaults "the ground within range of our muskets was literally covered with blue-coats."[9] The African American 1st and 3rd Louisiana Native Guards participated in the doomed charge, and while the assault failed, the bravery of the new recruits impressed observers in one of the first major instances of black Union soldiers entering combat in the Civil War. In his official report, Banks wrote, "It gives me pleasure to report that they answered every expectation. In many respects their conduct was heroic. No troops could be more determined or more daring."[10] The bloody failure of the first Federal assault on Port Hudson cost Banks 293 killed, 1,545 wounded, and 157 missing, while Gardner's army suffered only an estimated 350 casualties.[11] A second attack on June 14 achieved even less than the May 27 fiasco and resulted in Union losses of 216 killed, 1,401 wounded, and 188 missing. Like Grant at Vicksburg, Banks had no other option but to initiate a lengthy siege to starve the southerners out.[12]

While Banks besieged Port Hudson, Kirby Smith instructed Richard Taylor to attack Grant's supply bases on the west bank of the Mississippi River at Milliken's Bend, Young's Point, and Lake Providence opposite Vicksburg in northeastern Louisiana. Taylor doubted that his small force of roughly 5,000 men could do much to aid Pemberton's trapped army and would have instead preferred to operate against Union-occupied New Orleans. But, as he asserted in his memoirs, "Remonstrances were to no avail. I was informed that all the Confederate authorities in the east were urgent for some effort on our part in behalf of Vicksburg, and that public opinion would condemn us if we did not try to do something."[13] Unfortunately for Taylor and his men, the offensive could not threaten the Army of the Tennessee's supply lines because by this point Grant had established a more secure supply chain along the Yazoo River and no longer relied upon the Louisiana outposts.[14]

To accomplish his mission, Taylor commanded an expedition containing Major General John G. Walker's Texas Division along with two battalions of Louisiana cavalry. Walker, who had commanded a division in the Army of Northern Virginia at Antietam, now led the only division formed during the Civil War that consisted entirely of units from the same state. Walker's Texas Division consisted of the brigades of Brigadier Generals Henry E. McCulloch and James M. Hawes and Colonel Horace Randal supported by Brigadier General James C. Tappan's Arkansas brigade.[15]

Lieutenant Theophilus Perry, a Texan in Randal's brigade, depicted the ravaged countryside of northeastern Louisiana in a letter home as being as "desolate as can be." Perry portrayed the devastation as "fences and the houses broken in many places. Only a few old Negro women & children to be seen any where. Horses and cows and hogs all destroy[ed] and carried off. The most of the negroes, have been sent away to places of safety."[16]

Walker's division suffered greatly from the harsh environment of the Pelican State. On May 15, Captain Elijah P. Petty of the 17th Texas Infantry wrote to his wife that "the water is not healthy. The diarrhea prevails now extensively produced no doubt by the water. I have had it for two days and am somewhat weak & emaciated from it."[17] Other dangers lurked in this area of Louisiana as well. On June 5, Private Joseph Palmer Blessington of the 16th Texas Infantry recorded in his diary, "On our march through the swamps we beheld several large rattlesnakes, that had been killed by our advance guards. Very frequently, in the swamps of Louisiana, a soldier wakes up in the morning and finds that he has a rattlesnake for a sleeping partner."[18]

Although frustrated with his assignment, Taylor planned to seize the garrisons and capture badly needed provisions and equipment. Only a few midwestern regiments and newly organized African American units guarded the Union outposts, and the inexperienced black soldiers had received outdated weapons and little training. On June 6, Taylor directed McCulloch's brigade to storm Milliken's Bend while Hawes's brigade attacked Young's Point. Another force would capture Lake Providence while Randal's brigade and the artillery remained in reserve. The operation against Young's Point quickly fell behind schedule, and Hawes ordered a withdrawal when he discovered the unexpected strength of the defenses and the presence of three Union gunboats. The attack against Lake Providence likewise failed to materialize into a serious confrontation. Out of Taylor's elaborate battle plan, only McCulloch's brigade managed to attack its intended objective on June 7.[19]

Henry E. McCulloch, the younger brother of Confederate Brigadier General Ben McCulloch, deployed his men opposite Milliken's Bend under the cover of darkness. At 3:00 A.M., Union pickets initiated the battle by opening fire on the Rebel advance. McCulloch steadily drove his men forward toward the main Federal defensive line comprised of cotton bale breastworks positioned on a 10-foot-high levee. In the early light of dawn, the Texans stormed into the breastworks, and a brutal hand-to-hand struggle ensued.[20] Private Joseph Palmer Blessington recalled that when the Texans reached the Union defenses, "bayonets were crossed, and muskets clubbed, and the struggle indeed became a close and deadly one."[21] The African American recruits, who faced an uncertain fate if captured, fought with desperate courage. In his official report, McCulloch observed, "This charge was resisted by the negro portion of the enemy's force with considerable obstinacy, while the white or true Yankee portion ran like whipped curs almost as soon as the charge was ordered."[22] The retreating Federals sought safety behind a second levee and the large cannon of the gunboats *Choctaw* and *Lexington*. The naval artillery blasted the Texans, causing much confusion but few actual casualties. Well aware that his brigade could not defeat two Union gunboats, McCulloch reluctantly ordered a retreat.[23]

The successful defense of Milliken's Bend, though less well known than the major battles in the Vicksburg campaign, had a surprisingly high percentage of killed and wounded for the small number of soldiers involved. The Texans suffered 44 killed, 131 wounded, and 10 captured out of some 1,500 engaged, compared with reported Federal losses of 101 killed, 285 wounded, and 266 missing out of the 1,061-man garrison. The Battle of Milliken's Bend and the previous assault on Port Hudson contained the earliest significant combat in the Civil War involving African American units. The conduct of black soldiers in both battles deeply impressed observers in the U.S. Army.[24] Union official Charles Dana recalled that Milliken's Bend "completely revolutionized the sentiment of the army with regard to the employment of negro troops. I heard prominent officers who formerly in private had sneered at the idea of the negroes fighting express themselves after that as heartily in favor of it."[25] Grant, who would later command thousands of black troops during the final campaigns of the war in Virginia, observed in his memoirs, "This was the first important engagement of the war in which colored troops were under fire. These men were very raw, having all been enlisted since the beginning of the siege, but they behaved well."[26]

After the Battle of Milliken's Bend, rumors circulated that at least some African American soldiers and their white officers had been executed by the Confederate military. The existing sources are fragmentary and in conflict regarding the treatment of black prisoners, and it will never be known how many, if any, of the captured African Americans were put to death. McCulloch wrote in his official report of returning captured black soldiers to slavery, though some Federal eyewitnesses recorded that the Rebels shouted "no quarter" during the assault.[27] A large number of black prisoners must have survived, for on June 13, Kirby Smith wrote to Taylor, "I have been unofficially informed that some of your troops have captured negroes in arms. I hope this may not be so, and that your subordinates ... have recognized the propriety of giving no quarter to armed negroes and their officers." Smith informed Taylor that "in this way we may be relieved from a disagreeable dilemma."[28] The possibility of alleged war crimes at Milliken's Bend continues to be a contentious question among historians.

On June 16, Lieutenant Commander E. K. Owen notified Admiral Porter that a Confederate deserter, Thomas Cormal, stated that he had "witnessed the hanging at Richmond, La., of the white captain and negroes captured at Milliken's Bend. General Taylor and command were drawn up to witness the execution." According to Owen, Cormal also asserted "that the sergeant who commanded a company of contrabands, and who was captured by Harrison's cavalry some weeks ago, was also hung at Perkins' Landing."[29] When Grant learned of these alleged atrocities, he wrote directly to Taylor, stating, "I feel no inclination to retaliate for the offenses of irresponsible persons, but if it is the policy of any general intrusted with the command of any troops to show 'no quarter,' or to punish with death prisoners taken in battle, I will accept the issue."[30] On June 27, Taylor replied to Grant and vigorously denounced the report as "a fabrication" that would be "thoroughly investigated" and, if need be, dealt with "summary punishment." Taylor informed Grant that his orders were to turn African American prisoners of war over to "the civil authorities, to be dealt with according to the laws of the State wherein they were captured."[31] Grant accepted the denial but asserted in his reply to Taylor, "Having taken the responsibility of declaring slaves free and having authorized the arming of them, I cannot see the justice of permitting one treatment for them, and another for the white soldiers."[32] The subject of black prisoners of war continued to be controversial issue for the rest of the war and ultimately became one of the principal reasons that Grant ended the prisoner exchange system in 1864.

After their failure to capture the Louisiana outposts, Walker's Texas Division spent the rest of the summer in a frustrating campaign across the swamps, spending more time fighting heat, hunger, mosquitoes, malaria, and snakes than the Yankees. On June 15, Union Brigadier General Joseph Mower drove Walker's men from the small town of Richmond, Louisiana, in a brief skirmish. Mower then burned the town to the ground, leaving the residents to endure a precarious life as refugees.[33] One Federal participant, William Van Meter of the 47th Illinois Infantry, recorded that during the engagement, the Rebels "fired from windows and from behind houses, in which there were women and children, and we were compelled to charge them with bayonets or run the chance of killing women or children." Following the battle, Van Meter recalled that "after the inmates had taken all that was of value out of the houses, we were ordered to burn the village, most of the women and children went with us to Youngs Point where they were sheltered and feed [fed]."[34] The residents who escaped never rebuilt Richmond after the war. The blackened ruins of Richmond and other towns in the South served as a forbidding indication of the increasing harshness of the Union's hard war policies.[35]

Well aware that he lacked the strength to relieve Vicksburg, Taylor instead ordered his men to raid along the west bank of the Mississippi River to destroy the region's value to the Union and divert as much of Army of the Tennessee as possible. Taylor's men seared the landscape in a scorched earth campaign that equaled the Federal's hard war efforts. In this area of Louisiana, many abandoned plantations had been leased by the U.S. government to northern investors who paid former slaves to produce cotton, then exponentially expensive due to the wartime shortage. Walker's division burned cotton and plantations, seized dozens of acutely needed horses and mules, and captured some 2,000 African Americans who were returned to slavery. In his report, Walker acknowledged, "I am now engaged in burning all the cotton I can reach, from Lake Providence to the lower end of Concordia Parish, and shall endeavor to leave no spoil for the enemy." In addition, Walker declared, "I have also instructed the cavalry to destroy all subsistence and forage on abandoned plantations, that, from its proximity to the river, may give the enemy facilities for invasion."[36]

The destruction caused by Taylor's foray in Louisiana equaled that of the Union army. Observing the damage, Texan Theophilus Perry wrote his wife, "Our cavalry has destroyed the country between here and the Mississippi. They have burnt every thing I hear. It looks very silly to me for us to burn and destroy our own country. But this is the policy here."[37] A Confederate surgeon from Arkansas detailed, "The torch was applied to *every* building: Gin houses, cotton, fences, barns, cabins, residences, and stacks of fodder. Mules were taken from the plows where the Negroes had left them at the approach of danger, and driven off to the rear of our lines."[38] A Texans officer in Walker's division wrote home that the "enemy burns awhile then some of the planters take [the] oath of allegiance then our men [burn] them out and the plunderers and robbers end by sweeping what is left and the country once in the highest state of cultivation and pride of the South is nothing but a desert."[39] As historian Warren E. Grabau concluded, "Not even the Shenandoah Valley was scorched as thoroughly as this small region of Louisiana."[40]

At the same time, Kirby Smith's separate operation in Arkansas failed more dismally than his Louisiana debacles. In late June, Lieutenant

General Theophilus Holmes, the aged Confederate commander of the District of Arkansas, collected a small force of some 7,646 Arkansans and Missourians to strike at the Union supply base at Helena on the west bank of the Mississippi River. Much like Taylor at Milliken's Bend, Holmes intended to capture vital supplies, interrupt Federal navigation on the river, and threaten Grant's supply line at Vicksburg. Holmes and Taylor did not coordinate their offensives, and repeated delays postponed the Confederate attack until July. Finally, as the sun rose on the morning of July 4, Holmes launched several uncoordinated, piecemeal attacks on the elaborate defenses of Helena. The Union commander of the garrison, Major General Benjamin Prentiss, had constructed well-designed fortifications that included an abatis of felled trees, rifle pits, five heavily armed redoubts, the gunboat *Tyler*, and 4,000 Federal soldiers. Union artillery slaughtered the charging Rebels, and Prentiss's men swiftly repulsed the futile assaults. At 10:30 A.M, Holmes admitted defeat and ordered a retreat. Wasted Confederate valor at Helena cost Holmes 173 killed, 687 wounded, and 776 missing, for a total of 1,636 casualties, compared to Union losses of only 57 killed, 146 wounded, and 36 missing. The Battle of Helena ended in another catastrophe for the Confederacy. If Smith had commenced his offensives in April or early May, the expeditions might have seriously delayed or even defeated Grant's march to Vicksburg. The fruitless efforts of the Army of the Trans-Mississippi came too late to save Vicksburg, but at least Smith made the attempt, unlike Joseph E. Johnston and his poorly named Army of Relief.[41]

Despite Smith's endeavors, Johnston's army remained the only valid hope for the deliverance of John Pemberton and the Army of Vicksburg. Lida Lord, one of the civilians trapped inside the city, later recalled, "Joseph E. Johnston was our angel of deliverance in those days of siege, but alas! we were never even to touch the hem of his robe."[42] British observer Arthur Fremantle visited Johnston's headquarters on May 20 and recorded in his diary that Johnston "lives very plainly, and at present his only cooking utensils consisted of an old coffeepot and frying pan—both very inferior articles. There was only one fork (one prong deficient) between himself and staff, and this was handed to me ceremoniously as the 'guest.' "[43] According to Fremantle, the men in Johnston's army considered "the fall of Vicksburg as very possible, and its jeopardy was laid at the door of General Pemberton, for whom no language could be too strong. He was freely called a coward and a traitor." Pemberton, as Fremantle noted, had "the misfortune to be a Northerner by birth, which was against him in the opinion of all here."[44]

The soldiers under Johnston's command restlessly waited for orders to attack Grant's besieging army. One Texan officer, Major James C. Bates of the 9th Texas Cavalry, wrote to his wife on June 25, "We have more at stake in the coming contest at Vicksburgh, than any battle that has been fought during the war." Bates noted that Vicksburg "is the only artery that connects the two halves of the Confederacy—cut it & the lifeblood of either one or the other half will soon be drained."[45] The Confederate government in Richmond transferred as many reinforcements as possible to Johnston and sent a torrent of messages urging action. For reasons still debated today, Johnston ignored Richmond's pleas and refused to risk his hastily created army or his cherished reputation in any attempt to save the Army of Vicksburg. Johnston instead spent more time during May and June fighting with President Davis than with Grant's Army of the Tennessee. Johnston's earlier evacuation of Jackson had allowed the Federals to devastate the vital rail and supply center, making it much more difficult to transfer troops and equipment to Johnston's army. By June 4, Johnston's army had received its last major reinforcement, providing the Virginia aristocrat with a total of some 32,000 men. Still, Johnston failed to march to Pemberton's relief, while Grant's army steadily received reinforcements until the Union general commanded roughly 71,000 soldiers. When a desperate Pemberton inquired for relief from his superior, Johnston bleakly replied, "I am too weak to save Vicksburg; can do no more than attempt to save you and your garrison."[46] Johnston failed to act as siege continued, and on June 15, Johnston informed Richmond, "I consider saving Vicksburg hopeless."[47]

On June 26, Johnston complained to Kirby Smith, "It is impossible with the force the Government has put at my disposal to raise the siege of the city. The most that I can do is possibly to extricate the army, leaving the place in possession of the enemy." Ignoring the fact that he commanded a strong force within striking distance of Vicksburg, Johnston instead advised Smith that the "only hope of saving Vicksburg now depends on the operations of your troops on the other side of the river." Johnston was either unaware of the Texan blood shed at Milliken's Bend or simply unimpressed with the Trans-Mississippi offensives for the Virginian instead contended that if Smith would "contrive to plant artillery on the Mississippi banks, drive beef into Vicksburg, or join the garrison ... we may be able to save the city. Your troops up to this time have done nothing."[48]

While the siege of Vicksburg progressed through the summer, Grant dispatched 34,000 men under Sherman to prevent any possible attack from Johnston's army. In June, Sherman and his new Army of Maneuver fortified an "Exterior Line" from Haynes' Bluff in the north to the Big Black River in the south to defend against a Confederate relief expedition. At the same time, Federal soldiers in the appropriately named "Interior Line" tightened their siege lines and shoveled closer to Confederate defenses each day.[49] On June 16, Sherman received a copy of a congratulatory address written by McClernand to his XIII Corps that had been published in several newspapers. Written on May 30, "General Orders, No. 72" sought to magnify McClernand's role in the campaign and imply that both Sherman and McPherson failed to properly support that XIII Corps during the failed offensive on May 22. McClernand's fellow corps commanders in the Army of the Tennessee quickly protested about the address to Grant.[50] A furious Sherman labeled the order as "such a catalogue of nonsense—such an effusion of vain-glory and hypocrisy."[51] Grant had long been wary of his ambitious subordinate and had especially held McClernand responsible for the futile renewal of the bloody assaults on May 22. Two days after the attack, Grant had complained to Halleck that "Gen. McClernand's dispatches misled me as to the real state of facts, and caused much of this loss. He is entirely unfit for the position of corps commander, both on the march and on the battle-field." Grant further asserted that "looking after his corps gives me more labor and infinitely more uneasiness than all the remainder of my department."[52] The appearance of General Orders, No. 72 in several newspapers technically violated a War Department policy that forbad the publication of official letters and reports without prior permission. Although more of a press release than an actual order, Grant used the unauthorized circulation of General Orders, No. 72 to remove McClernand from command and replace him with Major General Edward O. C. Ord on June 18. An incensed McClernand requested a court of inquiry and fired off numerous angry letters to Washington, but neither Halleck nor President Lincoln intervened in the dispute, and the political general eventually returned home to Springfield.[53]

Within the surrounded fortress, the Army of Vicksburg held on throughout late June and early July while enduring ever-decreasing rations and an ever-increasing Federal bombardment. On June 20, Ohioan Osborn Oldroyd observed, "Even if the defenceless women and children in Vicksburg are protected, or feel as if they were, such a screeching of shot and shell must prove a terror to them, and my heart has not yet grown so hardened that I can not feel for them."[54] A few days later on June 26, Major Maurice Simons of the 2nd Texas Infantry inscribed in his diary how he entertained himself by recording the number of heavy shells that Union gunboats fired into Vicksburg during the preceding night, which he counted to be 166. From the estimated weight of the projectiles, Simons calculated that the total would "just make Thirty three Thousand two hundred pounds (33200) of iron that they fired at us last night Exclusive of the shot & shell thrown from their land Batteries." Simons ended his arithmetic by noting, "We have been under this fire for forty days which would make (3984000) three million nine hundred and Eighty four thousand pounds of Iron that the Morters have thrown at us which would require (498000) lbs of powder. This only the doings of the Morters which has not been half."[55]

Grant's artillery inflicted serious casualties in the Army of Vicksburg. Captain James Henry Jones of the 38th Mississippi Infantry recalled that after a large shell struck his position one night, "Four men were killed outright, and four others were seriously wounded, and all dreadfully mangled by that bursting shell. A bit of warm, quivering flesh fell on a soldier's hand a hundred yards distant. What a gruesome messenger of death that was."[56] The effects of the deadly missiles amazed eyewitnesses from both sides. Hoosier Thomas Wise Durham reported that one day, he and his comrades noticed a Confederate officer mounted on a parapet "brandishing his sword and cursing the Yankees." A Federal gunner decided to end the harangue with a cannon shot and fired at the reckless Rebel. Durham recorded that the projectile "struck the fellow midway of the body and bursted him like a glass ball. I have never seen pieces of flesh fly in so many directions as I saw there. It looked as though he was blown into mincemeat. I think the shell exploded just as it struck him."[57]

The ongoing bombardment affected civilian morale as well. Inside the caves, civilians sought any distraction possible from the terror of the shells exploding outside and the mounting hunger pains in their stomachs. Lida Lord recorded that one soldier who visited her cave "was an artist, and carved our profiles in bassorilievo [bas-relief] on the cave walls. A candle was held so as to throw a shadow, and with a penknife the work was very cleverly done. Even the baby in her nightgown was immortalized in clay."[58] William, her younger brother, wrote in his account of a young girl who had been slightly wounded from a spent minié ball. After medical authorities removed the bullet, "a clever convalescent soldier at the hospital transformed it later into a set of Lilliputian knives and forks, to the girl's infinite pride and delight." During the periods when the shelling ceased, William collected souvenirs from the siege, including one shell that failed to detonate after it "passed so near the top of my head as to stir my hair."[59] One day, when two shells exploded "almost simultaneously" near their cave, Margaret Lord reassured her youngest daughter, Louisa, by saying, " 'Don't cry, my darling. God will protect us.' 'But, mamma,' sobbed the little girl, 'I's so 'fraid God's killed, too!' "[60]

As the soldiers and citizens of Vicksburg approached the edge of starvation, any edible animal, including rats, became common Confederate cuisine. Lucy McRae remembered that late in the siege, "Our provisions were becoming scarce, and the Louisiana soldiers were eating rats as a delicacy, while mules were occasionally being carved up to appease the appetite. . . . Wheat bread was a rarity, and sweet-potato coffee was relished by the adults."[61] William Lord Jr. asserted that "fabulous prices were asked and paid for all kinds of food. Our own supply of provisions was reduced to a half-barrel of meal and about the same quantity of sugar; so that, like every one else, we began to look forward with anxiety to what might await us in the near future."[62] Mary Loughborough chronicled in her diary, "A certain number of mules are killed each day by the commissaries, and are issued to the men, all of whom prefer the fresh meat, though it be of mule, to the bacon and salt rations that they have eaten for so long without change." She observed, "There have already been some cases of scurvy: the soldiers have a horror of the disease; therefore, I suppose, the mule meat is all the more welcome."[63]

African American slaves in Vicksburg confronted hunger, disease, and death alongside their owners. At least one freedman in the city, William Newman, died when a shell struck his house on June 4, 1863.[64] Isaac Stier, a Jefferson County slave who witnessed the siege as a servant to his young master in the Army of Vicksburg, preserved an account of his experiences in an interview recorded for the WPA Slave Narratives. "De hongriest I ever been was at de Siege o' Vicksburg," he proclaimed. Stier described the 47-day siege as "a time I'd lak to forgit. De folks et up all de cats an' dogs an' den went to devourin' de mules an' hosses. Even de wimmin an' little chillun was a-starvin'. Dey stummicks was stickin' to dey backbones." Stier's interview presents a firsthand perspective on the hardships endured by slaves inside Vicksburg. He testified, "Us Niggers was sufferin' so us took de sweaty hoss blankets an' soaked 'em in mudholes where de hosses tromped. Den us wrung 'em out in buckets an' drunk dat dirty water for pot-likker. It tasted kinda salty an' was strength'nin', lak weak soup."[65]

Louisianan W. H. Tunnard detailed the final days of the siege in vivid imagery, observing that by that point "Vicksburg presented a fearful spectacle, having the appearance of being visited with a terrible scourge. Signs wretched from their fastenings; houses dilapidated and in ruins, rent and torn by shot and shell; the streets barricaded with earth-works, and defended by artillery, over which lonely sentinels kept guard." The second-largest city in Mississippi that had once been a booming river port now contained streets that "were almost deserted, save by hunger-pinched, starving and wounded soldiers . . . indifferent to the screaming and exploding shells. The stores, the few that were open, looked like the ghost of more prosperous times, with their empty shelves and scant stock of goods, held at ruinous prices." Tunnard grieved for the wrecked mansions "crumbling into ruins, the walks torn up by mortar-shells, the flower-beds, once blooming in all the regal beauty of spring loveliness, trodden down, the shrubbery neglected" while acknowledging that "even the enclosures around the remains of the revered dead, were destroyed, while wagons were parked around the grave-yard, horses tramping down the graves, and men using the tombstones as convenient tables for their scanty meals, or a couch for an uncertain slumber." Recalling the ravaged landscape in the era of Reconstruction, Tunnard declared, "Human language is impotent to portray the true situation of affairs."[66]

Throughout the month of June, Grant's men continued evacuating their approach trenches outside of Vicksburg. By June 23, Logan's Approach extended so close to the 3rd Louisiana Redan that Union soldiers from McPherson's Corps could began tunneling a mineshaft under the stronghold. Working night and day in shifts, a volunteer crew of 36 former coal and lead miners dug a tunnel under the fort 45 feet long with three separate smaller galleries, each extending out a further 15 feet. The Louisianans in the Redan could hear the sounds of digging from under their positions and commenced countermining operations, but the Rebels failed to discover the mine in time. On June 25, the volunteer miners completed their excavation and packed the galleries with 2,200 pounds of gunpowder borrowed from the U.S. Navy. Grant planned to detonate the mine at 3:00 P.M. and launch an attack through the crater spearheaded by Brigadier General Mortimer Leggett's brigade. As tensions mounted, 3:00 P.M. passed without incident. Soldiers waited in suspense as the minutes passed in eerie silence. Finally, at 3:28 P.M., the Redan erupted in an awe-inspiring explosion that killed at least six Mississippians working in the countermine.[67] Union Captain Andrew Hickenlooper described the sight as "an immense fountain of finely pulverized earth, mingled with flashes of fire and clouds of smoke, through which could occasionally be caught a glimpse of some dark objects,—men, gun-carriages, shelters, etc."[68] Illinoisan Sergeant Ira Blanchard recalled that after the explosion "all was dark with the clouds of smoke and dust; then came crashing down to earth again timbers, animals and men in one grand ruin; several bodies came down perfectly nude with every bone broken."[69]

Federal artillery blasted at the stunned Confederates as the 45th Illinois Infantry charged into a smoking crater 12 feet deep and 30 feet wide. The

Louisianans' brigade commander, Brigadier General Louis Hébert, had prepared for a possible attack by withdrawing most of the defenders to a newly constructed defensive line behind the Redan and requesting reinforcements from Pemberton. Union soldiers poured into the crater and into a maelstrom of rifle and cannon fire. Only a few regiments could occupy the crater at a time, and when each unit exhausted its ammunition, McPherson replaced it with fresh reserves. Colonel Francis Cockrell, commander of the reliable Missouri brigade, contributed first the 6th Missouri Infantry and later the 5th Missouri Infantry to reinforce the Louisianans. Colonel Eugene Erwin, a grandson of Henry Clay, led his veteran 6th Missouri Infantry into the melee and died after suffering two bullet wounds. In savage fighting, both sides blazed away at each other throughout the night with hand grenades and rifles at point-blank range. The following morning, Grant ended the assault after losing 34 killed and 209 wounded compared to the Confederates' 21 killed and 73 wounded. McPherson's men erected earthworks to hold their hard-won gains and on June 26 began tunneling a second mine under the new Confederate position. Once again, the Rebels commenced countermining, and, fearing discovery, McPherson exploded the second mine with 1,800 pounds of gunpowder at 3:00 P.M. on July 1.[70] In his postwar account, Louisianan W. H. Tunnard remembered that when the second mine detonated, "It seemed as if all hell had suddenly yawned upon the devoted band, and vomited forth its suphurous fire and smoke upon them."[71] Several Confederate soldiers died in the explosion, as did seven of the eight slaves working in the countermine. Incredibly, one African American named Abraham survived the eruption and landed relatively unscathed in Union lines. No Federal attack followed the explosion of the second mine, which destroyed much of what remained of the original redan. Instead, Grant began preparations for a final assault to end the siege and capture Vicksburg on July 6.[72]

Throughout the concluding days of the siege, Federal soldiers continued to mount foraging expeditions into the countryside outside of Vicksburg. Tired of battling heat and boredom as well as the Rebels, a few homesick Union soldiers sought consolation in the brown water of the Mississippi River. Wisconsin Private Chauncey Cooke recounted in a letter to his parents that while aboard a steamer on June 26, "The boys made a rush for the boiler deck to get a drink of the water that came from the lakes and springs of Wisconsin and Minnesota." Cooke admitted that while the water "was dirty and muddy and we saw dead mules and cattle floating by and knew that it was the sewer for all the filth of the northern states," he and his comrades, "whether we were dry or not, drank, and drank, until it ran out of our nose just because it came from the glorious North."[73] On

June 17, Emilie McKinley provided a woman's opinion of Federal foraging parties when she recorded in her diary, "The other day Mrs. Downs told a Yankee officer who was eating his dinner at her house, while his men were rushing furiously around the house shooting the poultry, that these were terrible times to live in." The officer asserted, " 'Yes, they are rather uncomfortable.' 'Uncomfortable!' exclaimed Mrs. Downs. 'That word does not give any idea of the times at all.' "[74]

On June 28, Pemberton received an anonymous petition entitled "Appeal for help." The letter, signed by "MANY SOLDIERS," affirmed confidence in Pemberton's leadership and the Confederate cause but declared, "A crisis has arrived in the midst of our siege. Our rations have been cut down to one biscuit and a small bit of bacon per day, not enough scarcely to keep soul and body together, much less to stand the hardships we are called upon to stand." The unnamed soldiers protested that "we are, and have been, kept close in the trenches day and night, not allowed to forage any at all, and, even if permitted, there is nothing to be had among the citizens." The note concluded with the warning, "If you can't feed us, you had better surrender us, horrible as the idea is, than suffer this noble army to disgrace themselves by desertion. . . . This army is now ripe for mutiny, unless it can be fed."[75] With no real hope of rescue from Johnston's forces and an army on the brink of exhaustion, Pemberton knew that his men could not hold Vicksburg much longer. The only unanswered question remaining was whether Pemberton would surrender before Grant could launch the final assault that both commanders knew would succeed.[76]

The Army of Vicksburg entered the month of July 1863 as a shadow of its former glory. Short of food and clean water, the steadfast defenders had been ravaged by siege, disease, and desertion. Each day, officers and men died who could not be replaced. Brigade commander Colonel Isham Garrott had been shot dead within the Square Fort on June 17, and a few days later on June 27, Pemberton lost another veteran subordinate when a Union sniper killed Brigadier General Martin E. Green.[77] On July 1, Pemberton issued a circular to his division commanders requesting a report on the condition of their commands and their opinion of whether the army should capitulate or fight to cut an escape route through Grant's lines. The replies were unanimous; every division commander in the Army of Vicksburg argued against an escape attempt and urged surrender. On the night of July 2, Pemberton called a council of war with his highest-ranking subordinates to discuss the bleak situation. All of the division and brigade commanders present, except for Brigadier Generals Stephen D. Lee and William E. Baldwin, voted in favor of laying down their arms.[78]

Pemberton, as a Pennsylvania-born Rebel, knew all too well the vilification he would endure for surrendering the "Gibraltar of the Confederacy."[79] After accepting the council's decision he confessed that "my own preference would be to put myself at the head of my troops and make a desperate effort to cut our way through the enemy. That is my only hope of saving myself from shame and disgrace."[80]

At 10:30 A.M. on July 3, 1863, white flags of truce appeared in front of Confederate earthworks. When the firing ceased, recently promoted Major General Bowen and Lieutenant Colonel Louis Montgomery from Pemberton's staff rode out with a message from their commander to Grant requesting to negotiate terms of surrender.[81] Grant, continuing the tactics that had made his famous, responded to Pemberton's proposal by declaring that he "had no terms other" than "the unconditional surrender of the city and garrison."[82] Bowen, who had been a neighbor of Grant's before the war in Missouri, realized that Pemberton might refuse an unconditional surrender and suggested that the two commanders should meet personally. At 3:00 P.M., Grant and Pemberton, accompanied by several officers and observers, met between the lines near a damaged oak tree.[83] After the war, Grant humorously conjectured that the famous tree had by that point "furnished as many cords of wood, in the shape of trophies, as 'The True Cross.' "[84]

When Grant reiterated his demand for an unconditional surrender, Pemberton threatened to end the conference and resume fighting unless Grant offered better terms. At that moment, Bowen proposed that he and one of Grant's subordinates meet separately to arrange a settlement acceptable to both sides. Grant, who had served with Pemberton in the Mexican War, agreed to the compromise. While Bowen, McPherson, Montgomery, and Brigadier General Andrew Jackson Smith discussed the capitulation, Pemberton and Grant reminisced about their service in the antebellum army. Upon resolving the last few details, both commanders approved the terms after midnight. The agreement permitted Pemberton's army to be paroled rather than transported to Union prison camps, and Confederate officers would be allowed to keep their sidearms, private baggage, and one horse each. Paroling the Army of Vicksburg would spare the Union the cost of transporting and supplying thousands of prisoners of war, and Grant realized that many of the Rebels who returned home on parole would remain there rather than take up arms again.[85]

When rumors of the surrender negotiations spread throughout the ranks, Union soldiers anxiously awaited official confirmation of their victory. On July 3, the usually serious Sherman wrote to his friend Grant, "If you are in Vicksburg, glory, hallelujah! the best Fourth of July since 1776. Of course,"

Sherman urged Grant, "we must not rest idle, only don't let us brag too soon."[86] Later, Sherman sent a second message to Grant that added, "If Vicksburg is ours, it is the most valuable conquest of the war, and the more valuable for the stout resistance it has made; if complete, we should follow up rapidly, but should leave nothing to chance. Of course we should instantly assume the offensive as against Johnston."[87]

Inside the doomed city, soldiers and civilians listened apprehensively as the cannon fell silent for the first time in weeks during the conference between Pemberton and Grant. Around 5:00 P.M. on July 3, both sides fired their last shells in the siege of Vicksburg.[88] That day, a Major Hauer from Bowen's staff called upon Margaret Lord to express the general's appreciation for her embroidering the "wreath round the stars" on his collar. Aware that Bowen had attended the negotiations to end the siege, Lord demanded that the major inform Bowen that she "had felt it an honor to be employed in such a manner for so brave a man, but if he had worn it in an interview with Gen. Grant for the surrender of Vicksburg I could only wish that I could take out every stitch I had put in."[89] Mrs. Lord had apparently not yet learned that Bowen had contracted dysentery during the siege, and this would claim his life shortly after the surrender on July 13. The death of Major General John Stevens Bowen, the last southern general to die in the Vicksburg campaign, cost the Confederacy an invaluable leader who could not be replaced. Initially interred near Raymond and reburied in 1881, Bowen's remains now rest alongside other Confederate soldiers in Vicksburg's Soldiers' Rest Confederate Cemetery.[90]

At 10:00 A.M. on July 4, 1863, the Army of Vicksburg officially surrendered. When Pemberton's men marched out of their trenches and laid down their arms, the epic 47-day siege was finally over. In the end, only 709 Confederate soldiers refused to sign a parole and instead chose to be transported north to be held as prisoners of war.[91] In his account of the momentous occasion, Indianan Thomas Wise Durham recalled, "The 2d Texas Rangers [Infantry] were in our front. We watched them march outside their works, form in line, their band played honors to their colors, then they stacked their arms. It was one of the most solemn and affecting scenes I have ever beheld." Instead of the expected exultation, Durham remembered that "there was no outburst of rejoicing on our part. In fact the scene was so solemn that nearly every one of our soldiers shed tears." According to his account, after the arms had been stacked, "the Union and rebel soldiers fraternized as if they had been fighting for the same cause. There was no enmity shown by either side." Durham conversed with the Texans and made the acquaintance of the "somewhat intoxicated" surgeon of the unit, who declared, " 'Well Captain, I am from Texas by G—. I suppose you want to see the city and I will pilot you through.' " Armed with a pair of canteens full of whiskey, the two former enemies toured the conquered southern citadel together.[92]

The sudden end of the siege stunned the civilians inside Vicksburg. Years later, Lida Lord remembered, "It was therefore a great shock to us all when the rector, pale as death, came into the cave, and said, with almost a sob, 'Take the children home. The town is surrendered, and the Union army will march in at ten o'clock.' " As the Lord family walked through the streets, they came upon the defeated remains of Pemberton's army. Lida wrote that during the encounter, "We were crying like babies, while tears rolled down their dusty cheeks, and eyes that had fearlessly looked into the cannon's mouth fell before our heartbroken glances. 'Ladies," the soldiers dejectedly announced, "we would have fought for you forever. Nothing but starvation whipped us.' " The Lords safely reached their damaged home, which Lida reported to be "almost uninhabitable" after the Union bombardment.[93] When the firing ceased, Mary Loughborough departed from her cave and discovered the enormous amount of debris created by the Federal cannonade. "On the hill above us," she observed, "the earth was literally covered with fragments of shell—Parrott, shrapnell, canister; besides lead in all shapes and forms, and a long kind of solid shot, shaped like a small Parrott shell." She noted that "minié balls lay in every direction, flattened, dented, and bent from the contact with trees and pieces of wood in their flight. The grass seemed deadened—the ground plowed into furrows in many places; while scattered over all, like giants' pepper, in numberless quantity, were the shrapnell balls."[94]

For many Confederates, Pemberton's decision to surrender on Independence Day appeared as an insult to southern honor for which the Pennsylvanian would never be forgiven. On July 8, Lettie Vick Downs wrote in her journal that Vicksburg had been "sold by a traitor, our brave men to have such a commander. Several have said (and no doubt they expressed the feelings of all) that rather than surrender to such thieving villains as the Yankees, they would fight three days after their provisions were out. Noble men."[95] In his official report, Pemberton explained his decision by arguing, "I believed that upon that day I should obtain better terms. Well aware of the vanity of our foes, I knew they would attach vast importance to the entrance on July 4," and on that day, "to gratify their national vanity they would yield then what could not be extorted from them at any other time."[96]

In a climatic celebration, the victorious Army of the Tennessee marched through Vicksburg and replaced the Confederate flag at the Warren County Courthouse with the Stars and Stripes. Lida Lord admitted that "the hardest trial of that bitter Fourth was the triumphant entrance of Grant's army, marching, with banners waving and drums beating, through streets plowed by their cannon-balls and strewn with the ruins of our homes."[97] Margaret Lord, Lida's mother, testified, "All that day tey [they] were streaming through town and in and out of my yard and *so* drunk."[98] Hoosier Thomas Wise Durham, who explored Vicksburg that day with two canteens of whiskey, wrote, "It was interesting, if not amusing, to see the women in hysterics, raving, pulling their hair, stamping their feet and cursing the Yankees." Durham asserted that the ladies of the city behaved as through the Earth "had come to an end and they wanted to die hard, but they mellowed down a little when we began to feed them. We not only fed the army that had surrendered but all the citizens of the city, for they were all quite hungry when the surrender was made."[99]

Upon entering Vicksburg, Grant's army began dispensing food to the starving residents and defenders of the city. One northern soldier, Ira Blanchard, recalled, "The inhabitants were in a famishing condition, and when we opened a bakery where we made fresh bread for our regiment, the women, those too who had been wealthy before, would come out and beg a loaf as we carried it through the streets."[100] Lida Lord expressed her embarrassment that her family had to plead for food from the Yankees when she detailed, "The day of the surrender we were in a pitiable plight, having neither food nor candles; but within twenty-four hours we were, with many others, receiving rations as 'a family in destitute circumstances'!"[101]

When the Army of the Tennessee occupied the town, some incidents of looting occurred until Grant's men restored order. On July 4, Texan Major Maurice Simons inscribed in his diary, "The yankees going in to every house. Plunder & pillage seems to be their fort."[102] Missourian Corporal Ephraim Anderson reported that none of the "dwellings in the place were disturbed except those from which the families had removed for safety; and the furniture in these was appropriated by the soldiers." Anderson did observe that "sugar belonging to the Confederate government, and also some that belonged to private parties, were rolled out into the streets by the Federal soldiery, the heads of the hogsheads knocked out, and the rebs around were invited to come up and help themselves."[103] Likewise, Lida Lord affirmed, "Just at first the Federal soldiers gave some trouble, trooping in and out of yards and houses, passing rough jokes with colored women, and bragging not a little." But she did concede that "the officers were uniformly kind and considerate, General McPherson especially exerting himself to make the lot of paroled prisoners and unfortunate people more endurable."[104]

The wreckage caused by the Union bombardment left many of Grant's soldiers awestruck. One Federal witness, Thomas Durham, stated, "There was hardly a house in the city that was not riddled by our cannon balls and shells," while another Hoosier, William Winters of the 67th Indiana Infantry, reported, "I saw one house that had 27 round shot holes in it and I don know how many from musket balls and fragments of shell, but it was an awful sight."[105] Lieutenant Joseph A. Savage of the 83rd Ohio Infantry wrote to his wife on July 4, "Vicksburg looks like it had been sowed with cannon balls. I dont think I saw a house that was not torn more or less with shot, some completely demolished the people all had caves in the Ground with carpeted floors and sides covered with canvas."[106]

Although the white citizens of Vicksburg considered Pemberton's surrender to be a disgraceful calamity, the newly freed African Americans in the city greeted Grant's army as liberators. The former slaves' social interaction with the conquering Army of the Tennessee astonished many white southerners. W. H. Tunnard noted that on July 7, "A new spectacle to the brave boys of the Third Louisiana was to-day witnessed in Vicksburg, which was the free intermingling between the Yankees and negroes on terms of equality." In addition to the more equal race relations, Tunnard wrote that he "saw a United States officer walking through the streets with a negro woman leaning on his arm. ... How such a scene affected a Southerner then can better be imagined than described. Now, it would scarce elicit a passing glance."[107]

On July 5, Sherman described the despondency southern civilians displayed when they learned of the fall of Vicksburg in a letter to his wife. "Oh the wail of these secesh Girls when Vicksburg surrendered," he proclaimed. "They cried and tore their hair, but I told them they had better not—they would survive the humiliating thought and eat whatever bread with as much relish as they ever did the corn dodgers of Aunt Dinah."[108] For the citizens of Vicksburg, the trauma of siege, shells, and starvation had ended. But the bitter troubles of military occupation and political Reconstruction had only just begun.

7

"The death knell of the beloved Confederacy"

After capturing Vicksburg, Grant directed Sherman to march 46,000 men to the east to confront Joseph E. Johnston's lingering Army of Relief. After weeks of bickering with President Davis, on July 1, Johnston had unenthusiastically begun maneuvering toward Vicksburg but quickly abandoned the operation when he learned of Pemberton's surrender on July 5. Johnston's men retreated to Jackson, leaving behind dead animal remains to contaminate the few sources of clean drinking water. The nauseating measure failed when Sherman ordered wagons of clean water hauled from the Big Black River to supply his men. On July 10, Sherman arrived at Jackson and began siege operations against the state capital of Mississippi.[1]

As a result of the severe foraging throughout the campaign, little sustenance survived in area between Vicksburg and Jackson. On July 4, Sherman informed Grant that "the farmers and families out here acknowledge the magnitude of this loss, and now beg to know their fate. All crops are destroyed and cattle eaten up."[2] On July 14, Sherman explained the extent of the devastation to Grant, writing, "Our foraging parties now go out about 15 miles. . . . We are absolutely stripping the country of corn, cattle, hogs, sheep, poultry, everything, and the new-growing corn is being thrown open as pasture fields or hauled for the use of our animals." In the dispatch, Sherman acknowledged that "the wholesale destruction to which this country is now being subjected is terrible to contemplate, but it is the scourge of war, to which ambitious men have appealed, rather than the judgment of the learned and pure tribunals which our forefathers

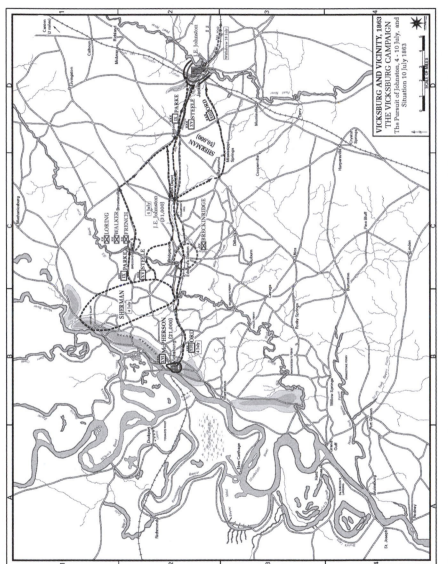

The Pursuit of Johnston, July 4–10, 1863. (Courtesy of the Department of History, United States Military Academy)

had provided for supposed wrongs and injuries." "Therefore," the Ohioan declared, "so much of my instructions as contemplated destroying and weakening the resources of our enemy are being executed with rigor, and we have also done much toward the destruction of Johnston's army."[3]

When Sherman's forces confronted the rebuilt defenses of Jackson that July, Johnston displayed no more vigor defending the city then than he did in May. Aside from a doomed charge by Union Colonel Isaac Pugh's brigade on July 12, only minor skirmishing and artillery shelling occurred during the brief siege. Private Samuel Barron of the 3rd Texas Cavalry reported that while passing a field hospital after Pugh's failed assault, "I looked into an old barrel and discovered it was nearly full of stumps of arms and legs, bloody and maimed, just as they had fallen under the knife and saw. This to me was so ghastly a sight that I never remember it without a shudder."[4] When a Confederate cavalry raid failed to destroy a critical Union supply train that provided Sherman with an adequate supply of ammunition for a sustained bombardment, Johnston once again ordered Jackson to be evacuated on July 16. For the second time, Johnston ordered the destruction of precious supplies and equipment that could not be retrieved and torched the last surviving bridges over the Pearl River. Sherman reoccupied Jackson on July 17 determined to finish the demolition of the city's war-making resources that he had commenced in May.[5]

That day, Sherman issued "General Orders, No. 59," in which he reminded his men, "One day's work of the Fifteenth Army Corps at Jackson in May prevented Johnston handling his troops and materials in the campaign, now made complete by the retreat from Jackson. Let us now so destroy this railroad that it cannot be used 'during the war.' "[6] Johnston's army had destroyed several buildings and houses to provide clear fields of fire, and other structures had been consumed when retreating Confederates burned their supplies. Union soldiers added to the ruin by systematically demolishing any rail or industrial resources that had escaped the first occupation or had since been repaired. On July 18, Sherman detailed to Grant, "The enemy burned great part of Jackson, and we have done some in that line. The place is ruined."[7] On the following day, Sherman explained to Admiral Porter that the Confederate army "set fire to a chief block of stores in which were commissary supplies, and our men, in spite of guards, have widened the circle of fire, so that Jackson, once the pride and boast of Mississippi, is now a ruined town."[8] In his official report of the brief siege, Sherman observed, "Indeed, the city, with the destruction committed by ourselves in May last and by the enemy during this siege, is one mass of charred ruins."[9]

One eyewitness, William R. Eddington of the 97th Illinois, documented his experiences during the second Federal occupation of Jackson. After Sherman's men added to the fires set during Johnston's evacuation, Eddington recalled that the "city was on fire in so many places, and what with the water mains, fire fighting apparatus pump and everything destroyed by our shells, there was only one way left to put the fire out, and that was to tear down the buildings ahead of the fire." Eddington's comrades attempted to control the inferno, but, as he reported, "The boys went to work and the more they worked, the worse the fire got. Some one would always throw a fiery board far enough to reach another house, thus causing the fire to start again." In the end, according the Eddington, Union officers "sent the boys all back to their company's and left the fire to burn itself out with what help the citizens could give. I saw the biggest portion of the city of Jackson, Mississippi burned up."[10]

Although Sherman's orders expressly forbade pillaging, some Federal soldiers seized the opportunity to ransack Jackson once again. On July 17, Private Henry Wilmer Franks of the 96th Ohio Infantry recorded that a "great excitement prevails this morning. Our men are stripping the town of all they can get and carrying it off and selling and speculating as fast as they can."[11] The next day, he concluded, "Well yesterday was a day of much excitement the boys made a play day of it, or rather a day of plundering for they carried off everything that was in the city."[12] In his official report, Sherman reluctantly admitted that "the conduct of the troops, so far as fighting is concerned, was all that any commander could ask ... but there was and is too great a tendency to plunder and pillage, confined to a few men, that reflects discredit on us all."[13]

Franks defended the behavior of Union soldiers as retribution for Johnston's employment of makeshift land mines hidden near water wells so that "when our boys went to get a drink they went off and killed some."[14] In his report of the siege, Sherman asserted that the Confederate army "burned all the bridges, and had placed loaded shells with torpedoes in the roads leading out from the river. The explosion of one of these wounded a citizen severely, and another killed a man and wounded two others of Lightburn's brigade."[15] Union observer John Merrilees reported that Federal soldiers forced captured Confederate prisoners to remove the hated mines at Jackson.[16] Historians have also theorized that Union soldiers from Indiana and Ohio devastated Jackson as a reprisal for the destruction inflicted by Confederate Brigadier General John Hunt Morgan's raid into those states during the same month.[17] On July 28, one Hoosier soldier, Darius Hall Dodd of the 83rd Indiana Infantry, wrote to his sister, "Some men in our Co had their houses in Ripley County [Indiana] plundered their horses stolen &c Wo! be unto the Rebs here after where the 83d goes. We have already made good Morgan's damage Even if he had of taken all Ind [iana]." Dodd declared that "there is ½ dozen horses left in Jackson every farm house almost between Vicks & there has been burned. The property all taken Negroes not excepted."[18]

On July 18, Grant instructed Sherman, "When you leave, leave nothing of value for the enemy to carry on war with. I would like the [rail]road destroyed east of Jackson as far as possible."[19] On the following day, Sherman informed Admiral Porter that his men tore up the rails "40 miles north and 60 south; also 10 miles east," while the "10-miles break west, of last May, is still untouched, so that Jackson ceases to be a place for the enemy to collect stores and men from which to threaten our great river." Indeed, the railroad has been so thoroughly wrecked that Sherman could proclaim that "the good folks of Jackson will not soon again hear the favorite locomotive whistle."[20] Sherman did observe that "State house, Governor's mansion and some fine dwellings, well within the lines of intrenchments, remain untouched," and while the business district of the city had been reduced to ashes, most residential homes survived.[21] After eliminating the military value of the capital of Mississippi, Sherman assured Grant that "Jackson will no longer be a point of danger. . . . The inhabitants are subjugated. They cry aloud for mercy. The land is devastated for 30 miles around."[22] Sherman remained in Jackson until July 23, leaving the capital city with a new name that would last for years: "Chimneyville."[23]

With Central Mississippi secured and Johnston's army in retreat, Grant could now concentrate on administering the conquered territory and restoring the loyalty of the civilian population. The destruction of the Vicksburg campaign had left Mississippians throughout the region in dire need of sustenance. Before returning to Clinton, Sherman provided "200 barrels of flour and 100 barrels of mess pork" for the starving citizens of Jackson and medical supplies for the Confederate sick and wounded left behind in hospitals.[24] Grant's army also supplied aid to residents in the rural areas that had been heavily foraged during the march to Vicksburg. As Grant noted in his memoirs, "Medicine and food were also sent to Raymond for the destitute families as well as the sick and wounded, as I thought it only fair that we should return to these people some of the articles we had taken while marching through the country."[25] Along with the provisions distributed in Raymond, Grant instructed that 15,000 rations be issued to the inhabitants of Clinton, Mississippi, in late July.[26] The Union commander affirmed that "provisions and forage, when called for by them, were issued to all the people, from Bruinsberg to Jackson and back to Vicksburg, whose resources had been taken for the supply of the army."[27]

Mississippians caught between the two armies urgently needed those provisions, as the wasted landscape had been stripped bare. Journalist Sylvanus Cadwallader reported, "No subsistence of any kind remained. Every growing crop had been destroyed when possible. Wheat was burned in the barn and stack whenever found. Provisions of every kind were brought away or destroyed. Livestock was slaughtered for use, or driven back on foot." Many proud southern families now found themselves in the humiliating position of relying on their enemies to provide rations. Cadwallader declared that "thousands were already applying for food to sustain life; and such heart-rending destitution had never been witnessed on the American Continent as in the region indicated."[28] On July 28, Sherman complained in a letter, "Our men are now all Expert thieves, sparing nothing not even the clothes of women, children & Negroes. Nothing is left between Vicksburg & Jackson so I can have peace here."[29]

Grant's new hard war policies proved to be extremely effective in reducing civilian support for the war. Correspondent Cadwallader asserted that "the people of that part of Mississippi were the worst-whipped communities on the face of the earth. They were completely humbled and begged for mercy on every hand." As Cadwallader noted, civilians in the area "acknowledged themselves thoroughly conquered; admitted their inability to longer oppose the Federal government; expressed their willingness to come into the Union again on any terms; and begged of him [Sherman] in the name of everything held sacred to oppress them no further."[30] Grant's masterful 98-day campaign virtually ended Mississippi's strategic role in the conflict, and its downfall foreshadowed the fate that would soon befall other southern states.

The surrender of Vicksburg shocked Mississippians throughout the state, and the city's fall on the Fourth of July only added to the anguish. On Independence Day, Emilie McKinley noted in her diary, "Report says Vicksburg has fallen, but I cannot and will not believe it." When confirmation of the disaster arrived, she inscribed on July 10 that "it is horrible to think that Vicksburg is really gone."[31] After the war, Ida Barlow Trotter recalled that "on July 4, 1863, Vicksburg was given over into the hands of the enemy, and a death blow fell upon the Confederacy for from that day those in authority knew that hope was vain and the cause for which so many brave men had given up their lives, was lost." Trotter declared the loss of Vicksburg to be "the death knell of the beloved Confederacy."[32]

One civilian family, the Lords, soon learned after Pemberton's surrender that Federal soldiers had ransacked the Flowers's plantation in the countryside where their most treasured belongings had been relocated.[33] Margaret Lord detailed with bitterness that within "an incredible short space of time after we left all was destroyed, scarcely a vestige left except the heaps of fragments of Dr. Lord's valuable books, torn from their covers and scattered around, even the trunks broken to pieces, carpets cut up into scripts with their pen knives" along with "china and glass dashed against the wall, barrels of molasses broken open that their contents might be wasted upon the ground, and last but not least to me, our clothing torn into strips not even a flannel skirt left us." In addition, the despairing diarist recorded that Union soldiers "passed into the rooms and dashed into fragments the large looking glass of my dressing table, and tearing the curtains from the windows with their bayonets[.] My bonnets were torn in two and the pieces tied to the posts of the bed." As a final insult, Margaret reported that the Federals "even went so far as to kill a sheep and bringing it into Mr. Flemin's [Flemens Granger] parlor cut it up in pieces on his carpet and on his handsome table; when they could do no more they left and this was but one of thousands of cases." In a rhetorical question, the minister's wife asked, "Can you wonder that our hearts were full of bitterness towards them? I had never believed the reports we heard of such outrages, looked upon them as men's paper stories gotten up for excitement, and as I knew our soldiers incapable of such conduct, believed the same of our enemies."[34]

The defeat at Vicksburg drastically affected the morale of Mississippi soldiers serving in the Confederate army and resulted in increased desertions from the state's military units. Jerome B. Yates, a Magnolia State Rebel in the 16th Mississippi Infantry, wrote to his sister from the Army of Northern Virginia, "What is the use of us fighting so hard and whipping the enemy up here when through the neglect of those down at home we are to lose everything that we are fighting for?" Although a member of the Confederacy's most illustrious army, Yates asserted, "I for one am wishing to stop the thing unless the Southern army will give us a little help."[35] Mississippi soldier James Johnson Kirkpatrick admitted in his diary, "Got Richmond papers of the 13th stating again and more positively that Vicksburg capitulated on the 4th. The news is very discouraging."[36] Another Mississippi Confederate, J. B. Crawford, complained, "News reached hear that vicksburg has gon up the spout. If it has wee had just as well quit and give up the Confederacy."[37] As historian Ben Wynne argues, "For some soldiers who had entered the service as part of a community enterprise, it was the successful federal invasion of their home state in 1863, not the subsequent fall of Richmond or the surrender at Appomattox, that marked the end of the war."[38]

The surrender of Vicksburg also decreased morale in Trans-Mississippi units as well.[39] On July 8, Vicksburg parolee Lieutenant Lewis Guion of the 26th Louisiana Infantry wrote in his diary that "I regret to say the La troops have in a great measure been demoralized by the Yankees in town it is said that many of the 27th & 26th went across the river this evening to try & get home but I understand they were turned back."[40] Private Samuel Farrow of the 19th Texas Infantry illustrated the significance of Grant's conquest when he lamented that the Union had secured "full control of the Mississippi river from its fountain head to where it empties into the Gulf and the Northwestern states now will pour down their forces upon us in such numbers that we will be compelled to retreat before them as far as they choose to follow."[41] On August 17, Captain Elijah Petty observed from Huntsville, Texas, "I find a general spirit of despondency prevailing all over the Country. People seem to be ready to give it up. ... Confederate Money is fast declining in consequence there of. "[42] Texas historian Charles Grear concludes, "Desertion became a major problem in Texan units only with the Union victory at Vicksburg" because that defeat "not only cut off Texans from communicating with their families in Texas but also dissolved the psychological barrier of the Mississippi River. Once the Federals controlled the river, Texans feared that their state would be vulnerable to invasion."[43]

When word Vicksburg's fall arrived, Franklin Gardner and the Port Hudson garrison capitulated on July 9, finally ending the Union's campaign to secure the Mississippi River.[44] On July 13, Lincoln wired a message of congratulations to Grant and confessed, "When you got below, and took Port-Gibson, Grand Gulf, and vicinity, I thought you should go down the river and join Gen. Banks; and when you turned Northward East of the Big Black, I feared it was a mistake." However, the president humbly admitted, "I now wish to make the personal acknowledgment that you were right, and I was wrong."[45] That August, Abraham Lincoln proudly announced, "The Father of Waters again goes unvexed to the sea."[46]

In Richmond, Jefferson Davis received word of Pemberton's surrender on July 7 and placed much of the blame for the calamity on the shoulders of Joseph E. Johnston.[47] On July 17, Confederate Chief of Ordinance Josiah Gorgas recorded in his journal that Davis "is bitter against Johnston." When Gorgas remarked "that Vicksburg fell apparently from want alone of provisions," Davis responded, " 'Yes, from want of provisions inside and a general outside who wouldn't fight.' "[48] In the spring of 1864, Davis wrote to Pemberton, "I thought, and still think, that you did right to risk an army for the purpose of keeping command of even a section of the Mississippi. Had you succeeded, none would have blamed; had you not made the attempt, few, if any, would have defended your course."[49] The disgrace of the surrender essentially ended Pemberton's military career, and when Confederate soldiers refused to serve under his command, the Pennsylvanian voluntarily accepted a demotion to lieutenant colonel in 1864. Pemberton led artillery batteries in Virginia and the Carolinas until the end of the war, after which he eventually returned to Philadelphia. He died in 1881, largely forgotten and never quite forgiven by most southerners for his performance in the Vicksburg campaign.[50]

The surrender of Vicksburg inflicted a fatal wound on the infant Confederacy. Grant's victory, along with the simultaneous Union triumph at Gettysburg, caused northern morale to soar and drastically diminished support for the region's antiwar Copperheads. The conquest of the Mississippi Valley provided a key propaganda victory for Lincoln that further eroded any lingering chance of European recognition of the Confederacy. As the Union gained control of the South's most important river, the Confederacy's ability to transport supplies from the vital Trans-Mississippi supply line ended forever.[51] In his memoirs, William T. Sherman observed that the victories at Vicksburg and Gettysburg "should have ended the war; but the rebel leaders were mad, and seemed determined that their people should drink of the very lowest dregs of the cup of war, which they themselves had prepared."[52]

The fall of Vicksburg cost the Confederacy an army of 29,491 men, many of whom never returned to duty after being exchanged.[53] The capture of Port Hudson produced another 6,404 Rebel prisoners; this, when added to the casualties inflicted during the campaign in Mississippi, Louisiana, and Arkansas, resulted in an appalling loss of manpower that the South could not recover from.[54] An estimate of the Confederacy's overall killed, wounded, and captured during the campaign from May 1 to July 17, including casualties suffered at Port Hudson and in the Trans-Mississippi theater, surpasses 46,000. That figure far exceeds General Robert E. Lee's losses at Gettysburg and does not include the increasing number of desertions that resulted from the repeated defeats. The Confederate army also lost an astounding amount of irreplaceable war equipment and munitions in the campaign. In the surrender of Vicksburg, Grant's Army of the Tennessee captured 172 artillery pieces, 38,000 artillery rounds, 58,000 pounds of gunpowder, 4,800 artillery carriages, 50,000 small arms, 600,000 rounds of ammunition, and 350,000 percussion caps. Banks seized 51 cannon and 7,500 small arms at Port Hudson, while Sherman acquired three cannon, 1,396 weapons, and 23,245 artillery rounds in the Siege of Jackson. Most of this weaponry would later be used in battle against their previous owners. Altogether, Federal forces captured 254 cannon in the Vicksburg campaign, including 85 pieces of heavy artillery. In contrast, Lee's Army of Northern Virginia did not lose a single gun in the Gettysburg campaign and actually captured three cannon in the battle.[55] According to historian Terry Winschel, the number of Confederate artillery pieces lost in the Vicksburg campaign represented "more than 11% of the total number of cannon cast by the Confederacy from 1861–1865," an amount the South could never hope to replace.[56]

The agricultural, economic, and psychological ruin imposed on the region by the extensive foraging, the burnings of Jackson, and the liberation of a vast number of slaves is immeasurable. In addition to securing a mountain of military supplies, the conquest of Vicksburg forever altered the way the war impacted southern civilians. In their march across Mississippi, Grant's Army of the Tennessee perfected the methods of hard war that would later be used against other states in the Confederacy and ultimately win the war for the North by destroying the South's ability and will to continue the struggle. Indeed, historian Mark Grimsley asserts that the Mississippi River valley was the "Cradle of Hard War."[57] In 1864, William T. Sherman would introduce the lessons of hard war to Georgia in his infamous "March to the Sea" and continue these policies with brutally effective results during the Carolinas campaign in 1865.[58]

Ulysses S. Grant achieved all of this after launching an amphibious landing deep into enemy territory with no clear avenue of retreat and confronted by two hostile armies that would outnumber his own when combined. Amazingly, the Army of the Tennessee suffered only 10,142 casualties during the campaign, a stunningly small price to pay for such a decisive victory.[59] Abraham Lincoln declared the Vicksburg campaign to be "one of the most brilliant in the world" and the triumph secured Grant's future military career.[60] In 1864, Grant received a promotion to lieutenant general and appointment as the Union's general in chief, ultimately leading to Robert E. Lee's surrender at Appomattox Courthouse. Although the conflict did not end at Vicksburg, Grant recognized the campaign as the turning point of the entire war. In his memoirs, Grant proclaimed that "the fate of the Confederacy was sealed when Vicksburg fell. Much hard fighting was to be done afterwards and many precious lives were to be sacrificed; but the *morale* was with the supporters of the Union ever after."[61] Ultimately, after years of reflection on the struggle for Vicksburg, Grant would conclude, "It looks now as though Providence had directed the course of the campaign while the Army of the Tennessee executed the decree."[62]

For the Texans who remained in the ranks after the fall of Vicksburg, the war continued for almost two more tragic years. After valiantly defending their state through the bloodiest conflict American history, Texan veterans returned home to help reconstruct a divided nation. In 1899, Congress created the Vicksburg National Military Park, but it would not be until nearly a century after the Civil War that the State of Texas erected a monument to its soldiers who fought in the defense of the "Gibraltar of the Confederacy." In 1961, Vicksburg received the first and largest Texas monument on a Civil War battlefield at the site where Waul's Texas Legion sealed the breach in Confederate lines during the May 22 assault at the Railroad Redoubt.[63] The inscription on the monument honors the service of Texans in the most influential campaign of the war and declares appropriately,

They were terrible in battle. They were generous in victory. They rose up from defeat to fight again and while they lived they were formidable. The heritage they left, of valor and devotion, is treasured by a united country.[64]

Notes

CHAPTER 1

1. William C. Davis, *Jefferson Davis: The Man and His Hour* (New York: HarperCollins, 1991), 504–7.

2. Terrence J. Winschel, *Vicksburg: Fall of the Confederate Gibraltar* (Abilene, TX: McWhiney Foundation Press, 1999), 22, 124; Steven E. Woodworth, *Jefferson Davis and His Generals: The Failure of Confederate Command in the West* (Lawrence: University Press of Kansas, 1990), 109.

3. Woodworth, *Jefferson Davis and His Generals*, 214–21.

4. William L. Shea and Terrance J. Winschel, *Vicksburg Is the Key: The Struggle for the Mississippi River* (Lincoln: University of Nebraska Press, 2003), 17–18; Warren E. Grabau, *Ninety-Eight Days: A Geographer's View of the Vicksburg Campaign* (Knoxville: University of Tennessee Press, 2000), 9; Terrence J. Winschel, *Triumph and Defeat: The Vicksburg Campaign*, vol. 2 (New York: Savas Beatie, 2006), 141–58. For an excellent discussion of the strategic role of the Trans-Mississippi theater, see Robert G. Tanner, *Retreat to Victory? Confederate Strategy Reconsidered* (Wilmington, DE: Scholarly Resources, 2001), 23–46.

5. David Dixon Porter, "The Opening of the Mississippi," in *Battles and Leaders of the Civil War*, vol. 2, ed. Robert Underwood Johnson and Clarence Clough Buel (1887; reprint, New York: Thomas Yoseloff, 1956), 24.

6. *The War of the Rebellion: A Compilation of the Official Records of the Union and Confederate Armies* (Washington, DC: Government

Printing Office, 1880–1901), ser. 1, vol. 17, pt. 2, 100 (hereinafter cited as OR).

7. Thomas L. Connelly, "Vicksburg: Strategic Point or Propaganda Device?," *Military Affairs* 34, no. 2 (April 1970): 49–53.

8. OR, vol. 31, pt. 3, 459.

9. W. H. Getzendaner, *A Brief and Condensed History of Parsons' Texas Cavalry Brigade Composed of Twelfth, Nineteenth, Twenty-First, Morgan's Battalion, and Pratt's Battery of Artillery of the Confederate States, Together with the Roster of the Several Commands as far as Obtainable—Some Historical Sketches—General Orders and a Memoranda of Parsons' Brigade Association* (1892; reprint, Waco, TX: W. M. Morrison, 1962), 17.

10. Getzendaner, *A Brief and Condensed History*, 17; Charles David Grear, *Why Texans Fought in the Civil War* (College Station: Texas A&M University Press, 2010), 117.

11. Winschel, *Fall of the Confederate Gibraltar*, 13.

12. Ibid., 130–40; Grabau, *Ninety-Eight Days*, 605–10. The figures vary based on how historians categorize Confederate military forces. For example, by the Vicksburg campaign, several Confederate regiments had been consolidated due to battle losses, disease, and attrition, which some authors may count as one combined unit or two separate regiments. Also, during the campaign, certain Confederate regiments had various detachments stationed in different locations, which also may affect the total numbers for each state.

13. Douglas Lee Braudaway, "A Texan Records the Civil War Siege of Vicksburg, Mississippi: The Journal of Maj. Maurice Kavanaugh Simons, 1863," *Southwestern Historical Quarterly* 105, no. 1 (July 2001): 96.

14. Shea and Winschel, *Vicksburg Is the Key*, 17.

15. Ibid.; Michael B. Ballard, *Vicksburg: The Campaign That Opened the Mississippi* (Chapel Hill: University of North Carolina Press, 2004), 5–12; A. A. Hoehling and the editors of Army Times Publishing Company, *Vicksburg: 47 Days of Siege* (New York: Fairfax Press, 1969), 1–11.

16. David Dixon Porter, *Incidents and Anecdotes of the Civil War* (1885; reprint, Harrisburg, PA: The Archive Society, 1997), 95–96; Winschel, *Fall of the Confederate Gibraltar*, 14.

17. Terrence J. Winschel, *Triumph and Defeat: The Vicksburg Campaign* (Mason City, IA: Savas Publishing Company, 1999), 2.

18. Shea and Winschel, *Vicksburg Is the Key*, 1–2; John E. Stanchak, "Anaconda Plan," in *Historical Times Illustrated Encyclopedia of the Civil War*, ed. Patricia L. Faust (New York: HarperPerennial, 1986), 12–13.

19. James M. McPherson, *Battle Cry of Freedom: The Civil War Era* (New York: Oxford University Press, 1988), 313; Gary D. Joiner,

Mr. Lincoln's Brown Water Navy: The Mississippi Squadron (New York: Rowman & Littlefield, 2007), 1–29; Shea and Winschel, *Vicksburg Is the Key*, 2.

20. Woodworth, *Jefferson Davis and His Generals*, 19–33; Shea and Winschel, *Vicksburg Is the Key*, 3–5.

21. Woodworth, *Jefferson Davis and His Generals*, 34–60; Spencer C. Tucker, *Unconditional Surrender: The Capture of Forts Henry and Donelson* (Abilene, TX: McWhiney Foundation Press, 2001), 47–51.

22. Woodworth, *Jefferson Davis and His Generals*, 34–60; Shea and Winschel, *Vicksburg Is the Key*, 5–6.

23. Woodworth, *Jefferson Davis and His Generals*, 71–79; Tucker, *Unconditional Surrender*, 22–27; William L. Shea and Earl J. Hess, *Pea Ridge: Civil War Campaign in the West* (Chapel Hill: University of North Carolina Press, 1992), 23–25.

24. Woodworth, *Jefferson Davis and His Generals*, 61–70; Wiley Sword, "Mill Springs (Beech Grove; Fishing Creek; Logan's Cross Roads; Somerset), Ky., Battle of," in Faust, *Historical Times Illustrated Encyclopedia of the Civil War*, 495.

25. Tucker, *Unconditional Surrender*, 51; Woodworth, *Jefferson Davis and His Generals*, 17–33; Steven Nathaniel Dossman, *Campaign for Corinth: Blood in Mississippi* (Abilene, TX: McWhiney Foundation Press, 2006), 14.

26. Edward G. Longacre, "Grant, Ulysses Simpson," in Faust, *Historical Times Illustrated Encyclopedia of the Civil War*, 320; Grady McWhiney, "Grant's Military Model," in *Confederate Crackers and Cavaliers* (Abilene, TX: McWhiney Foundation Press, 2002), 64–76; Steven E. Woodworth, *This Great Struggle: America's Civil War* (New York: Rowman & Littlefield, 2011), 60; Wiley Sword, *Shiloh: Bloody April* (Dayton, OH: Morningside Bookshop, 1988), 18; Tucker, *Unconditional Surrender*, 16–17.

27. Woodworth, *Jefferson Davis and His Generals*, 61–80; Tucker, *Unconditional Surrender*, 47–60; Shea and Winschel, *Vicksburg Is the Key*, 7.

28. Tucker, *Unconditional Surrender*, 60–92; Woodworth, *Jefferson Davis and His Generals*, 79–82.

29. Tucker, *Unconditional Surrender*, 93–104; Woodworth, *Jefferson Davis and His Generals*, 82–85.

30. Tucker, *Unconditional Surrender*, 115.

31. Dossman, *Campaign for Corinth*, 20; Woodworth, *Jefferson Davis and His Generals*, 79.

32. Shea and Winschel, *Vicksburg Is the Key*, 7; William L. Shea, *War in the West: Pea Ridge and Prairie Grove* (Abilene, TX: McWhiney Foundation Press, 2001), 13–72.

33. Peter Cozzens, *The Darkest Days of the War: The Battles of Iuka and Corinth* (Chapel Hill: University of North Carolina Press, 1997), 18.

34. Woodworth, *Jefferson Davis and His Generals*, 86–108; Dossman, *Campaign for Corinth*, 21; Sword, *Shiloh*, 460–61.

35. Albert Marrin, *Unconditional Surrender: U.S. Grant and the Civil War* (New York: Atheneum, 1994), 74–75.

36. *Personal Memoirs of Ulysses S. Grant* (1885; reprint, New York: Barnes & Noble Publishing, 2005), 211.

37. *Memoirs of General W. T. Sherman* (1875; reprint, New York: The Library of America, 1990), 270.

38. Ibid.

39. Alexander K. McClure, *Abraham Lincoln and Men of War-Times: Some Personal Recollections of War and Politics during the Lincoln Administration*, 4th ed. (Philadelphia: The Times Publishing Company, 1892), 196.

40. Joiner, *Mr. Lincoln's Brown Water Navy*, 57–74; Woodworth, *Jefferson Davis and His Generals*, 109–10.

41. Joiner, *Mr. Lincoln's Brown Water Navy*, 77–87; Shea and Winschel, *Vicksburg Is the Key*, 12–15; Woodworth, *Jefferson Davis and His Generals*, 109–11; Winschel, *Triumph and Defeat*, vol. 2, 148.

42. Shea and Winschel, *Vicksburg Is the Key*, 1–32; *Official Records of the Union and Confederate Navies in the War of the Rebellion*, vol. 18 (Washington, DC: Government Printing Office, 1894–1922), 492.

43. Shea and Winschel, *Vicksburg Is the Key*, 2–4,15–20; Woodworth, *Jefferson Davis and His Generals*, 109–12; Joiner, *Mr. Lincoln's Brown Water Navy*, 82–84; Grabau, *Ninety-Eight Days*, 14–50; Winschel, *Triumph and Defeat*, vol. 2, 147.

44. Shea and Winschel, *Vicksburg Is the Key*, 20–22; Woodworth, *Jefferson Davis and His Generals*, 112–17; Joiner, *Mr. Lincoln's Brown Water Navy*, 84–85; National Park Service, "Grant's Canal," Vicksburg National Military Park, http://www.nps.gov/vick/historyculture/grants-canal.htm (accessed September 4, 2012).

45. Shea, and Hess, *Pea Ridge*, 22; Shea and Winschel, *Vicksburg Is the Key*, 20–25; Woodworth, *Jefferson Davis and His Generals*, 112–16; Joiner, *Mr. Lincoln's Brown Water Navy*, 82–84; Dossman, *Campaign for Corinth*, 20; William N. Still Jr., "*Arkansas*, CSS," in Faust, *Historical Times Illustrated Encyclopedia of the Civil War*, 22–23; Isaac N. Brown, "The

Confederate Gun-Boat 'Arkansas,'" in Johnson and Buel, *Battles and Leaders of the Civil War*, vol. 3, 572–80.

46. Shea and Winschel, *Vicksburg Is the Key*, 25–27; Woodworth, *Jefferson Davis and His Generals*, 116–17; Joiner, *Mr. Lincoln's Brown Water Navy*, 85–86.

47. Shea and Winschel, *Vicksburg Is the Key*, 28–32; Woodworth, *Jefferson Davis and His Generals*, 117–21; Joiner, *Mr. Lincoln's Brown Water Navy*, 86–87; Dossman, *Campaign for Corinth*, 45–46.

48. *Personal Memoirs of Ulysses S. Grant*, 213–14.

49. Dossman, *Campaign for Corinth*, 40–54; McPherson, *Battle Cry of Freedom*, 515–17; Shelby Foote, *The Civil War: A Narrative, Fort Sumter to Perryville* (New York: Random House, 1958), 571–77.

50. Dossman, *Campaign for Corinth*, 76–138; Joseph E. Chance, *From Shiloh to Vicksburg: The Second Texas Infantry* (Austin, TX: Eakin Press, 1984), 63–77.

51. Dossman, *Campaign for Corinth*, 133–38.

52. *Memoirs of General W. T. Sherman*, 284.

53. Edwin H. Fay, *This Infernal War: The Confederate Letters of Sgt. Edwin H. Fay*, ed. Bell Irvin Wiley (Austin: University of Texas Press, 1958), 165.

54. Foote, *The Civil War*, 650–744.

55. *Personal Memoirs of Ulysses S. Grant*, 234.

56. John E. Stanchak, "Tennessee, Union Department of the," in Faust, *Historical Times Illustrated Encyclopedia of the Civil War*, 747; Shea and Winschel, *Vicksburg Is the Key*, 33–43; Winschel, *Fall of the Confederate Gibraltar*, 23–25.

CHAPTER 2

1. John C. Pemberton, *Pemberton: Defender of Vicksburg* (1942; reprint, Chapel Hill: University of North Carolina Press, 1976), 1–60; Woodworth, *Jefferson Davis and His Generals*, 169–85; Cozzens, *The Darkest Days of the War*, 307–10; Shea and Winschel, *Vicksburg Is the Key*, 36–37; James I. Robertson, "Pemberton, John Clifford," in Faust, *Historical Times Illustrated Encyclopedia of the Civil War*, 569; Michael B. Ballard, *Pemberton: A Biography* (Jackson: University Press of Mississippi, 1991), 83–113.

2. Woodworth, *Jefferson Davis and His Generals*, 116–85; Shea and Winschel, *Vicksburg Is the Key*, 48–50; Edwin C. Bearss, "Holmes, Theophilus Hunter," in Faust, *Historical Times Illustrated Encyclopedia of the Civil War*, 366; Edward G. Longacre, "Department No. 2, Confederate," in Faust, *Historical Times Illustrated Encyclopedia of the Civil War*, 216.

3. Archer Jones, *Confederate Strategy from Shiloh to Vicksburg* (1961; reprint, Baton Rouge: Louisiana State University Press, 1991), 104–10; Winschel, *Fall of the Confederate Gibraltar*, 130–40; Grabau, *Ninety-Eight Days*, 604–10; Dean E. Smith, "Vicksburg, Confederate Army of," in Faust, *Historical Times Illustrated Encyclopedia of the Civil War*, 781; Ballard, *Pemberton*, 114–21.

4. Fay, *This Infernal War*, 179.

5. Ibid., 184.

6. Winschel, *Triumph and Defeat*, 5.

7. Samuel H. Lockett, "The Defense of Vicksburg," in Johnson and Buel, *Battles and Leaders of the Civil War*, vol. 3, 484.

8. Ibid.

9. Shea and Winschel, *Vicksburg Is the Key*, 37–38; Winschel, *Fall of the Confederate Gibraltar*, 21–22; Grabau, *Ninety-Eight Days*, 39–50.

10. Shea and Winschel, *Vicksburg Is the Key*, 38–39; Winschel, *Fall of the Confederate Gibraltar*, 23–25; McPherson, *Battle Cry of Freedom*, 577.

11. John Y. Simon, "McClernand, John Alexander," in Faust, *Historical Times Illustrated Encyclopedia of the Civil War*, 456–57; Roy P. Basler, ed., *The Collected Works of Abraham Lincoln*, vol. 5 (New Brunswick, NJ: Rutgers University Press, 1953), 468–69.

12. John Y. Simon, ed., *The Papers of Ulysses S. Grant*, vol. 6 (Carbondale: Southern Illinois University Press, 1977), 288; Shea & Winschel, *Vicksburg Is the Key*, 41.

13. Shea and Winschel, *Vicksburg Is the Key*, 39–40.

14. Ira Blanchard, *I Marched with Sherman: Civil War Memoirs of the 20th Illinois Volunteer Infantry* (San Francisco: D. Huff and Company, 1992), 73.

15. Ibid.

16. Shea and Winschel, *Vicksburg Is the Key*, 41–43; Winschel, *Fall of the Confederate Gibraltar*, 24–25; McPherson, *Battle Cry of Freedom*, 577; *Personal Memoirs of Ulysses S. Grant*, 239–40.

17. Brooks D. Simpson and Jean V. Berlin, eds., *Sherman's Civil War: Selected Correspondence of William T. Sherman, 1860–1865* (Chapel Hill: University of North Carolina Press, 1999), 339.

18. Samuel B. Barron, *The Lone Star Defenders: A Chronicle of the Third Texas Cavalry Regiment in the Civil War* (1908; reprint, Washington, DC: Zenger Publishing, 1983), 135.

19. John E. Stanchak, "Forrest's Second Raid, Tenn.," in Faust, *Historical Times Illustrated Encyclopedia of the Civil War*, 270–71; Edwin C. Bearss, "Holly Springs, Miss., Raid on," in Faust, *Historical Times Illustrated Encyclopedia of the Civil War*, 365–66; William R. Brooksher and

David K. Snider, *Glory at a Gallop: Tales of the Confederate Cavalry* (New York: Brassey's, 1993), 71–98; Shea and Winschel, *Vicksburg Is the Key*, 43–45.

20. *Personal Memoirs of Ulysses S. Grant*, 242.

21. Shea and Winschel, *Vicksburg Is the Key*, 43–45.

22. Ibid., 44–45; Winschel, *Fall of the Confederate Gibraltar*, 25; Shea and Hess, *Pea Ridge*, 301.

23. Thomas W. Knox, *Camp-Fire and Cotton-Field: Southern Adventure in Time of War. Life with the Union Armies, and Residence on a Louisiana Plantation* (New York, 1865), Project Gutenberg e-book, http://www.gutenberg.org/files/12068/12068-h/12068-h.htm (accessed August 25, 2011).

24. *Personal Memoirs of Ulysses S. Grant*, 243.

25. Shea and Winschel, *Vicksburg Is the Key*, 46–51; Woodworth, *Jefferson Davis and His Generals*, 181–84; Davis, *Jefferson Davis*, 482–88.

26. *Jefferson Davis: The Essential Writings*, ed. William J. Cooper Jr. (New York: Modern Library, 2003), 275–76.

27. Shea and Winschel, *Vicksburg Is the Key*, 48–51; Woodworth, *Jefferson Davis and His Generals*, 181–85; Davis, *Jefferson Davis*, 482–88; William L. Shea, "'A Continual Thunder,'" in *Rugged and Sublime: The Civil War in Arkansas*, ed. Mark K. Christ (Fayetteville: University of Arkansas Press, 1994), 38–39; Jones, *Confederate Strategy from Shiloh to Vicksburg*, 111–30.

28. Joiner, *Mr. Lincoln's Brown Water Navy*, 89–101; Shea and Winschel, *Vicksburg Is the Key*, 46–47; Ballard, *Vicksburg*, 120–21; William N. Still Jr., "Cairo, USS," in Faust, *Historical Times Illustrated Encyclopedia of the Civil War*, 104–5.

29. Shea and Winschel, *Vicksburg Is the Key*, 47–53; John E. Stanchak, "Chickasaw Bluffs, Miss., Battle of," in Faust, *Historical Times Illustrated Encyclopedia of the Civil War*, 138–39; Richard M. McMurry, "Lee, Stephen Dill," in Faust, *Historical Times Illustrated Encyclopedia of the Civil War*, 431.

30. George W. Morgan, "The Assault on Chickasaw Bluffs," in Johnson and Buel, *Battles and Leaders of the Civil War*, vol. 3, 462–71; Shea and Winschel, *Vicksburg Is the Key*, 51–53; Steven E. Woodworth, *Sherman*, The Great Generals Series (New York: Palgrave Macmillan, 2009), 62–63.

31. Morgan, "The Assault on Chickasaw Bluffs," 467.

32. Ibid.

33. Ibid., 468.

34. Shea and Winschel, *Vicksburg Is the Key*, 54–55; Woodworth, *Sherman*, 63–64; Morgan, "The Assault on Chickasaw Bluffs," 468–70.

35. Susan T. Puck, ed., *Sacrifice at Vicksburg: Letters from the Front* (Shippensburg, PA: Burd Street Press, 1997), 43.

36. Simpson and Berlin, *Sherman's Civil War*, 351.

37. McPherson, *Battle Cry of Freedom*, 620–25.

38. Simpson and Berlin, *Sherman's Civil War*, 269–70.

39. OR, vol. 17, pt. 2, 330.

40. Ibid., 337.

41. Ibid., 421–22.

42. Ibid., 424.

43. Jean Edward Smith, *Grant* (New York: Simon & Schuster, 2001), 225.

44. Edward G. Longacre, "Grant's 'Anti-Jew Order' (General Orders No. 11, Holly Springs, Miss.)," in Faust, *Historical Times Illustrated Encyclopedia of the Civil War*, 320–21; McPherson, *Battle Cry of Freedom*, 620–25; Marrin, *Unconditional Surrender*, 77–78.

45. Darius Hall Dodd to Hatty Dodd, January 8, 1863, Civil War Miscellany, 1848–1927 (bulk 1860–1865), Indiana Historical Society, Indianapolis.

46. Robert M. Harsch, *Ninety-Seventh Regiment, Indiana Volunteer Infantry, 1862–1865*, 1967, Indiana Historical Society, Indianapolis.

47. Mildred Throne, ed., *The Civil War Diary of Cyrus F. Boyd, Fifteenth Iowa Infantry, 1861–1863* (Baton Rouge: Louisiana State University Press, 1998), 118–19.

48. Quoted in Rossiter Johnson, *Campfires and Battlefields: A Pictorial Narrative of the Civil War* (New York: Gallant Books, 1960), 279.

49. Grabau, *Ninety-Eight Days*, 507–10; Larry Gara, "Black Soldiers," in Faust, *Historical Times Illustrated Encyclopedia of the Civil War*, 62–63.

50. Stephen V. Ash, *When the Yankees Came: Conflict and Chaos in the Occupied South, 1861–1865* (Chapel Hill: University of North Carolina Press, 1995), 1–37; Mark Grimsley, *The Hard Hand of War: Union Military Policy toward Southern Civilians, 1861–1865* (Cambridge: Cambridge University Press, 1995), 3–22.

51. Ash, *When the Yankees Came*, 13–38.

52. Grimsley, *The Hard Hand of War*, 3.

53. Ibid., 23–95; Ash, *When the Yankees Came*, 13–37.

54. Grimsley, *The Hard Hand of War*, 3.

55. Ash, *When the Yankees Came*, 13–18.

56. Grimsley, *The Hard Hand of War*, 118.

57. Ash, *When the Yankees Came*, 13–18, 50–56; Grimsley, *The Hard Hand of War*, 96–142; Ballard, *Vicksburg*, 210–11.

58. Blanchard, *I Marched with Sherman*, 82.

59. Ibid.

60. Patricia L. Faust, "Foraging," in *Historical Times Illustrated Encyclopedia of the Civil War*, 266.

61. Michael Fellman, "Women and Guerilla Warfare," in *Divided Houses: Gender and the Civil War*, ed. Catherine Clinton and Nina Silber (Oxford: Oxford University Press, 1992), 147–65; Drew Gilpin Faust, *Mothers of Invention: Women of the Slaveholding South in the American Civil War* (Chapel Hill: University of North Carolina Press, 1996), 200; Jacqueline Glass Campbell, *When Sherman Marched North from the Sea: Resistance on the Confederate Home Front* (Chapel Hill: University of North Carolina Press, 2003), 44–57.

62. Gordon A. Cotton, ed., *From the Pen of a She-Rebel: The Civil War Diary of Emilie Riley McKinley* (Columbia: University of South Carolina Press, 2001), 13–16.

63. Thomas P. Lowry, *The Story the Soldiers Wouldn't Tell: Sex in the Civil War* (Mechanicsburg, PA: Stackpole Books, 1994), 31–32, 129–30.

64. Throne, *The Civil War Diary of Cyrus F. Boyd, Fifteenth Iowa Infantry, 1861–1863*, 125.

65. Ash, *When the Yankees Came*, 50–56.

66. Brett J. Derbes, "Arkansas Post," in *Handbook of Texas Online*, http://www.tshaonline.org/handbook/online/articles/qea04 (accessed September 30, 2012); James M. McCaffrey, *This Band of Heroes: Granbury's Texas Brigade, C.S.A.* (College Station: Texas A&M University Press, 1996), 27–36; Thomas L. Snead, "The Conquest of Arkansas," in Johnson and Buel, *Battles and Leaders of the Civil War*, vol. 3, 441–61; Shea and Winschel, *Vicksburg Is the Key*, 55–57; Joiner, *Mr. Lincoln's Brown Water Navy*, 105–6; Virgil Carrington Jones, "Arkansas Post, Ark., eng. at.," in Faust, *Historical Times Illustrated Encyclopedia of the Civil War*, 23.

67. Bell Irvin Wiley, ed., *Fourteen Hundred and 91 Days in the Confederate Army. A journal kept by W. W. Heartsill for four years, one month, and one day. Or, Camp life, day by day, of the W. P. Lane Rangers from April 19, 1861, to May 20, 1865* (Jackson, TN: McCowat-Mercer Press, 1954), 85.

68. Derbes, "Arkansas Post"; McCaffrey, *This Band of Heroes*, 36–37; Shea and Winschel, *Vicksburg Is the Key*, 57.

69. Norman D. Brown, ed., *One of Cleburne's Command: The Civil War Reminiscences and Diary of Capt. Samuel T. Foster, Granbury's Texas Brigade, CSA* (Austin: University of Texas Press, 1980), 20.

70. Derbes, "Arkansas Post."

71. Derbes, "Arkansas Post"; McCaffrey, *This Band of Heroes*, 37–43; Shea and Winschel, *Vicksburg Is the Key*, 57–59; Jones, "Arkansas Post, Ark., eng. at.," 23.

72. John Y. Simon, ed., *The Papers of Ulysses S. Grant*, vol. 7 (Carbondale: Southern Illinois University Press, 1979), 209; *Personal Memoirs of Ulysses S. Grant*, 245–46.

73. *Personal Memoirs of Ulysses S. Grant*, 249.

74. Henry Clemons to wife Anna, February 20, 1863, Henry Clemons Civil War Letters, 1862–1863, Wisconsin Historical Society, Madison.

75. Shea and Winschel, *Vicksburg Is the Key*, 63; Joiner, *Mr. Lincoln's Brown Water Navy*, 122.

76. Simpson and Berlin, *Sherman's Civil War*, 377.

77. OR, vol. 24, pt. 3, 38.

78. Shea and Winschel, *Vicksburg Is the Key*, 63.

79. Ibid., 68–72; Joiner, *Mr. Lincoln's Brown Water Navy*, 122–26; John E. Stanchak, "Yazoo Pass Expedition, Miss.," in Faust, *Historical Times Illustrated Encyclopedia of the Civil War*, 846.

80. Shea and Winschel, *Vicksburg Is the Key*, 68–72; Joiner, *Mr. Lincoln's Brown Water Navy*, 122–26; Stanchak, "Yazoo Pass Expedition, Miss.," 846; *Personal Memoirs of Ulysses S. Grant*, 251–52; Chance, *From Shiloh to Vicksburg*, 95–100.

81. Herman Hattaway, "Loring, William Wing," in Faust, *Historical Times Illustrated Encyclopedia of the Civil War*, 446.

82. Ralph J. Smith, *Reminiscences of the Civil War and Other Sketches* (1911; reprint, Waco, TX: W. M. Morrison, 1962), 22.

83. Shea and Winschel, *Vicksburg Is the Key*, 71–72.

84. Luther H. Cowan to Harriet, March 17, 1863, Civil War letters and diary of Luther H. Cowan, Wisconsin Historical Society, Madison.

85. Earl J. Hess, ed., *A German in the Yankee Fatherland: The Civil War Letters of Henry A. Kircher* (Kent, OH: Kent State University Press, 1983), 89.

86. Shea and Winschel, *Vicksburg Is the Key*, 72–74; John E. Stanchak, "Steele's Bayou Expedition, Miss.," in Faust, *Historical Times Illustrated Encyclopedia of the Civil War*, 716.

87. Shea and Winschel, *Vicksburg Is the Key*, 74–75; Stanchak, "Steele's Bayou Expedition, Miss.," 716.

88. *Personal Memoirs of Ulysses S. Grant*, 253.

89. Shea and Winschel, *Vicksburg Is the Key*, 64–68; Joiner, *Mr. Lincoln's Brown Water Navy*, 110–18; Virgil Carrington Jones, "*Queen of*

the West, USS," in Faust, *Historical Times Illustrated Encyclopedia of the Civil War*, 607.

90. Shea and Winschel, *Vicksburg Is the Key*, 81–83; Joiner, *Mr. Lincoln's Brown Water Navy*, 118–22.

91. *Personal Memoirs of Ulysses S. Grant*, 254–63; Ballard, *Vicksburg*, 206–11; Shea and Winschel, *Vicksburg Is the Key*, 90–91.

92. Simpson and Berlin, *Sherman's Civil War*, 446.

93. OR, vol. 24, pt. 3, 186–87.

94. Shea and Winschel, *Vicksburg Is the Key*, 91–92; Grabau, *Ninety-Eight Days*, 60–64.

95. *The Journal of Lettie Vick Downs in the Year 1863*, Downs (Lettie) Collection, Mississippi Department of Archives and History, Jackson, 6.

96. Stewart Bennett and Barbara Tillery, eds., *The Struggle for the Life of the Republic: A Civil War Narrative by Brevet Major Charles Dana Miller, 76th Ohio Volunteer Infantry* (Kent, OH: Kent State University Press, 2004), 90–91.

97. OR, vol. 24, pt. 3, 208.

98. *Personal Memoirs of Ulysses S. Grant*, 254–76; Ballard, *Vicksburg*, 206–11; Shea and Winschel, *Vicksburg Is the Key*, 92–93; Edwin C. Bearss, "Grierson's Raid," in Faust, *Historical Times Illustrated Encyclopedia of the Civil War*, 326; Fred L. Schultz, "Streight's Raid," in Faust, *Historical Times Illustrated Encyclopedia of the Civil War*, 726–27; Pemberton, *Pemberton*, 89–104.

99. Bernard Schmerhorn collection, April 19, 1863, Bernard Schmerhorn papers, Indiana Historical Society, Indianapolis.

100. William Warren Rogers Jr., " 'The Prospects of Our Country in This Quarter Are Gloomy Indeed': Stephens Croom at Vicksburg (April 1863)," *Journal of Mississippi History* 59, no. 1 (Spring 1997): 48.

101. Braudaway, "A Texan Records the Civil War Siege of Vicksburg, Mississippi," 103.

102. George B. Carter to his brother Bill, April 13, 1863, George B. Carter Civil War Letters, 1861–1864, Wisconsin Historical Society, Madison.

103. OR, vol. 24, pt. 3, 213.

CHAPTER 3

1. Shea and Winschel, *Vicksburg Is the Key*, 93–94; Grabau, *Ninety-Eight Days*, 10–13.

2. Shea and Winschel, *Vicksburg Is the Key*, 83; Grabau, *Ninety-Eight Days*, 34–38.

3. Smith, *Reminiscences of the Civil War and Other Sketches*, 23–24.

4. Ibid., 25.

5. W. H. Tunnard, *A Southern Record: The History of the Third Regiment Louisiana Infantry* (1866; reprint, Fayetteville: University of Arkansas Press, 1997), 197.

6. Winschel, *Triumph and Defeat*, 17–24.

7. Ephraim Anderson, *Memoirs: Historical and Personal; Including the Campaigns of the First Missouri Confederate Brigade*, 2nd ed. rev. (1868; reprint, Dayton, OH: Morningside Bookshop, 1972), 284–85.

8. OR, vol. 24, pt. 3, 730.

9. Shea and Winschel, *Vicksburg Is the Key*, 94–95; Grabau, *Ninety-Eight Days*, 67–73; OR, vol. 24, pt. 1, 250–51.

10. Shea and Winschel, *Vicksburg Is the Key*, 90–101; Winschel, *Fall of the Confederate Gibraltar*, 48–49; Joiner, *Mr. Lincoln's Brown Water Navy*, 129–33.

11. Simpson and Berlin, *Sherman's Civil War*, 458.

12. Shea and Winschel, *Vicksburg Is the Key*, 102–5; Joiner, *Mr. Lincoln's Brown Water Navy*, 133–34.

13. *Personal Memoirs of Ulysses S. Grant*, 266.

14. Shea & Winschel, *Vicksburg is the Key*, 104–5.

15. *Personal Memoirs of Ulysses S. Grant*, 269.

16. Winschel, *Triumph and Defeat*, 59; Grabau, *Ninety-Eight Days*, 143–49.

17. Shea and Winschel, *Vicksburg Is the Key*, 109–10; Grabau, *Ninety-Eight Days*, 150–54; OR, vol. 24, pt. 3, 806.

18. OR, vol. 24, pt. 1, 32.

19. Winschel, *Triumph and Defeat*, 59–63; Grabau, *Ninety-Eight Days*, 162–64; Shea and Winschel, *Vicksburg Is the Key*, 109–16; OR, vol. 24, pt. 1, 657–67.

20. Winschel, *Triumph and Defeat*, 63–75; Grabau, *Ninety-Eight Days*, 154–67; Shea and Winschel, *Vicksburg Is the Key*, 110–15.

21. Winschel, *Triumph and Defeat*, 65–74; Grabau, *Ninety-Eight Days*, 154–67; Shea and Winschel, *Vicksburg Is the Key*, 111–12; OR, vol. 24, pt. 1, 664.

22. Winschel, *Triumph and Defeat*, 78–84; Grabau, *Ninety-Eight Days*, 154–67; Shea and Winschel, *Vicksburg Is the Key*, 112–14; OR, vol. 24, pt. 1, 664.

23. George W. Covell diary, quoted in Robert S. Bevier, *History of the First and Second Missouri Confederate Brigades: 1861–1865 and from Wakarusa to Appomattox, a Military Anagraph* (St. Louis, MO: Bryan, Brand, & Company, 1879), 179.

24. Bevier, *History of the First and Second Missouri Confederate Brigades*, 180.

25. *OR*, vol. 24, pt. 1, 659.

26. Winschel, *Triumph and Defeat*, 84–88; Grabau, *Ninety-Eight Days*, 154–67; Shea and Winschel, *Vicksburg Is the Key*, 114–16; Philip Thomas Tucker, *The South's Finest: The First Missouri Confederate Brigade from Pea Ridge to Vicksburg* (Shippensburg, PA: White Mane Publishing Company, 1993), 121–47.

27. *Personal Memoirs of Ulysses S. Grant*, 273.

28. Ibid.

29. Jeffrey L. Patrick, ed., *Three Years with Wallace's Zouaves: The Civil War Memoirs of Thomas Wise Durham* (Macon, GA: Mercer University Press, 2003), 151–52.

30. Blanchard, *I Marched with Sherman*, 86.

31. *The Civil War Diary of a Common Soldier: William Wiley of the 77th Illinois Infantry*, ed. Terrence J. Winschel (Baton Rouge: Louisiana State University Press, 2001), 44.

32. Leo M. Kaiser, ed., "The Civil War Diary of Florison D. Pitts," *Mid-America: An Historical Quarterly* 40, no. 29 (January 1958): 38.

33. Winschel, *Triumph and Defeat*, vol. 2, 2–3.

34. Ibid., 3–12.

35. *OR*, vol. 24, pt. 3, 269.

36. Charles A. Wilson, *Reminiscences of a Boy's Service with the 76th Ohio* (Huntington, WV: Blue Acorn Press, 1995), 52.

37. Patrick, *Three Years with Wallace's Zouaves*, 125.

38. *OR*, vol. 24, pt. 3, 249.

39. Winschel, *Triumph and Defeat*, vol. 2, 13–15.

40. *Personal Memoirs of Ulysses S. Grant*, 275.

41. Ibid., 276.

42. Grabau, *Ninety-Eight Days*, 33.

43. James R. Arnold, *Grant Wins the War: Decision at Vicksburg* (New York: John Wiley & Sons, 1997), 126; Shea and Winschel, *Vicksburg Is the Key*, 120.

44. Simpson and Berlin, *Sherman's Civil War*, 468.

45. *Personal Memoirs of Ulysses S. Grant*, 276.

46. Benjamin P. Thomas, ed., *Three Years with Grant: As Recalled by War Correspondent Sylvanus Cadwallader* (New York: Alfred A. Knopf, 1956), 72.

47. Simpson and Berlin, *Sherman's Civil War*, 470.

48. *OR*, vol. 24, pt. 1, 259.

49. "Amount of Stock & Property Consumed & taken off by Gen. U. S. Grant's Army, 1863," Miscellaneous Civil War Documents, Mississippi Department of Archives and History, Jackson, 1–4.

50. Ibid.

51. Thomas, *Three Years with Grant*, 72.

52. U.S. Treasury Department, "Claim of Rosetta L. Newsom," in the *Southern Claims Commission Approved Claims, 1871–1880*, at Fold3.com, http://www.fold3.com/browse.php#34 | h-knXjBbfBBQt_jMEUQpsE-tle4uWWtS8P2vP4F9W (accessed March 17, 2012).

53. Thomas, *Three Years with Grant*, 72.

54. Rebecca Blackwell Drake, ed., *A Soldier's Story of the Siege of Vicksburg: From the Diary of Osborn H. I. Oldroyd* (1885; reprint, Raymond, MS: Friends of Raymond, 2001), 21.

55. Shea and Winschel, *Vicksburg Is the Key*, 106–26.

56. OR, vol. 24, pt. 3, 266.

57. Blanchard, *I Marched with Sherman*, 87.

58. OR, vol. 24, pt. 3, 808.

59. Ibid., 842.

60. Ibid., 814–28; Shea and Winschel, *Vicksburg Is the Key*, 117–25; Grabau, *Ninety-Eight Days*, 200–49.

61. OR, vol. 24, pt. 1, 238.

62. Woodworth, *Jefferson Davis and His Generals*, 217–21.

63. OR, vol. 24, pt. 3, 297.

64. Shea and Winschel, *Vicksburg Is the Key*, 106–23.

65. OR, vol. 24, pt. 3, 856; Jeffry D. Wert, "Gregg, John," in Faust, *Historical Times Illustrated Encyclopedia of the Civil War*, 325; Grabau, *Ninety-Eight Days*, 221–38; Shea and Winschel, *Vicksburg Is the Key*, 106–23.

66. Grabau, *Ninety-Eight Days*, 221–38; Shea and Winschel, *Vicksburg Is the Key*, 106–23; Edwin C. Bearss, "Raymond, Miss., eng. at.," in Faust, *Historical Times Illustrated Encyclopedia of the Civil War*, 617.

67. Henry Otis Dwight, "The Affair on the Raymond Road," *New York Semi-Weekly Tribune*, 1886, James and Rebecca Drake, http://battleofraymond.org/dwight.htm (accessed March 2, 2013).

68. Dwight, "The Affair on the Raymond Road," http://battleofraymond.org/dwight.htm (accessed March 2, 2013).

69. *Force without Fanfare: The Autobiography of K. M. Van Zandt*, ed. Sandra L. Myres (Fort Worth: Texas Christian University Press, 1968), 99.

70. Drake, *A Soldier's Story of the Siege of Vicksburg*, 23.

71. OR, vol. 24, pt. 1, 736–48; Shea and Winschel, *Vicksburg Is the Key*, 121–24; Grabau, *Ninety-Eight Days*, 221–38; Winschel, *Triumph and Defeat*, vol. 2, 21–30.

72. Blanchard, *I Marched with Sherman*, 89.

73. Shea and Winschel, *Vicksburg Is the Key*, 117–24; Winschel, *Fall of the Confederate Gibraltar*, 62–67.

74. Drake, *A Soldier's Story of the Siege of Vicksburg*, 24.

75. Shea and Winschel, *Vicksburg Is the Key*, 124; Winschel, *Triumph and Defeat*, vol. 2, 30–35.

CHAPTER 4

1. Shea and Winschel, *Vicksburg Is the Key*, 124; Winschel, *Triumph and Defeat*, vol. 2, 31–36.

2. OR, vol. 24, pt. 3, 870.

3. OR, vol. 24, pt. 1, 215.

4. Davis, *Jefferson Davis*, 502.

5. Shea and Winschel, *Vicksburg Is the Key*, 124–26; Winschel, *Triumph and Defeat*, vol. 2, 35–36; Grabau, *Ninety-Eight Days*, 239–49.

6. Shea and Winschel, *Vicksburg Is the Key*, 124–26.

7. Timothy B. Smith, "Jackson: The Capital City and the Civil War," *Mississippi History Now: An Online Publication of the Mississippi Historical Society*, http://mshistory.k12.ms.us/articles/337/jackson-the-capital-city-and-the-civil-war (accessed March 20, 2012).

8. Michael B. Dougan, "Herrmann Hirsh and the Siege of Jackson," *Journal of Mississippi History* 43 (February 1991): 21–23; Winschel, *Triumph and Defeat*, vol. 2, 31–48.

9. Junius Henri Browne, *Four Years in Secessia* (1865; reprint, New York: Arno and the *New York Times*, 1970), 248.

10. Shea and Winschel, *Vicksburg Is the Key*, 124–26.

11. Browne, *Four Years in Secessia*, 248.

12. Ibid., 248–49.

13. Thomas Frank Gailor, *Some Memories* (Kingsport, TN: Southern Publishers, 1937), 7–13, quoted in James W. Silver, *Mississippi in the Confederacy: As Seen in Retrospect* (Baton Rouge: Louisiana State University Press, 1961), 186.

14. Shea and Winschel, *Vicksburg Is the Key*, 126.

15. *Personal Memoirs of Ulysses S. Grant*, 283–84.

16. OR, vol. 24, pt. 3, 312.

17. Ben Wynne, *Mississippi's Civil War: A Narrative History* (Macon, GA: Mercer University Press, 2006), 111–12.

18. *Personal Memoirs of Ulysses S. Grant*, 284.

19. Wynne, *Mississippi's Civil War*, 111.

20. Thomas, *Three Years with Grant*, 74.

21. Dougan, "Herrmann Hirsh and the Siege of Jackson," 22–23; Wynne, *Mississippi's Civil War*, 110–11.

22. Thomas, *Three Years with Grant*, 74–75.

23. Dana, *Recollections of the Civil War*, 53.

24. Thomas, *Three Years with Grant*, 74–75.

25. Blanchard, *I Marched with Sherman*, 90.

26. Charles A. Wilson, *Reminiscences of a Boy's Service with the 76th Ohio* (Huntington, WV: Blue Acorn Press, 1995), 53–54.

27. Winschel, *Triumph and Defeat*, vol. 2, 44–48.

28. OR, vol. 24, pt. 1, 754.

29. Wynne, *Mississippi's Civil War*, 111; Dougan, "Hermann Hirsh and the Siege of Jackson," 22–23.

30. Edward P. Stanfield to his father, May 22, 1863, Edward P. Stanfield papers, Indiana Historical Society, Indianapolis.

31. George M. Lucas diary, 1863, Abraham Lincoln Presidential Library, Springfield, Illinois, 18.

32. Kathleen Davis, ed., *Such Are the Trials: The Civil War Diaries of Jacob Gantz* (Ames: Iowa State University Press, 1991), 26.

33. Hess, *A German in the Yankee Fatherland*, 107.

34. Bennett and Tillery, *The Struggle for the Life of the Republic*, 95.

35. Drake, *A Soldier's Story of the Siege of Vicksburg*, 16.

36. Greenman, *Greenman Diary*, 91–92.

37. Drake, *A Soldier's Story of the Siege of Vicksburg*, 29.

38. Dunbar Rowland, ed., *Jefferson Davis, Constitutionalist: His Letters, Papers, and Speeches*, vol. 6 (Jackson, MS: Printed for the Mississippi Department of Archives and History, 1923), 2–6, quoted in John K. Bettersworth, *Mississippi in the Confederacy: As They Saw It* (Baton Rouge: Louisiana State University Press, 1961), 204.

39. Rufus W. Cater to Cousin Fannie, June 2, 1863, Douglas Cater and Rufus W. Cater papers, 1859–1865, Library of Congress, Washington, D.C.

40. Dougan, "Hermann Hirsh and the Siege of Jackson," 23–24; Wynne, *Mississippi's Civil War*, 111.

41. OR, vol. 24, pt. 3, 314–15.

42. Elizabeth K. Miller, ed., *The Diary of John Merrilees 1st Lieutenant Battery E (Waterhouse's Battery) Illinois Light Artillery (In 3 books)*, bk. 1 (Chicago: Chicago Historical Society), 45–46.

43. OR, vol. 24, pt. 3, 315

44. Miller, *The Diary of John Merrilees*, 46.

45. *Memoirs of General W. T. Sherman*, 347–48.

46. Bennett and Tillery, *The Struggle for the Life of the Republic*, 95.

47. Miller, *The Diary of John Merrilees*, 46–47.

48. Ibid., 47.

49. Walter Lord, ed., *The Fremantle Diary: Being the Journal of Lieutenant Colonel James Arthur Lyon Fremantle, Coldstream Guards, on*

His Three Months in the Southern States (Boston: Little, Brown, 1954), 87–88.

50. Ibid., 87.

51. Ibid., 91–92.

52. Wynne, *Mississippi's Civil War*, 111.

53. Thomas, *Three Years with Grant*, 124.

54. Winschel, *Fall of the Confederate Gibraltar*, 74–75; Shea and Winschel, *Vicksburg Is the Key*, 127–28; Winschel, *Triumph and Defeat*, 89–96; Grabau, *Ninety-Eight Days*, 244–62; Herman Hattaway, "Loring, William Wing," in Faust, *Historical Times Illustrated Encyclopedia of the Civil War*, 446.

55. Winschel, *Fall of the Confederate Gibraltar*, 74–75; Shea and Winschel, *Vicksburg Is the Key*, 128; Winschel, *Triumph and Defeat*, 95; Grabau, *Ninety-Eight Days*, 261–62.

56. Winschel, *Fall of the Confederate Gibraltar*, 75; Shea and Winschel, *Vicksburg Is the Key*, 128; Winschel, *Triumph and Defeat*, 95; Grabau, *Ninety-Eight Days*, 249–63.

57. OR, vol. 24, pt. 1, 269.

58. Winschel, *Fall of the Confederate Gibraltar*, 75; Shea and Winschel, *Vicksburg Is the Key*, 128; Winschel, *Triumph and Defeat*, 95; Grabau, *Ninety-Eight Days*, 249–63.

59. OR, vol. 24, pt. 1, 261.

60. Ibid.

61. Winschel, *Fall of the Confederate Gibraltar*, 75; Shea and Winschel, *Vicksburg Is the Key*, 128–29; Winschel, *Triumph and Defeat*, 95–96; Grabau, *Ninety-Eight Days*, 262–63.

62. Winschel, *Fall of the Confederate Gibraltar*, 75; Shea and Winschel, *Vicksburg Is the Key*, 129–31; Winschel, *Triumph and Defeat*, 96–101; Grabau, *Ninety-Eight Days*, 263–65; OR, vol. 24, pt. 2, 93.

63. Blanchard, *I Marched with Sherman*, 90–91.

64. *Personal Memoirs of Ulysses S. Grant*, 284–86; OR, vol. 24, pt. 1, 51–52, 263; Shea and Winschel, *Vicksburg Is the Key*, 131; Winschel, *Triumph and Defeat*, 98–99; Grabau, *Ninety-Eight Days*, 270–73.

65. OR, vol. 24, pt. 1, 263.

66. Lockett, "The Defense of Vicksburg," 487.

67. Winschel, *Fall of the Confederate Gibraltar*, 75; Shea and Winschel, *Vicksburg Is the Key*, 132–33; Winschel, *Triumph and Defeat*, 99–100; Grabau, *Ninety-Eight Days*, 265–75; OR, vol. 24, pt. 1, 263; OR, vol. 24, pt. 2, 75–94.

68. Winschel, *Fall of the Confederate Gibraltar*, 76–77; Shea and Winschel, *Vicksburg Is the Key*, 133; Winschel, *Triumph and Defeat*, 101–3; Grabau, *Ninety-Eight Days*, 278–85.

69. *Personal Memoirs of Ulysses S. Grant*, 287.

70. OR, vol. 24, pt. 2, 95.

71. Winschel, *Fall of the Confederate Gibraltar*, 77; Shea and Winschel, *Vicksburg Is the Key*, 133–35; Winschel, *Triumph and Defeat*, 103–5; Grabau, *Ninety-Eight Days*, 278–93; OR, vol. 24, pt. 2, 95; OR, vol. 24, pt. 1, 264.

72. Winschel, *Fall of the Confederate Gibraltar*, 77; Shea and Winschel, *Vicksburg Is the Key*, 135; Winschel, *Triumph and Defeat*, 105; Grabau, *Ninety-Eight Days*, 290–97; OR, vol. 24, pt. 2, 75–76; OR, vol. 24, pt. 1, 264.

73. Anderson, *Memoirs*, 312.

74. Ibid.

75. Winschel, *Fall of the Confederate Gibraltar*, 77; Shea and Winschel, *Vicksburg Is the Key*, 135; Winschel, *Triumph and Defeat*, 105; Grabau, *Ninety-Eight Days*, 290–97.

76. Anderson, *Memoirs*, 313.

77. OR, vol. 24, pt. 1, 264.

78. Winschel, *Fall of the Confederate Gibraltar*, 77–78; Shea and Winschel, *Vicksburg Is the Key*, 135–36; Winschel, *Triumph and Defeat*, 105–6; Grabau, *Ninety-Eight Days*, 294–305; *Personal Memoirs of Ulysses S. Grant*, 290–91.

79. OR, vol. 24, pt. 1, 265.

80. Winschel, *Fall of the Confederate Gibraltar*, 78; Shea and Winschel, *Vicksburg Is the Key*, 136–37; Winschel, *Triumph and Defeat*, 108–10; Grabau, *Ninety-Eight Days*, 303–5; OR, vol. 24, pt. 1, 265.

81. Winschel, *Fall of the Confederate Gibraltar*, 78; Shea and Winschel, *Vicksburg Is the Key*, 137; Winschel, *Triumph and Defeat*, 110–11; Grabau, *Ninety-Eight Days*, 308–12; OR, vol. 24, pt. 2, 77–78.

82. Winschel, *Fall of the Confederate Gibraltar*, 78; Shea and Winschel, *Vicksburg Is the Key*, 137; Winschel, *Triumph and Defeat*, 111–12; Grabau, *Ninety-Eight Days*, 312.

83. *Personal Memoirs of Ulysses S. Grant*, 291.

84. Blanchard, *I Marched with Sherman*, 93.

85. Winschel, *Fall of the Confederate Gibraltar*, 80–81; Shea and Winschel, *Vicksburg Is the Key*, 138; Grabau, *Ninety-Eight Days*, 326–28; Anderson, *Memoirs*, 318–20; OR, vol. 24, pt. 1, 267.

86. Drake, *A Soldier's Story of the Siege of Vicksburg*, 33.

87. Winschel, *Fall of the Confederate Gibraltar*, 80–81; Shea and Winschel, *Vicksburg Is the Key*, 138–39; Grabau, *Ninety-Eight Days*, 328–34; Anderson, *Memoirs*, 318–20; OR, vol. 24, pt. 1, 266–67.

88. Anderson, *Memoirs*, 320.

89. OR, vol. 24, pt. 2, 73.

90. OR, vol. 24, pt. 1, 267.

91. Shea and Winschel, *Vicksburg Is the Key*, 127–139; National Park Service, "Battle of Big Black River Bridge (May 17)," Vicksburg National Military Park, http://www.nps.gov/vick/historyculture/bigblack.htm (accessed September 15, 2011).

92. Lockett, "The Defense of Vicksburg," 487.

93. Ibid., 488.

94. Scott Bowden and Bill Ward, *Last Chance for Victory: Robert E. Lee and the Gettysburg Campaign* (El Dorado Hills, CA: Savas Publishing, 2001), 10–36.

95. Ibid., 11.

96. Ibid., 10–36.

97. Mary Loughborough, *My Cave Life in Vicksburg: With Letters of Trial and Travel* (1864; reprint, Wilmington, NC: Broadfoot Publishing, 1989), 34–35.

98. Winschel, *Triumph and Defeat*, vol. 2, 93–96.

99. William W. Lord Jr., "A Child at the Siege of Vicksburg," *Harper's Monthly Magazine*, December 1908, 53.

100. Lida Lord Reed, "Woman's Experiences during the Siege of Vicksburg," *Century* 61 (April 1901): 922–28, quoted in *The Women's War in the South: Recollections and Reflections of the American Civil War*, ed. Charles G. Waugh and Martin H. Greenberg (Nashville, TN: Cumberland House Publishing, 1999), 82.

101. Winschel, *Triumph and Defeat*, vol. 2, 96–99.

102. Reed, "Woman's Experiences during the Siege of Vicksburg," 82.

103. Shea and Winschel, *Vicksburg Is the Key*, 142; Grabau, *Ninety-Eight Days*, 340–46; *Personal Memoirs of Ulysses S. Grant*, 293.

104. Thomas, *Three Years with Grant*, 82.

105. Wynne, *Mississippi's Civil War*, 116; *Memoirs of General W. T. Sherman*, 348–49.

106. Bennett and Tillery, *The Struggle for the Life of the Republic*, 95.

107. W. S. Morris, L. D. Hartwell Jr., and J. B. Kuykendall, *History 31st Regiment: Illinois Volunteers Organized by John A. Logan* (Carbondale: Southern Illinois University Press, 1998), 68.

108. Drake, *A Soldier's Story of the Siege of Vicksburg*, 34.

109. VOL 401 F. J. Thackara diary, May 18, 1863, entry, Ohio Historical Society, Columbus.

110. Shea and Winschel, *Vicksburg Is the Key*, 142–43.

111. Winschel, *Triumph and Defeat*, 9–10; *Personal Memoirs of Ulysses S. Grant*, 298–99.

112. Quoted in Shea and Winschel, *Vicksburg Is the Key*, 143.

CHAPTER 5

1. OR, vol. 24, pt. 1, 272.

2. Ibid., 273.

3. OR, vol. 24, pt. 3, 842.

4. OR, vol. 24, pt. 1, 273.

5. Smith, *Reminiscences of the Civil War and Other Sketches*, 25.

6. *Personal Memoirs of Ulysses S. Grant*, 296; Anderson, *Memoirs*, 326.

7. Loughborough, *My Cave Life in Vicksburg*, 25; Winschel, *Fall of the Confederate Gibraltar*, 96.

8. Loughborough, *My Cave Life in Vicksburg*, 25.

9. Shea and Winschel, *Vicksburg Is the Key*, 141–42; John E. Stanchak, "Smith, Martin Luther," in Faust, *Historical Times Illustrated Encyclopedia of the Civil War*, 697.

10. OR, vol. 24, pt. 1, 271–73; Grabau, *Ninety-Eight Days*, xxviii, 45–48; Shea and Winschel, *Vicksburg Is the Key*, 141–42; Hoehling and the editors of Army Times Publishing Company, *Vicksburg*, 9; Allan C. Richard Jr. and Mary Margaret Higginbotham Richard, *The Defense of Vicksburg: A Louisiana Chronicle* (College Station: Texas A&M University Press, 2004), 151.

11. Emma Harrison Balfour, *Vicksburg, A City under Siege: Diary of Emma Balfour May 16, 1863–June 2, 1863* (N.p.: Philip C. Weinberger, 1983), 6.

12. Wynne, *Mississippi's Civil War*, 125–26; Vicksburg National Military Park, "Tour Stop 2-Shirley House," http://www.nps.gov/vick/history-culture/tour-stop-2-shirley-house.htm (accessed August 21, 2013).

13. Shea and Winschel, *Vicksburg Is the Key*, 143–47.

14. Richard and Richard, *The Defense of Vicksburg*, 153.

15. Shea and Winschel, *Vicksburg Is the Key*, 146; Grabau, *Ninety-Eight Days*, 354–66; Richard and Richard, *The Defense of Vicksburg*, 152; Winschel, *Triumph and Defeat*, 118–24.

16. Shea and Winschel, *Vicksburg Is the Key*, 146–47; Winschel, *Fall of the Confederate Gibraltar*, 87–88.

17. Shea and Winschel, *Vicksburg Is the Key*, 147; OR, vol. 24, pt. 1, 274; Ballard, *Vicksburg*, 332.

18. Reed, "Woman's Experiences during the Siege of Vicksburg," 83.

19. *Personal Memoirs of Ulysses S. Grant*, 296–97.

20. Ibid., 297.

21. OR, vol. 24, pt. 3, 333–34.

22. Chance, *The Second Texas Infantry*, 21–81; Thomas W. Cutrer, "Waul's Texas Legion," in *Handbook of Texas Online* (Austin: Texas State

Historical Association), http://www.tshaonline.org/handbook/online/ articles/qkw02 (accessed August 12, 2013). Published by the Texas State Historical Association.

23. Chance, *The Second Texas Infantry*, 103–5; Grabau, *Ninety-Eight Days*, 46.

24. Winschel, *Fall of the Confederate Gibraltar*, 20, 90–92.

25. Balfour, *Balfour Diary*, 11.

26. *Memoirs of General W. T. Sherman*, 352.

27. Shea and Winschel, *Vicksburg Is the Key*, 149.

28. Drake, *A Soldier's Story of the Siege of Vicksburg*, 39–41.

29. Shea and Winschel, *Vicksburg Is the Key*, 149–50; Ballard, *Vicksburg*, 339–40.

30. Steven E. Woodworth, *Nothing but Victory: The Army of the Tennessee, 1861–1865* (New York: Alfred A. Knopf, 2005), 415–19; Chance, *The Second Texas Infantry*, 103–8; Arnold, *Grant Wins the War*, 248–53.

31. Smith, *Reminiscences of the Civil War and Other Sketches*, 25–26.

32. Chance, *The Second Texas Infantry*, 105–6; Ballard, *Vicksburg*, 340–43; Shea and Winschel, *Vicksburg Is the Key*, 150; Michelle Riter, "Vicksburg Medal of Honor Recipients," Vicksburg National Military Park, http://www.nps.gov/vick/historyculture/vicksburg-medal-of-honor-recipients.htm (accessed August 17, 2013).

33. Chance, *The Second Texas Infantry*, 105–8; Arnold, *Grant Wins the War*, 248–53; Ballard, *Vicksburg*, 340–43.

34. Grabau, *Ninety-Eight Days*, 46, 375–76; Chance, *The Second Texas Infantry*, 103–5.

35. Grabau, *Ninety-Eight Days*, 375–82.

36. Shea and Winschel, *Vicksburg Is the Key*, 151; Grabau, *Ninety-Eight Days*, 375–82.

37. *Memoirs of General W. T. Sherman*, 352.

38. Grabau, *Ninety-Eight Days*, 369–75.

39. Byron Cloyd Bryner, *Bugle Echoes: The Story of Illinois 47th* (Springfield, IL: Phillip Bros., Printers, 1905), 85.

40. Grabau, *Ninety-Eight Days*, 369–75; Winschel, *Fall of the Confederate Gibraltar*, 91–93.

41. Bryner, *Bugle Echoes*, 86.

42. E. W. Pettus, "Heroism of Texans at Vicksburg," *Confederate Veteran* 15 (May 1907): 211–12; Grabau, *Ninety-Eight Days*, 381–82; Ballard, *Vicksburg*, 347.

43. Pettus, "Heroism of Texans at Vicksburg," 212.

44. Arnold, *Grant Wins the War*, 248–55; Ballard, *Vicksburg*, 340–48.

45. Ballard, *Vicksburg*, 348.

46. Chance, *The Second Texas Infantry*, 108–16.

47. OR, vol. 24, pt. 1, 55.

48. *Memoirs of General W. T. Sherman*, 353.

49. *Personal Memoirs of Ulysses S. Grant*, 298.

50. OR, vol. 24, pt. 3, 343.

51. OR, vol. 24, pt. 1, 276–77.

52. Blanchard, *I Marched with Sherman*, 97.

53. Braudaway, "The Journal of Maj. Maurice Kavanaugh Simons, 1863," 110.

54. Drake, *A Soldier's Story of the Siege of Vicksburg*, 45.

55. Anderson, *Memoirs*, 334.

56. Shea and Winschel, *Vicksburg Is the Key*, 153–55; Winschel, *Triumph and Defeat*, 129–33; Grabau, *Ninety-Eight Days*, 408–12.

57. Winschel, *Triumph and Defeat*, vol. 2, 74–91; Joiner, *Mr. Lincoln's Brown Water Navy*, 136–37.

58. Tunnard, *A Southern Record*, 211.

59. Winschel, *Triumph and Defeat*, vol. 2, 92.

60. Grabau, *Ninety-Eight Days*, 408–10.

61. Braudaway, "The Journal of Maj. Maurice Kavanaugh Simons, 1863," 107.

62. Winschel, *Fall of the Confederate Gibraltar*, 102; Shea and Winschel, *Vicksburg Is the Key*, 156–57; Winschel, *Triumph and Defeat*, 133–35.

63. "Camels and Eagles and Bears ... Oh My!," Vicksburg National Military Park, http://www.nps.gov/vick/forteachers/loader.cfm?csModule=security/getfile&PageID=348155 (accessed September 17, 2013).

64. Winschel, *Fall of the Confederate Gibraltar*, 97–101.

65. OR, vol. 24, pt. 3, 401.

66. Winschel, *Fall of the Confederate Gibraltar*, 97.

67. Stephen E. Ambrose, "A Wisconsin Boy at Vicksburg: The Letters of James K. Newton," *Journal of Mississippi History* 23 (January 1961): 5.

68. Drake, *A Soldier's Story of the Siege of Vicksburg*, 57–58.

69. Reed, "Woman's Experiences during the Siege of Vicksburg," 83.

70. Peter F. Walker, *Vicksburg: A People at War, 1860–1865* (1960; reprint, Wilmington, NC: Broadfoot Publishing, 1987), 144–46.

71. Loughborough, *My Cave Life in Vicksburg*, 64.

72. Ibid., 53.

73. Anderson, *Memoirs*, 325.

74. Winschel, *Fall of the Confederate Gibraltar*, 104.

75. Reed, "Woman's Experiences during the Siege of Vicksburg," 84.

76. Lucy McRae Bell, "A Girl's Experiences in the Siege of Vicksburg," *Harper's Weekly* 56 (June 8, 1912): 12–13, http://app.harpweek.com/viewarticletext.asp?webhitsfile=hw19120608000046.htm&xpath=%2FTEI.2[1]%2Ftext[1]%2Fbody[1]%2Fdiv1[15]&xml=HW\1912\19120608.xml&titleid=HW&volumeid=1912&issueid=0608&pagerange=0012ad-0013a&restriction=&pageIDs=|HW-1912-06-08-0012|HW-1912-06-08-0013 (accessed April 25, 2012).

77. Lord, "A Child at the Siege of Vicksburg," 46.

78. Balfour, *Balfour Diary*, 6.

79. Reed, "Woman's Experiences during the Siege of Vicksburg," 85–86.

80. OR, vol. 24, pt. 3, 913.

81. Joseph Dill Alison Diary, Manuscript Collection, Mississippi Department of Archives and History, Jackson, Mississippi, 15–16.

82. Ibid.

83. Simpson and Berlin, *Sherman's Civil War*, 491.

84. Walker, *Vicksburg*, 193.

85. Balfour, *Balfour Diary*, 10–16.

86. Loughborough, *My Cave Life in Vicksburg*, 64.

87. Reed, "Woman's Experiences during the Siege of Vicksburg," 86.

88. Lord, "A Child at the Siege of Vicksburg," 50.

89. Cotton, ed., *From the Pen of a She-Rebel*, 41.

90. Grabau, *Ninety-Eight Days*, 501.

91. OR, vol. 24, pt. 3, 367.

92. OR, vol. 24, pt. 2, 41.

93. Ida Barlow Trotter, *The Siege of Vicksburg, and Some Personal Experiences Connected Therewith*, Ida Barlow Trotter Papers, Mississippi Department of Archives and History, Jackson, 2.

94. Ibid., 3.

95. Ibid., 4.

96. *The Journal of Lettie Vick Downs in the Year 1863*, 7.

97. Cotton, *From the Pen of a She-Rebel*, 1–9.

98. Ibid., 9–29.

99. Ibid., 20–29.

100. Tryphena. B. Fox letter to her mother, July 3, 1863, T. Fox Papers, Mississippi Division of Archives and History, Jackson, 93.

101. Ibid.

102. [Max Kuner?], "Vicksburg, and After: Being the Experience of a Southern Merchant and Non-Combatant during the Sixties," arranged by Edwin L. Sabin, *Sewanee Review* 15, no. 4 (October 1907): 490.

103. Walker, *Vicksburg: A People at War*, 194.

104. Walker, *Vicksburg*, 194–96; Tunnard, *A Southern Record*, 231–58.

105. Tunnard, *A Southern Record*, 212.

106. Anderson, *Memoirs*, 337.

107. Reed, "Woman's Experiences during the Siege of Vicksburg," 86–88; Winschel, *Fall of the Confederate Gibraltar*, 95–104.

108. Loughborough, *My Cave Life in Vicksburg*, 52–53.

109. Chance, *The Second Texas Infantry*, 112–13.

110. Reed, "Woman's Experiences during the Siege of Vicksburg," 88.

111. Ibid.

112. "Copy of a Journal Kept by Mrs. W. W. Lord, during the Siege of Vicksburg by the forces of General U. S. Grant May and July, 1863," Library of Congress, Washington, D.C., 4.

113. Reed, "Woman's Experiences during the Siege of Vicksburg," 84–88.

114. Tunnard, *A Southern Record*, 215; Anderson, *Memoirs*, 340.

115. Tunnard, *A Southern Record*, 256.

116. Walker, *Vicksburg: A People at War*, 179.

117. J. H. Jones, "The Rank and File at Vicksburg," in *Publications of the Mississippi Historical Society*, vol. 7, ed. Franklin L. Riley (Oxford: Mississippi Historical Society, 1903), 23.

118. *Personal Memoirs of Ulysses S. Grant*, 303.

119. Reed, "Woman's Experiences during the Siege of Vicksburg," 87–88.

120. Lord, "A Child at the Siege of Vicksburg," 51.

121. Tunnard, *A Southern Record*, 231.

CHAPTER 6

1. John C. Waugh, *Sam Bell Maxey and the Confederate Indians* (Fort Worth, TX: Ryan Place Publishers, 1995), 16.

2. Winschel, *Fall of the Confederate Gibraltar*, 107–12.

3. Shea and Winschel, *Vicksburg Is the Key*, 76–88.

4. Ibid., 87–88.

5. Ibid., 89.

6. Shea and Winschel, *Vicksburg Is the Key*, 78–80, 187–92; Lawrence Lee Hewitt, *Port Hudson, Confederate Bastion on the Mississippi* (Baton Rouge: Louisiana State University Press, 1987), 96–138; John E. Stanchak, "Gardner, Franklin," in Faust, *Historical Times Illustrated Encyclopedia of the Civil War*, 298.

7. Edward Young McMorries, *History of the First Regiment Alabama Volunteer Infantry C.S.A.* (Montgomery, AL: The Brown Printing Company, 1904), 58.

8. Shea and Winschel, *Vicksburg Is the Key*, 192–97; Hewitt, *Port Hudson, Confederate Bastion on the Mississippi*, 140–72.

9. McMorries, *History of the First Regiment Alabama Volunteer Infantry C.S.A.*, 63.

10. *OR*, vol. 26, pt. 1, 45.

11. Shea and Winschel, *Vicksburg Is the Key*, 197.

12. Ibid., 201; Hewitt, *Port Hudson, Confederate Bastion on the Mississippi*, 171.

13. Richard Taylor, *Destruction and Reconstruction: Personal Experiences of the Late War*, ed. Richard B. Harwell (1879; reprint, New York: Longmans, Green, 1955), 165.

14. Richard Lowe, *Walker's Texas Division, C.S.A.: Greyhounds of the Trans-Mississippi* (Baton Rouge: Louisiana State University Press, 2004), 80–81.

15. Grabau, *Ninety-Eight Days*, 383–407; Winschel, *Triumph and Defeat*, 157–62.

16. M. Jane Johansson, ed., *Widows by the Thousands: The Civil War Letters of Theophilus and Harriet Perry, 1862–1864* (Fayetteville: University of Arkansas Press, 2000), 139.

17. Norman D. Brown, ed., *Journey to Pleasant Hill: The Civil War Letters of Captain Elijah P. Petty, Walker's Texas Division, CSA* (San Antonio: University of Texas Institute of Texan Cultures, 1982), 217.

18. Joseph Palmer Blessington, *The Campaigns of Walker's Texas Division* (Austin, TX: State House Press, 1994), 93.

19. Grabau, *Ninety-Eight Days*, 383–407; Shea and Winschel, *Vicksburg Is the Key*, 163–64.

20. Grabau, *Ninety-Eight Days*, 390–407; Shea and Winschel, *Vicksburg Is the Key*, 164; Winschel, *Triumph and Defeat*, 157–70.

21. Blessington, *The Campaigns of Walker's Texas Division*, 97.

22. *OR*, vol. 24, pt. 2, 467.

23. Shea and Winschel, *Vicksburg Is the Key*, 164–65; Grabau, *Ninety-Eight Days*, 397–407; Lowe, *Walker's Texas Division, C.S.A.*, 87–101.

24. Shea and Winschel, *Vicksburg Is the Key*, 164–65; Grabau, *Ninety-Eight Days*, 397–407; Lowe, *Walker's Texas Division, C.S.A.*, 96–101.

25. Dana, *Recollections of the Civil War*, 86.

26. *Personal Memoirs of Ulysses S. Grant*, 305.

27. *OR*, vol. 24, pt. 2, 469; *OR*, vol. 24, pt. 2, 447.

28. *OR*, ser. 2, vol. 6, 21–22.

29. *OR*, vol. 24, pt. 3, 425.

30. Simon, *The Papers of Ulysses S. Grant*, 400; *OR*, vol. 24, pt. 3, 425–26.

31. OR, vol. 24, pt. 3, 443–44.

32. Simon, *The Papers of Ulysses S. Grant*, 468.

33. Lowe, *Walker's Texas Division*, C.S.A, 79–106; Grabau, *Ninety-Eight Days*, 383–407.

34. William H. Van Meter, "A Condensed History of the 47th Regiment of Illinois Vol. Infantry," John Nelson Cromwell Papers, 1861–1925, Abraham Lincoln Presidential Library, Springfield, Illinois, 13–14.

35. Lowe, *Walker's Texas Division*, C.S.A, 79–106; Grabau, *Ninety-Eight Days*, 383–407.

36. OR, vol. 24, pt. 2, 466.

37. Johansson, *Widows by the Thousands*, 149.

38. Junius Newport Bragg, *Letters of a Confederate Surgeon, 1861–1865*, ed. Mrs. T. J. Gaughan (Camden, AR: Hurley, 1960), 143, quoted in Lowe, *Walker's Texas Division*, C.S.A., 107.

39. John T. Stark to Martha, June 14, 1863, Stark Letters and Diary (13th Texas Cavalry file), Confederate Research Center, Hill College, Hillsboro, Texas, quoted in Lowe, *Walker's Texas Division*, C.S.A., 107.

40. Grabau, *Ninety-Eight Days*, 396.

41. Ibid., 477–91; Shea and Winschel, *Vicksburg Is the Key*, 165–67; OR, vol. 22, pt. 1, 411.

42. Reed, "Woman's Experiences during the Siege of Vicksburg," 89.

43. Lord, *The Fremantle Diary*, 93.

44. Ibid., 92.

45. Richard Lowe, ed., *A Texas Cavalry Officer's Civil War: The Diary and Letters of James C. Bates* (Baton Rouge: Louisiana State University Press, 1999), 254–55.

46. OR, vol. 24, pt. 3, 965–66.

47. OR, vol. 24, pt. 1, 227.

48. OR, vol. 24, pt. 3, 979.

49. Shea and Winschel, *Vicksburg Is the Key*, 167–69; Grabau, *Ninety-Eight Days*, 447–67.

50. Shea and Winschel, *Vicksburg Is the Key*, 152; Winschel, *Triumph and Defeat*, vol. 2, 49–66.

51. Simpson and Berlin, *Sherman's Civil War*, 485.

52. OR, vol. 24, pt. 1, 37.

53. Winschel, *Triumph and Defeat*, vol. 2, 66–72; John Y. Simon, "McClernand, John Alexander," in Faust, *Historical Times Illustrated Encyclopedia of the Civil War*, 456–57.

54. Drake, *A Soldier's Story of the Siege of Vicksburg*, 69.

55. Braudaway, "The Journal of Maj. Maurice Kavanaugh Simons, 1863," 118.

56. Jones, "The Rank and File at Vicksburg," 24.

57. Patrick, *Three Years with Wallace's Zouaves*, 146.

58. Reed, "Woman's Experiences during the Siege of Vicksburg," 89.

59. Lord, "A Child at the Siege of Vicksburg," 50.

60. Ibid., 49.

61. Bell, "A Girl's Experiences in the Siege of Vicksburg," 13.

62. Lord, "A Child at the Siege of Vicksburg," 51.

63. Loughborough, *My Cave Life in Vicksburg*, 109.

64. U.S. Treasury Department, "Claim of Candis Newman," in the *Southern Claims Commission Approved Claims, 1871–1880*, http://www.fold3.com/browse.php#34|h-knXjBbfBBQt_jMEgO5-zlvfe4uWWtS8wn3PdAmh (accessed June 10, 2012).

65. George F. Ranwick, gen. ed., *Oklahoma and Mississippi Narratives*, vol. 7 of *The American Slave: A Composite Autobiography*, pt. 2 (1941; reprint, Westport, CT: Greenwood Publishing, 1972), 146–47.

66. Tunnard, *A Southern Record*, 228–29.

67. Grabau, *Ninety-Eight Days*, 428–31; Shea and Winschel, *Vicksburg Is the Key*, 157–58; Winschel, *Triumph and Defeat*, 135–36; Andrew Hickenlooper, "The Vicksburg Mine," in Johnson and Buel, *Battles and Leaders of the Civil War*, vol. 3, 539–42.

68. Hickenlooper, "The Vicksburg Mine," 542.

69. Blanchard, *I Marched with Sherman*, 100.

70. Grabau, *Ninety-Eight Days*, 431–38; Shea and Winschel, *Vicksburg Is the Key*, 158–60; Winschel, *Triumph and Defeat*, 136–38.

71. Tunnard, *A Southern Record*, 234.

72. Grabau, *Ninety-Eight Days*, 433–38; Shea and Winschel, *Vicksburg Is the Key*, 159–60; Winschel, *Triumph and Defeat*, 137–38.

73. William H. Mulligan, ed., *A Badger Boy in Blue: The Civil War Letters of Chauncey H. Cooke* (Detroit: Wayne State University Press, 2007), 71.

74. Cotton, *From the Pen of a She-Rebel*, 31.

75. OR, vol. 24, pt. 3, 982–83.

76. Grabau, *Ninety-Eight Days*, 444–46.

77. John E. Stanchak, "Garrott, Isham Warren," in *Historical Times Illustrated Encyclopedia of the Civil War*, ed. Patricia L. Faust (New York: HarperPerennial, 1986), 300; John E. Stanchak, "Green, Martin Edwin," in Faust, *Historical Times Illustrated Encyclopedia of the Civil War*, 323.

78. Shea and Winschel, *Vicksburg Is the Key*, 172–73; Winschel, *Triumph and Defeat*, 176–77; Lockett, "The Defense of Vicksburg," 492; OR, vol. 24, pt. 1, 281–83.

79. Winschel, *Fall of the Confederate Gibraltar*, 20.

80. Lockett, "The Defense of Vicksburg," 492.

81. Shea and Winschel, *Vicksburg Is the Key*, 173–74.

82. OR, vol. 24, pt. 1, 283–84.

83. Shea and Winschel, *Vicksburg Is the Key*, 173–78; Winschel, *Triumph and Defeat*, 176–84; *Personal Memoirs of Ulysses S. Grant*, 312–15; OR, vol. 24, pt. 1, 283–85.

84. *Personal Memoirs of Ulysses S. Grant*, 313.

85. Shea and Winschel, *Vicksburg Is the Key*, 173–78; Winschel, *Triumph and Defeat*, 176–84; *Personal Memoirs of Ulysses S. Grant*, 312–15; OR, vol. 14, pt. 1, 283–85.

86. OR, vol. 24, pt. 3, 461.

87. Ibid., 461–63.

88. Winschel, *Triumph and Defeat*, 181.

89. "Copy of a Journal Kept by Mrs. W. W. Lord, during the Siege of Vicksburg by the forces of General U. S. Grant May and July, 1863," Library of Congress, Washington, D.C., 7–8.

90. Winschel, *Triumph and Defeat*, 189.

91. Shea and Winschel, *Vicksburg Is the Key*, 178; Grabau, *Ninety-Eight Days*, 498–503.

92. Patrick, *Three Years with Wallace's Zouaves*, 147–48.

93. Reed, "Woman's Experiences during the Siege of Vicksburg," 90–91.

94. Loughborough, *My Cave Life in Vicksburg*, 130–31.

95. *The Journal of Lettie Vick Downs in the Year 1863*, 8.

96. OR, vol. 24, pt. 1, 285.

97. Reed, "Woman's Experiences during the Siege of Vicksburg," 91.

98. Mrs. W. W. Lord journal, 10.

99. Patrick, *Three Years with Wallace's Zouaves*, 147.

100. Blanchard, *I Marched with Sherman*, 106.

101. Reed, "Woman's Experiences during the Siege of Vicksburg," 91.

102. Braudaway, "The Journal of Maj. Maurice Kavanaugh Simons, 1863," 124.

103. Anderson, *Memoirs*, 358–59.

104. Reed, "Woman's Experiences during the Siege of Vicksburg," 91.

105. Patrick, *Three Years with Wallace's Zouaves*, 148; Steven E. Woodworth, ed., *The Musick of the Mocking Birds, the Roar of the Cannon: The Civil War Diary and Letters of William Winters* (Lincoln: University of Nebraska Press, 1998), 63.

106. Joseph A. Savage Papers, 1863, Pearce Civil War Collection, Navarro College, Corsicana, Texas.

107. Tunnard, *A Southern Record*, 245.

108. Simpson and Berlin, *Sherman's Civil War*, 502.

CHAPTER 7

1. Winschel, *Fall of the Confederate Gibraltar*, 112–13; Shea and Winschel, *Vicksburg Is the Key*, 179–86.

2. OR, vol. 24, pt. 3, 474.

3. OR, vol. 24, pt. 2, 526.

4. Barron, *The Lone Star Defenders*, 163–64.

5. Shea and Winschel, *Vicksburg Is the Key*, 179–86; Winschel, *Triumph and Defeat*, vol. 2, 137–39.

6. OR, vol. 24, pt. 3, 525.

7. OR, vol. 24, pt. 2, 529.

8. OR, vol. 24, pt. 3, 531–32; Simpson and Berlin, *Sherman's Civil War*, 505.

9. OR, vol. 24, pt. 2, 536.

10. *My Civil War Memoirs, and Other Reminiscences as Written by my Father, W. R. Eddington*, ed. Norman O. Eddginton (Brigton, IL: 1934?), 13.

11. VFM 4891 Henry Wilmer Franks Civil War Letters [photocopy], Letter to Cous, July 17, 1863, Ohio Historical Society, Columbus.

12. VFM 4891 Henry Wilmer Franks Civil War Letters [photocopy], Letter to Cous, July 18, 1863, Ohio Historical Society, Columbus.

13. OR, vol. 24, pt. 2, 537.

14. VFM 4891 Henry Wilmer Franks Civil War Letters [photocopy], Letter to Cous, July 18, 1863, Ohio Historical Society, Columbus.

15. OR, vol. 24, pt. 2, 536.

16. Miller, *The Diary of John Merrilees*, 86.

17. Grimsley, *The Hard Hand of War*, 160–62.

18. Darius Hall Dodd to Sister, July 28, 1863, Civil War Miscellany, 1848–1927 (bulk 1860–1865), Indiana Historical Society, Indianapolis.

19. OR, vol. 24, pt. 3, 528.

20. Ibid., 531; Simpson and Berlin, *Sherman's Civil War*, 505.

21. Ibid.

22. OR, vol. 24, pt. 2, 529.

23. Shea and Winschel, *Vicksburg Is the Key*, 186.

24. OR, vol. 24, pt. 2, 537–39; Shea and Winschel, *Vicksburg Is the Key*, 186.

25. *Personal Memoirs of Ulysses S. Grant*, 324.

26. OR, vol. 24, pt. 3, 546.

27. *Personal Memoirs of Ulysses S. Grant*, 324.

28. Thomas, *Three Years with Grant*, 124–25.

29. Simpson and Berlin, *Sherman's Civil War*, 508.

30. Thomas, *Three Years with Grant*, 124.

31. Cotton, *From the Pen of a She-Rebel*, 39–41.

32. Trotter, *The Siege of Vicksburg*, 7.

33. Lord, "A Child at the Siege of Vicksburg," 52–53.

34. Mrs. W. W. Lord journal, 11–12.

35. Robert G. Evans, ed., *The 16th Mississippi Infantry: Civil War Letters and Reminiscences* (Jackson: University of Mississippi Press, 2002), 160.

36. Ibid., 181.

37. Ibid., 182.

38. Wynne, *Mississippi's Civil War*, 138.

39. John D. Winters, *The Civil War in Louisiana* (Baton Rouge: Louisiana State University Press, 1963), 301–6.

40. Richard and Richard, *The Defense of Vicksburg*, 235.

41. S. W. Farrow to Josephine, July 11, 1863, Farrow Papers, Center for American History, University of Texas at Austin, Austin, Texas, quoted in Lowe, *Walker's Texas Division, C.S.A.*, 110.

42. Brown, *Journey to Pleasant Hill*, 245–46.

43. Grear, *Why Texans Fought in the Civil War*, 134.

44. Shea and Winschel, *Vicksburg Is the Key*, 203–4.

45. Basler, *The Collected Works of Abraham Lincoln*, vol. 6, 326.

46. Ibid., 409.

47. Davis, *Jefferson Davis*, 506–12.

48. Sarah Woolfolk Wiggins, ed., *The Journals of Josiah Gorgas, 1857–1878* (Tuscaloosa: University of Alabama Press, 1995), 74.

49. OR, vol. 51, pt. 2, 833–34.

50. Ballard, *Pemberton*, 184–202.

51. Shea and Winschel, *Vicksburg Is the Key*, 205.

52. *Memoirs of General W. T. Sherman*, 359.

53. Winschel, *Triumph and Defeat*, 185.

54. Hewitt, *Port Hudson, Confederate Bastion on the Mississippi*, 181.

55. Shea and Winschel, *Vicksburg Is the Key*, 178–204; Grabau, *Ninety-Eight Days*, 502–6; Winschel, *Triumph and Defeat*, vol. 2, 145–46; Harold B. Simpson, *Hood's Texas Brigade: Lee's Grenadier Guard* (1970; reprint, Fort Worth, TX: Landmark Publishing, 1999), 279.

56. Winschel, *Triumph and Defeat*, vol. 2, 145–46.

57. Grimsley, *The Hard Hand of War*, 153.

58. Ibid., 142–70.

59. Winschel, *Triumph and Defeat*, 185.

60. Basler, *The Collected Works of Abraham Lincoln*, vol. 6, 230.

61. *Personal Memoirs of Ulysses S. Grant*, 319–23.

62. Ibid., 323.

63. Thomas E. Alexander and Dan K. Utley, *Go Where the Fighting Was Fiercest: The Guide to the Texas Civil War Monuments* (Abilene, TX: State House Press, 2013), 108–16.

64. Ibid., 108.

Bibliographical Essay

There is a growing library of excellent scholarly works on the Vicksburg campaign. These works have greatly increased our knowledge of the decisive campaign of the Civil War that secured Union control of the Mississippi River and saved the career of the North's most brilliant commander, Ulysses S. Grant.

Although the conquest and siege of Vicksburg was one of the longest and most significant military operations of the war, the campaign is often overshadowed in general histories of the war by the more popular and bloodier battles that took place in the eastern theater between the Union capital at Washington, D.C., and the Confederate capital at Richmond, Virginia. Two large studies of the war that best describe the fall of Vicksburg and its significance include Shelby Foote's multivolume *The Civil War: A Narrative* (1958, 1963, 1974) and James M. McPherson, *Battle Cry of Freedom: The Civil War Era* (1988). A helpful state history of the Civil War in Mississippi that includes the fall of Vicksburg is Ben Wynne's *Mississippi's Civil War: A Narrative History* (2006).

Numerous well-written biographies of the major commanders have been published in the century and a half since the fall of Vicksburg. Excellent scholarly studies of Grant include Brooks D. Simpson, *Ulysses S. Grant: Triumph over Adversity, 1822–1865* (2000), and Jean Edward Smith, *Grant* (2001). William T. Sherman has also been the subject of multiple high-quality biographies, including John F. Marszalek's authoritative *Sherman:*

A Soldier's Passion for Order (1993) and Stephen E. Woodworth's *Sherman* (2009).

Fewer biographies of the senior Confederate commanders of the Vicksburg campaign have been written, but worthwhile studies of the most important figures have been published. It was not until 1942, almost a century after the war, that a biography of John C. Pemberton appeared in print with the publication of *Pemberton: Defender of Vicksburg* (1942), authored by the general's grandson and namesake, John C. Pemberton. The book presented a much-needed defense of Pemberton's record during the Vicksburg campaign but failed to fully restore the general's reputation among scholars and military historians. Vicksburg historian Michael Ballard produced the definitive examination of the commander of the Army of Vicksburg in *Pemberton: A Biography* (1991). A useful but perhaps too forgiving evaluation of Joseph E. Johnston's role in the campaign is provided in Craig L. Symonds, *Joseph E. Johnston: A Civil War Biography* (1992). While there are many biographies of Jefferson Davis, the best one- volume treatment of the Confederacy's lone president is William C. Davis, *Jefferson Davis: The Man and His Hour* (1991).

Several outstanding military studies of the campaign are available. Helpful resources on the early phases of the Union's struggle to control the rivers of the Western Theater include Benjamin F. Cooling, *Forts Henry and Donelson: The Key to the Confederate Heartland* (1987); Wiley Sword, *Shiloh: Bloody April* (1988); and Spencer C. Tucker, *Unconditional Surrender: The Capture of Forts Henry and Donelson* (2001). The siege and Battle of Corinth, Mississippi, is best described in Peter Cozzens, *The Darkest Days of the War: The Battles of Iuka and Corinth* (1997); Steven Nathaniel Dossman, *Campaign for Corinth: Blood in Mississippi* (2006); and Timothy B. Smith, *Corinth 1862: Siege, Battle, Occupation* (2012).

The first modern military study of the Vicksburg campaign appeared in Earl Schenk Miers's *The Web of Victory: Grant at Vicksburg* (1955). The role of civilians during the siege is described in Peter F. Walker, *Vicksburg: A People at War, 1860–1865* (1960), and A. A. Hoehling, *Vicksburg: 47 Days of Siege* (1969). Other useful collections of primary sources are Richard Wheeler's *The Siege of Vicksburg* (1978) and *Guide to the Vicksburg Campaign* (1998), edited by Leonard Fullenkamp, Leonard, Stephen Bowman, and Jay Luvaas. *Guide to the Vicksburg Campaign* also contains a driving tour of the various Vicksburg campaign battlefields and historic sites.

Informative single- volume histories of the Vicksburg campaign include Samuel Carter III, *The Final Fortress: The Campaign for Vicksburg 1862– 1863* (1980); James R. Arnold, *Grant Wins the War: Decision at Vicksburg,* (1997); Michael Ballard, *Vicksburg: The Campaign That Opened the*

Mississippi (2004); and Winston Groom, *Vicksburg, 1863* (2009). The most detailed tactical study of the campaign is the excellent three- volume series *The Vicksburg Campaign* (1985–1986), authored by National Park Service historian Edwin C. Bearss. Warren E. Grabau's *Ninety-Eight Days: A Geographer's View of the Vicksburg Campaign* (2000) offers an exceptional analysis of the geographical and terrain features of the lower Mississippi Valley and their effects on the campaign. Vicksburg National Military Park historian Terrence J. Winschel's multiple publications are all outstanding, including *Vicksburg: Fall of the Confederate Gibraltar* (1999), *Triumph and Defeat: The Vicksburg Campaign* (1999), and *Triumph and Defeat: The Vicksburg Campaign*, vol. 2 (2006). Winschel and William L. Shea coauthored the superb study *Vicksburg Is the Key: The Struggle for the Mississippi River* (2003), which examines the Union's entire effort to control the Mississippi River.

Few major scholarly studies have been written on the battles of Port Gibson, Raymond, Jackson, and the Big Black River Bridge, but Timothy B. Smith's *Champion Hill: Decisive Battle for Vicksburg* (2004) is the authoritative survey of the climactic battle of the Vicksburg campaign. Other historical have studied the simultaneous consequences of the surrender of Vicksburg and the Battle of Gettysburg, including Duane Schultz, *The Most Glorious Fourth: Vicksburg and Gettysburg, July 4, 1863* (2002), and Edwin C. Bearss, with J. Parker Hills, *Receding Tide: Vicksburg and Gettysburg, the Campaigns That Changed the Civil War* (2010).

Many valuable unit histories have been published that analyze famous units from both sides in the Vicksburg campaign. Confederate unit sources include Joseph E. Chance, *From Shiloh to Vicksburg: The Second Texas Infantry* (1984); Philip Thomas Tucker, *The South's Finest: The First Missouri Confederate Brigade from Pea Ridge to Vicksburg* (1993); Allan C. Richard Jr. and Mary Margaret Higginbotham Richard, *The Defense of Vicksburg: A Louisiana Chronicle* (2004); Richard Lowe, *Walker's Texas Division, C.S.A.: Greyhounds of the Trans-Mississippi* (2004); and William D. Taylor, *"A Fit Representation of Pandemonium": East Tennessee Confederate Soldiers in the Campaign for Vicksburg* (2008). Charles D. Grear's *Why Texans Fought in the Civil War* (2010) details the motivations of Texas soldiers and the impact of the defeat at Vicksburg upon their morale. There are several solid sources for Union units, but the most thorough large-scale examination of Grant's army is Steven E. Woodworth's *Nothing but Victory: The Army of the Tennessee, 1861–1865* (2005). The crucial role played by the U.S. Navy and the Mississippi Squadron at Vicksburg is concisely described in Gary D. Joiner, *Mr. Lincoln's Brown Water Navy: The Mississippi Squadron* (2007). Steven E.

Woodworth and Charles D. Grear also edited a brief but well-written series of essays concerning the maneuver phase of the campaign collected in *The Vicksburg Campaign, March 29–May 18, 1863* (2013).

A revisionist study of postwar Vicksburg and the campaign's memory is found in Christopher Waldrep's *Vicksburg's Long Shadow: A Legacy of Race and Remembrance* (2005). Essential resources detailing the treatment of southern civilians during the war and the evolution of the Union's hard war policy include Stephen V. Ash, *When the Yankees Came: Conflict and Chaos in the Occupied South, 1861–1865* (1995); Mark Grimsley, *The Hard Hand of War: Union Military Policy toward Southern Civilians, 1861–1865* (1995); and Jacqueline Glass Campbell, *When Sherman Marched North from the Sea: Resistance on the Confederate Home Front* (2003). A valuable study of the social revolution and changing labor relations in this area of Mississippi during and after the Civil War is found in Michael Wayne's *The Reshaping of Plantation Society: The Natchez District, 1860–1880* (1983).

Index

Adams, Wirt, 80
African Americans: in Civil War, 119, 121; and Emancipation Proclamation, 30; execution of, 121; and loss of livestock, 58–59; regiments, 30; as slaves, 121–23, 128
Alison, Joseph Dill, 107
"Anaconda Plan," 4
Anderson, Ephraim M.: and Army of Tennessee, 135; and Big Black River, 86; and Champion Hill, 82; and Dunbar's plantation, 48; and May 22 assault, 102; and "Pea bread," 112; war after Vicksburg, 105
Anti-Semitism, 29
Appalachian Mountains, 2, 6
Arkansans, 6; batteries, 35; battle of Pea Ridge, 9; cattle and corn supply from, 4; and Champion Hill, 82; and fall of Island No. 10, 36; and Farragut attack, 14; and Fort Pemberton, 39; and Holmes power, 26; provisions and forage from, 25; and Union armies, 3, 11

Arkansas Post, 34–36
Arkansas River, 34–35
Army, Union. See Union army
Army of Cumberland, 47
Army of Maneuver, 125. See also Sherman, William T.
Army of Mississippi, 10, 11, 13, 15, 19, 34
Army of Northern Virginia, 15, 27, 119; and critical supplies, 2; and Johnston, 20. See also Johnston, Joseph E.
Army of Potomac, 15
Army of Relief, 109, 115, 117, 124, 137. See also Johnston, Joseph E.
Army of Tennessee (See photo essay), 1, 49, 54, 71, 79, 95, 100, 102, 105; Achilles' heel of, 56; at battle of Shiloh, 96; "Blitzkrieg through Mississippi," 57; and Bragg, 43–44, 49; at Bruinsburg, 88; casualties of, 38, 54, 84, 100–101, 146; at Corinth, Mississippi, 9–10; and critical supplies, 2; flow of critical supplies to, 2; and Grant, 21–22;

"hard war," 32–33, 39–40, 146; and
    Jackson, 68, 75; and Johnston,
    25–26; logistical situation of, 89;
    mobility of, 24–25; and Port
    Gibson, 55, 90; rations for, 49; and
    resources of Jackson, 67; slaves as
    spies and guides for, 31; soldiers of,
    50, 55, 56, 77; and Steele's
    Greenville Expedition, 42–45; and
    Vicksburg campaign, 21, 63, 66,
    77–79, 84, 89, 92, 104–5, 109, 123,
    135, 145; victory over Army of
    Vicksburg, 135; XIII, XV, XVII
    Corps in, 61, 70–71, 96, 118, 126.
    See also Grant, Ulysses S.
Army of the Gulf (See photo essay),
    42, 47, 109, 117–18. See also Banks,
    Nathaniel P.
Army of Trans-Mississippi, 117, 124.
    See also Confederate army
Army of Vicksburg: African
    American slaves in, 128; attack at
    Big Black River, 61–62; and Bakers
    Creek, 83; and battles of
    Champion's Hill, 80–82, 87, 92;
    casualties of, 84–85, 127; divisions
    of, 20; at Edwards Station, 75;
    estimated force of, 52; and Federal
    bombardment, 126; fighting ability
    of, 93–94; during July 1863,
    131–32; marching to Clinton,
    75–82; pea bread to, 112;
    Pemberton restoring fighting ability
    of, 93–94; and Rodney Road,
    53; Smith vs. Johnston, 125;
    surrender of, on July 4, 1863, 133;
    and transfer of soldiers, 49;
    transportation of prisoners of, 132;
    and Van Dorn's Holly Springs
    raid, 25. See also Pemberton,
    John C.
Atlanta, Georgia, 6, 68
Atlantic Ocean., 2
Autrey, James L., 12

Bagnell plantation, 58
Bakers Creek, 80, 83–84
Baldwin, William E., 50–51, 52, 53,
    85, 94, 131
Baldwin's Ferry Road, 93, 96
Balfour, Emma, 93, 96, 106, 108
Banks, Nathaniel P., 42,
    109, 117
Barron, Samuel, 24, 139
Barton, Seth, 27, 80
Bates, James C., 125
Baton Rouge, 14–15
Battery Robinette, 16–17, 96
Battle(s): of Belmont, 6; Big Black
    River, 86, 88–90; Chancellorsville,
    87; of Chickasaw Bayou, 27, 40, 75;
    of Corinth, 16–17; Gettysburg,
    145–46; of Helena, 124; Iuka, 16;
    Jackson, 67–68; Memphis, 11; of
    Milliken's Bend, 121; of Mill
    Springs, 6; of Pea Ridge, 9, 13–14;
    of Port Gibson, 54–55; of Prairie
    Grove, 26; of Raymond, 63–64; of
    Second Manassas, 16; of Shiloh,
    10, 22, 29, 96; of Stone's River, 26.
    See also Wars/warfare; specific types
Beauregard, Pierre G. T., 10, 15, 19
Belmont, battle of, 6
Benton, William P., 54, 98
Big Black River, 92; battle of, 85–88;
    and Confederate casualties, 86; and
    Pemberton defenses, 61–62, 75–76,
    84–85; Sherman's XV Corps at, 61;
    Union army victory at, 88; and
    Vicksburg campaign, 111, 126, 137;
    XVII Corps camped at, 58
Bissel, J. W., 11
Black Hawk War, 22
Blair, Frank P., Jr., 79
Blanchard, Ira: and battle of
    Raymond, 63; and foraging
    expeditions, 60; in Jackson, 69; and
    May 22 assault, 101; memoirs, 33;
    and Port Gibson, 55; 20th Illinois

Infantry, 22; and Vicksburg
    Campaign, 77–79, 84–85, 129, 135
Bledsoe, Hiram, 62
Blessington, Palmer, 120–21
"Blitzkrieg through Mississippi," 57
Blue Wing, 35
Botetourt Virginia Artillery, 53, 54
Bowden, Scott, 87
Bowen, John S. (See photo essay), 75,
    84, 133; army of, 52; at Big Black
    River Bridge, 85; and casualties
    report, 54; at Champion Hill, 82;
    and Cockrell's regiments, 49; at
    Grand Gulf, 50–55; Grant vs.,
    60–61; and Port Gibson, 52;
    Rodney Road counterattack, 53;
    and Vicksburg Campaign, 52.
    See also Army of Vicksburg
Bowling Green, Kentucky, 8
Boyd, Cyrus F., 30, 34
Bragg, Braxton, 15, 24, 43–44, 49
Breckinridge, John C., 14
Brown, Isaac, 14
Browne, Junius Henri, 66
Brown-water navy, 4, 13, 26
Bruinsburg, road transport at, 50
Bruinsburg Road, 52–54; Army of the
    Tennessee at, 88; Osterhaus's
    division at, 54; Tracy's brigade
    on, 53
Buchannan administration, 8
Buckner, Simon B, 8
Buell, Don Carlos, 8
Buford, Abraham, 80
Burbridge, Stephen G., 98
Bush, Andrew, 30
Butler, Benjamin, 12

Cadwallader, Sylvanus, 57, 58,
    74, 88, 142
Camels, in wars/warfare, 104. See also
    Old Douglas
Carr, Eugene A., 52, 79
Cater, Rufus W., 71

Cave shelters, trade of, 105–6
Champion Hill (See photo essay), 77,
    80–81, 85; Bowen's brigades on, 82;
    Confederate disaster at, 84; and
    Missourians, 82; Union soldiers
    on, 81
Champion House, 82
Chancellorsville, battle of, 87
Chase, Salmon P., 29
Chattanooga, 6, 15
Chicago Mercantile Battery, 55, 99
Chicago Times, 57
Chickasaw Bayou, battle of, 27, 40, 75
Chickasaw Bluffs, and Sherman,
    88–89
Chimneyville. See Jackson
    (Mississippi)
Churchill, Thomas, 34
Civilians of Vicksburg: and shelling,
    104–8, 127–28; and sickness,
    112–13, 128; and starvation,
    109–14, 128
Civil War, 10, 31, 96; African
    Americans in, 119, 121; foraging
    in, 33; and Grant's campaign for
    Vicksburg, 4; Mississippi River and,
    2, 31; outbreak of, 4; and rapes, 33–
    34; rapes by soldiers in, 33–34
Clemons, Henry, 38
Cockrell, Francis M., 48, 52,
    53, 80, 130
Columbus, 5, 6, 9
Commerce and trade. See Trade and
    commerce
Confederate army: battle of Pea
    Ridge, 9; at Corinth, 16–17; and
    economy, 32; and "General Orders,
    No. 59," 139–40; and Mississippi
    river, 1, 143; needs of, 28, 59, 117;
    and Vicksburg campaign, 59,
    76, 145
Confederate friends, 68–69
"Confederate House," 72
Cooke, Chauncey, 130–31

"Coonskin's Tower," 103
Corinth, Battle of, 16–17, 19, 96
Cormal, Thomas, 122
Cotton, 57–59, 70, 85; burning of,
    68–69, 123; price of, 58; and
    Walker's division, 123
Cottonclads warships, 11
Cotton trade, 28–29, 43
Covell, George W., 54
Cowan, Luther H, 39
Crawford, J. B., 143; Arkansas
    Battalion, 35
Crocker, Marcellus M., 62, 79
Croom, C. Stephens, 44
CSS *Arkansas*, 14–15
Cumberland Gap, 6
Cumberland River, 5
Cumming, Alfred, 80
Curtis, Samuel R., 9

Daily Citizen, 112–13
Dana, Charles, 69
Davis, Charles H., 10, 11
Davis, Jefferson, 1, 4–5, 19, 25, 86,
    144–45
Davis, Joseph, 89
Davis, William C, 65–66
De Courcy, John F., 27
Dennis, Elias S., 54, 62
Denson's company, of Louisiana
    cavalry, 35
Department Number Two, 6
Deshler, James, 35
De Soto Point, 12, 13, 38,
    49, 102
Dodd, Darius Hall, 30, 140–41
Donelson, Daniel S., 5
Dot (steamer), 85
Downs, Lettie Vick, 43, 110, 134
Dunnington, John W., 35
Durham, Thomas Wise, 55, 56, 127,
    133, 135
Dwight, Henry Otis, 62
Dysentery, 112–13

Eads, James Buchanan, 4
Echelon assault, 62
Economy: Confederate, 32; and
    Mississippi River, 3, 36; and Union
    armies, 59. *See also* Trade and
    commerce
Eddington, William R., 140
Edwards Station, 80, 84
18th Texas Cavalry, 35
Emancipation Proclamation, 30
Episcopal Church, prayers at, 114–15
Erwin, Eugene, 130
"Exterior Line," 126

Farragut, David G., 12, 26; and Arkansas,
    14; and New Orleans, 12, 13
Farrow, Samuel, 144
Fay, Edwin H., 21, 178
Featherston, Winfield S., 40, 80
Federal attack, 91–92
Federal foraging parties, 33
Ferguson, Samuel, 40
"First at Vicksburg," 94
Floyd, John B., 8
Food and food supplies: and African
    Americans, 59; "Blitzkrieg through
    Mississippi, 57; in Civil War, 33;
    and Grand Gulf, 60; and Grant
    determination, 60, 101; and
    Vicksburg Campaign, 66, 89,
    109–14, 128, 131, 135, 142
Foote, Andrew H., 7
Foraging expeditions, Grant's
    determination for, 60
Foraging parties, authorized/
    unauthorized, 33
Force, Manning F., 30
"Forlorn hope," 96, 98
Forney, John H. (*See* photo essay), 20,
    44, 75, 92
Forrest, Nathan Bedford, 8, 15, 24, 43
Fort De Russy, 41
Fort Donelson, 5, 6–9, 22, 29, 62, 63
Fort Donelson No. 2, 35

Fort Henry, 5, 6, 7, 9, 11, 29
Fort Hill, 93
Fort Hindman, 35–36
Fort Jackson, 11
Fort Nogales, 3
Fort Pemberton, 39
Fort Pillow, 11
Fort Taylor. *See* Fort De Russy
Foster, Samuel T., 36
Fox, Tryphena B., 111
Franks, Henry Wilmer, 140
Fremantle, Arthur, 73, 124

Gailor, Thomas Frank, 67
Gantz, Jacob, 70
Gardner, Franklin, 118, 144
Garland, Robert, 35
Garrott, Isham, 53, 131
General Orders (Sherman): No. 11,
    29, 30; No. 59, 139; No. 72, 126
Gibraltar of Confederacy, 96
Grabau, Warren E., 57, 123
Granbury, Hiram, 62
Grand Gulf, Mississippi, 21, 49–52,
    55–57; attack on April 29, 50–51;
    Bowen's evacuation from, 55–56;
    description about Port Gibson, 52;
    and Grant's forces, 49–50, 56–57;
    transportation at, 49–50
Grand Junction, 21
Grant, Ulysses S.: anti-Semitism, 29;
    Bowen's *vs*., 60–61; conquest of
    Vicksburg, 3; counterattack by, 8;
    course of action into interior of
    Mississippi, 56–57; 98-day
    campaign, 1–142; decision to
    destroy Jackson's resources, 67, 69;
    devastation of Jackson and, 137;
    early life of, 7; ended prisoner
    exchange system, 122; fall of
    Vicksburg and, 137–47; and
    Grierson's raid, 44; and hard war,
    32; and illegal flow of goods, 29;
    and media/press, 10; as national

hero, 8–9; new hard war policies,
    142; and Port Gibson, 61; reentry,
    to possess Mississippi, 15; and
    residents of Mississippi, 141–42;
    retreat in North Mississippi, 28; and
    Special Orders, No. 110, 44; and
    "Ulysses Surprise Grant," 10; and
    "Unconditional Surrender," 9;
    unconditional surrender and,
    131–32; and Union war effort, 6;
    and Vicksburg campaign, 84;
    Vicksburg venture, 49–50; victory
    over Army of Vicksburg, 133–35;
    and war operations, 19–45
Graveyard Road, 93
Great Redoubt, 98
Green, Martin E., 80, 131
Green, William Siege, 105
Greenville Expedition, 42–43, 47, 52
Gregg, John (*See* photo essay), 27, 61
Grierson, Benjamin, 43, 44
Griffin, John, 24
Grimsley, Mark, 33
Guerilla conflict, 30, 32
Guion, Lewis, 144
Gulf, Army of, 42
Gunboats and Ships, 4, 6–8, 11–14, 26,
    35, 36, 38–41. *See also* specific types

Haines Bluff, 89
Haldeman's Texas battery, 35
Halleck, Henry W., 2
"Hard war," 32, 34
Hawes, James M., 119
Haynes' Bluff, 126
Herbert, Louis T., 94, 130
Hickenlooper, Andrew, 129
Higgins, Edward, 20
Higgins, Thomas J., 99
HMS *Diligent*, 40
Holmes, Theophilus, 20, 124
Hovey, Alvin P., 21, 52, 79
Howe, Orion P., 21, 52, 79, 95
Hurlbut, Stephen, 29

Infernal machine, 26
"Interior Line," 126
Island No. 10 (waterway), 9, 11, 12, 36
Iuka, battle of, 16

Jackson (Mississippi), 66–67; battle
    of, 67; burnings of, 139–40, 141;
    destruction in, 74–75; fall of, 66;
    Johnston's defense of, 67–68;
    location of, 66; people's relocation
    from, 66–67; population of, 66;
    resources of, 67; second Federal
    occupation of, 140; Sherman's
    capture of, 68; and Sherman's
    neckties, 68–70; textile industry in,
    68–69; Union occupation of, 68–69
Jackson, Battle of, 67
Jackson Road, 80, 83, 93
Jews, 28–29
John A., Logan, 79
Johnston, Albert Sidney, 6, 10, 20
Johnston, Joseph E. (See photo essay),
    15, 44, 73, 137, 144; army in
    retreat, 69, 141; and Army of
    Northern Virginia, 20; and Army of
    Tennessee, 25; and Canton, 76;
    casualties, 67; and Davis, 26;
    deliverance in siege, 124; and
    "General Orders, No. 59," 139; as
    hero in 1861, 20; and Jackson, 61,
    65–67, 84, 125, 139; and Kirby
    Smith, 125; and Loring, 84–85; and
    marching of soldiers, 25, 44, 49, 79;
    orders, 80, 91, 125, 139; and Pearl
    River railroad bridge, 70; pursuit of,
    137–39; reinforcement, 93–94, 125;
    and Vicksburg campaign, 73, 125.
    See also Army of Northern Virginia
Jones, James Henry, 127

Killgore, Gabriel, 94
Kircher, Henry A., 39, 70
Kirkpatrick, James Johnson, 143
Knox, Thomas W., 25

Lake Providence waterway, 38, 39
Landrum, William, 99
Lawler, Michael, 86, 99
Lay, Benjamin D., 107
Lee, Robert E., 15, 16, 86–87, 145
Lee, Stephen Dill, 27, 43, 80–81, 100,
    106, 131
Leggett, Mortimer, 129
Lincoln, Abraham, 2, 30, 144
Livestock, loss of, 2, 32, 43, 58–59
Lockett, Samuel H., 21, 80, 83, 86
Logan, John A., 54, 102
Logan's Approach, 102, 103, 129
Lord, William, Jr., 106
Loring, William W., 20, 39, 75, 83
Loughborough, Mary, 87, 92
Louisiana cavalry, 35
Lucas, George M, 70

Malaria, 112–13
Malnutrition, 112
May 19 attack, 84, 93–95
May 22 attack, 70, 96, 100–101, 118,
    126, 147
McClellan, George, 15
McClernand, John (See photo essay),
    8, 22, 30; mismanagement, 100;
    and XIII Corps, 42
McCulloch, Benjamin, 9
McCulloch, Henry E., 119
McKay, Gil, 35
McKinley, Emilie, 34, 110,
    131, 142
McMorries, Edward Young, 119
McPherson, James B. (See photo
    essay), 36, 42
Medal of Honor, 103; "forlorn hope"
    won, 98; to Higgins, Thomas J., 99;
    to Howe, Orion P., 95
Memphis, battle of, 11
Merrilees, John, 71
Mexican War, 7, 19, 75
Middle Road, 83
Miller, Charles Dana, 70, 72, 89

Milliken's Bend, and McCulloch's brigade, 120–21

Mississippi, state of: crayfish soup at, 48; population of, 3; and Union war efforts, 6–7; voting, 3

Mississippi River: and battle of Corinth, 17; and Breckinridge's defensive barrier, 14; and Confederate supremacy, 1, 4; conquest of, 145; defenses, 2, 3; and economy, 3, 36; and European trade, 2; Federal transports in, 48–49; and Grant, 15, 19–45; and guerilla war, 33; and leaders opinions, 2, 3–4; McClernand's conquest of, 22, 34–35; and navigation, 36; roads and railroads, 5, 9; Southern Railroad of, 56; and trade, 2; and transportation, 1–2, 9, 20; and Union Army, 1–2, 3, 4; Western Gunboat Flotilla and, 4, 7, 11, 13, 14, 26; XV Corps crossing, 56

Mississippi rock. See Gibraltar of Confederacy

Mississippi State Troops, 67

Mississippi Valley. See Mississippi River

Missourians, 24; and Champion Hill, 82; and Federal reinforcements, 48; from Grand Gulf, 53–54; at Helena, 139; in plantation house, 48

Mobile railroads, 24

Monroe, Louisiana, 12

Moon Lake, 38

Moore, John C., 16, 96

Morgan, George W., 27

Morgan, John Hunt, 15, 140

Mortar schooner, Farragut's, 12

Mower, Joseph A., 71–72, 100, 122

National Military Park (See photo essay), 147

Neutrality policy, of Kentucky, 5–6

New Orleans: devastating loss of, 15; and Farragut's attack, 12, 13; population of, 11; trade and commerce, 11–12, 28

Newsom, Rosetta L, 59

Newton, James K., 104

New York Herald, 25

New York Tribune, 66

19th Arkansas Infantry, 35

Northern Virginia, army of. See Army of Northern Virginia

Nutt's company, of Louisiana cavalry, 35

Ohio railroads, 24

"Old Abe," 100

"Old Blizzards," 83, 84

Old Douglas (camel), 104

Oldroyd, Osborn H., 60, 63, 70–71, 85, 98, 102, 126

Ord, Edward O. C., 126

Osterhaus, Peter J., 53, 79

Owen, E. K., 122

Pragmatic phase, of war, 32

Parsons, William H., 2–3

Pea bread, 112

Pea Ridge, battle of, 9

Pearl River, 70, 71, 139

Pemberton, John C. (See photo essay), 19, 47, 83; abysmal lack of cavalry, 76–77; and Bowne's Brigade, 52; early life of, 19; efforts to destroy Union gunboat, 103; petition from soldier of, 131; unconditional surrender and, 131–32

Pennsylvania Rebel, 47

Perry, Theophilus, 120, 123

Pettus, E. W., 100

Pettus, John Jones, 66, 71

Pettus Flying Artillery, 52

Petty, Elijah P., 120, 144

Pillow, Gideon J., 8

Pitts, Florison D, 55

Pittsburg Landing, 9–10
Plantation crops, and Grant's army, 58
Polk, Leonidas, 5
Pook, Samuel, 4
"Pook Turtles," 4
Pope, John, 11
Population: Jackson, 66; Mississippi, 3; New Orleans, 11
Porter, David Dixon (*See* photo essay), 13, 26
Port Gibson, 50, 52–53, 54, 60; battle of, 54–55; Grant's landing and fighting at, 61
Port Hudson, 88, 91, 109, 144; and Bank's campaign, 47, 56, 88, 118–19, 124, 145; batteries, 42; casualties, 145; Confederate fortress attack at, 118; Confederate garrison at, 1, 60; and Davis order, 91; and Van Dorn, 15
Prairie Grove, battle of, 26
Prentiss, Benjamin, 124
Price, Sterling, 16
Prisoner exchange system, 122
Pugh, Isaac, 139

"Quaker gun," 41

Railroad Redoubt, 98, 99–100
Railroads and roads. *See* Roads and railroads
Randal, Horace, 119
Rapes, and Civil War, 33–34
Ratliff Road, 77, 82
Raymond, battle of, 63–64
Raymond-Edwards Road, 77
Raymond Road, 79, 80, 83
Rebel skirmish line, 62
Rebel Yell, 53
Rector, Henry M., 26
Red River, 3, 13, 15, 24, 38, 41, 48
Reynolds, Alexander W, 80
River Road, 93

Roads and railroads: at Bruinsburg, 50; in Mississippi River, 5. *See also* Transport/transportation; specific types
Rodney Road, 52–54
Roman Catholic Church, 73
Rosecrans, William S., 16
Ross, Leonard, 38

Savage, Joseph A., 136
Schmerhorn, Bernard, 44
Scott, Winfield, 4
Second Manassas, battle of, 16
2nd Texas Infantry, 20, 27
Seddon, James A, 61, 65
17th Texas Cavalry, 35
Shea, William L., 117–18
Shelling, Vicksburg's civilians and, 104–8, 127–28
Sherman, William T. (*See* photo essay), 2, 145, 146; and Chickasaw Bluffs, 88–89; and Jackson, 139; neckties, 70; XV Corps, 42
Shiloh, battle of, 10, 22, 29, 96
"Shock troops," 52
Shoup, Francis, 94
Sickness, Vicksburg's civilians and, 112–13, 128
Simons, Maurice K., 44, 100–101, 103, 126, 135
6th Texas Infantry, 35
Slack, James R., 54
Slaveocracy, 32
Slaves/slavery, 30–31; and Bagnell plantation, 58; in orgy of destruction, 118; in Union Army, 31, 32
Smith, Andrew J., 27, 36, 52, 79, 86
Smith, Charles F., 8
Smith, Edmund Kirby, 16, 117
Smith, Giles A., 40, 94
Smith, Jean Edward, 29
Smith, John E., 54, 62
Smith, Martin Luther (*See* photo essay), 12, 20, 21, 75, 92

Smith, Morgan L., 27
Smith, Ralph J., 39, 48, 92, 98–99
Smith, Thomas Kilby, 95
Smith, Watson, 38
"Special Orders, No. 110," 44
"Spinal column of America," 3
Square Fort, 93
St. Philip brick fort, 11
Stanfield, Edward, 70
Starvation, Vicksburg's civilians and, 109–14, 128
State of Kentucky, 5
State of Mississippi. See Mississippi, state of
State of Texas, 2
Steele, Frederick, 27, 36
Steele's Bayou Expedition, 40
Stevenson, Carter L. (See photo essay), 20, 25, 75
Stevenson, John D., 54
Stockade Redan, 93, 94, 96, 98, 100
Stone, William M, 50
Stone's River, battle of, 26
Streight, Abel D., 43

Tallahatchie River, 21, 38, 39
Tappan, James C., 119
Taylor, Richard, 117
Taylor, Zachery, 7
Tennessee, army of. See Army of Tennessee
Tennessee River, 5, 10
10th Texas Infantry, 35
Thackara, Flavius J., 89
3rd Louisiana Infantry, 20
Thomas, Allen, 27
Thomas, George, 6
Tilghman, Lloyd, 7, 80
Tobacco in Jackson, 69
Todd, David, 98
Tracy, Edward D., 27, 50–51, 52–53
Trade and commerce: of cave shelters, 105; cotton, 28–29, 43; Mississippi, 2; New Orleans, 11–12. See also Economy
Trans-Mississippi, 60, 115, 117; and fall of Vicksburg, 144; and Mississippi River, 1–2, 9, 20; war and warfare, 13, 15; and waterways, 3
Transport/transportation: at Grand Gulf, Mississippi, 49–50; and Mississippi River, 2, 5; of war prisoners, 132. See also Roads and railroads; Waterway(s)
Trotter, Ida Barlow, 109, 142
Tunnard, William H., 48, 103, 112, 128–29, 130, 136
Turkey Creek Road, 77
Tuttle, James, 100
25th Texas Cavalry, 35
24th Arkansas Infantry, 35
24th Texas Cavalry, 35

"Ulysses Surprise Grant," 10
"Unconditional Surrender" Grant, 9
Union army: bombardment in Vicksburg by, 108–9; brown-water navy, 26; coal and lead mining by, 129; dangers of shells of, 105; and economic devastation, 59; and Emancipation Proclamation, 30; and foraging expeditions, 60; as foreign immigrants, 31; and Frank, 140; and Grant victories, 8–9; and Grierson's raid, 44; and guerilla war, 33; gunboats and ships, 4, 6–8, 11–14, 26, 35, 36, 38–41; hard war policies of, 122–23; invasions, 9; military policies of, 31–32; and Mississippi River, 1–2, 3; river steamer, purchase of, 3; and slavery, 31, 32; and Vicksburg capture attempts, 22–24; Vicksburg periodically bombardment by, 105; and war efforts, 6; warships, 12, 14
USS Albatross, 42
USS Beatty, 41

USS *Benton*, 49, 50, 102
USS *Cairo*, 26
USS *Carondelet*, 11, 14, 40, 49, 102
USS *Choctaw*, 121
USS *Cincinnati*, 40, 102–3
USS *Eastport*, 7
USS *General Price*, 49, 102
USS *Hartford*, 42
USS *Henry Clay*, 49
USS *Indianola*, 41–42
USS *Lafayette*, 49
USS *Lexington*, 121
USS *Louisiana*, 12
USS *Louisville*, 40, 49
USS *Mississippi*, 12
USS *Mound City*, 40, 102
USS *Pittsburg*, 11, 40, 49
USS *Queen of the West*, 14, 41
USS *Star of the West*, 39
USS *Switzerland*, 42
USS *Tigress*, 49
USS *Tuscumbia*, 49
USS *Tyler*, 14, 124
USS *Varuna*, 12

Van Dorn, Earl, 6, 9, 13–15, 19, 24;
    and Holly Springs raid, 25
Van Meter, William, 122
Van Zandt, Khleber Miller, 62
Vaughn, John C., 27, 85
Vick, Reverend Newitt, 3
Vicksburg campaign, 59–60, 63, 64,
    66, 68, 73, 74, 84; death rates, 84;
    destruction of, 141
Vicksburg National Military Park, 147
Voters/voting, and Mississippi, 3

Wage war, 2, 32, 34
Wagon train, 80
Walker, John G., 119
Walker, Leroy, 9
Walker, Peter F., 108, 114
Walnut Hills, 26–27
Ward, Bill, 87

Warrenton Road, 93
Wars/warfare: animals in, 55; camels
    usage in, 104; and Grant
    operations, 19–45; gunboats and
    ships in, 4, 6–8, 11–14, 26, 35, 36,
    38–41; and hard war, 32, 34;
    horrors of, 111–12; loss of livestock
    due to, 58–59; pragmatic phase of,
    32; prayers by soldiers, 114–15;
    Trans-Mississippi's strategic role in,
    3; and Union Army, 6; wage, 2, 32,
    34; and waterways, 3, 5. *See also*
    specific battles
Washburne, Elihu, 7
Washington, Edward, 94
Waterway(s): Lake Providence,
    38, 39; role in war and warfare, 3, 5.
    See also Transport/transportation
Waul's Texas Legion, 96, 99
Webb, William H., 41
Western Gunboat Flotilla, 4, 7, 11,
    13, 14, 26
West Gulf Blockading Squadron, 13
Wild honey, 48
Wiley, William, 55
Williams, Thomas, 13
Wilson, Charles A, 56, 69
Winschel, Terrence J., 117–18
Winschel, Terry, 146
Withers, William T., 27
Women: attempts to secure property,
    110–11; and bombardment in
    Vicksburg, 107–9; mental issues to,
    107–9
Wynne, Ben, 143

Yalobusha River, 22, 39
Yankees, 10, 67, 102
Yates, Jerome B., 143
Yates, Richard, 7
Yazoo River, 4, 14, 22, 26, 27, 38, 40,
    89, 119
Young's Point, 120

About the Author

STEVEN NATHANIEL DOSSMAN, PhD, earned his master's and doctoral degrees in history from Texas Christian University in Fort Worth, Texas, where his dissertation examined soldier and civilian interaction during the Vicksburg campaign. Originally from Gatesville, Texas, he received a bachelor's degree in history and political science from McMurry University in Abilene, Texas, in 2006. He is the author of *Campaign for Corinth: Blood in Mississippi*, published in 2006 by the McWhiney Foundation Press, Abilene, Texas.